D0190704

1.00

WITHDRAWN

Festivals in
World Religions

Festivals in World Religions

Edited by Alan Brown

on behalf of
The Shap Working Party on World Religions in Education

LONGMAN
London and New York

LONGMAN GROUP LIMITED
Longman House
Burnt Mill, Harlow, Essex CM20 2JE, England
and Associated Companies throughout the World

Published in the United States of America
by Longman Inc., New York

© Longman Group Limited, 1986

All rights reserved. No part of this publication
may be reproduced, stored in a retrieval system,
or transmitted in any form or by any means, electronic,
mechanical, photocopying, recording or otherwise,
without the prior written permission of the Publisher.

First published 1986
ISBN 0 582 36196 6

Set in 10/12pt Palatino Roman, Linotron 202

Printed in Great Britain
by Mackays of Chatham

291.3
505,792
2025697

British Library Cataloguing in Publication Data

Festivals in world religions.
  1. Fasts and feasts.
  I. Brown, Alan, *1944–*   II. Shap Working Party
on World Religions in Education
  291.3′6   BL590

  ISBN 0–582–36196–6

Library of Congress Cataloging in Publication Data

Festivals in world religions.
  Bibliography: p.
  Includes index.
  1. Fasts and feasts. 2. Festivals. 3. Fasts and
feasts – Study and teaching – Great Britain. 4. Festivals
– Study and teaching – Great Britain. I. Brown, Alan,
1944–   II. Shap Working Party on World Religions in
Education.
BL590.F47 1985   291.3′6   85–23189
ISBN 0–582–36196–6

Contents

WITHDRAWN

Preface   ix
Alan Brown

1 Introduction   1
Geoffrey Parrinder

Feasts and festivals   2
Natural cycles and festivals   4
Sacred history   6
Sacred times   8
Sacred places   10
The Gregorian Calendar   17

2 Baha'i Festivals   19
Philip Hainsworth

Introduction   19
The festivals   23
Table of Baha'i festivals   29

3 Buddhist Festivals   31
Richard Gombrich

Buddhism   31
The festivals   39
Table of Buddhist festivals   58

Contents

4 Chinese Festivals   60
   Douglas Jones

   Religion in China   60
   The Chinese calendar   64
   The festivals   66
   Table of Chinese festivals   73

5 Christian Festivals   74
   John Rankin

   Christianity   74
   The Church's Year   77
   The festivals   82
   Table of Christian festivals   102

6 Hindu Festivals   104
   Robert Jackson

   Hinduism   104
   The festivals   106
   Table of Hindu festivals   139

7 Jaina Festivals   140
   Padmanabh S Jaini

   Jainism   140
   The Jaina era and calendar   142
   The festivals   142
   Table of Jaina festivals   149

8 Japanese Festivals   150
   Michael Pye

   Introduction   150
   The festivals   153
   Table of Japanese festivals   168

9 Jewish Festivals   170
   Angela Wood and Hugo Gryn

   The Jewish calendar   170
   The festivals   172
   Table of Jewish festivals   209

10   Muslim Festivals   211
     Riadh el-Droubie

     Islam   211
     The Muslim calendar   213
     The festivals   215
     Table of Muslim festivals   232

11   Sikh Festivals   234
     W Owen Cole

     Sikhism   234
     The festivals   236
     Table of Sikh festivals   242

12   Zoroastrian (Parsi) Festivals   245
     Mary Boyce

     Zoroastrianism   245
     The festivals   246
     Table of Zoroastrian holy days of obligation   255
     Table of the obligatory and other festivals according
       to the Fasli calendar   255

13   National and Secular Festivals   256
     Ninian Smart

     National celebrations   256
     Other secular festivals   261
     Summary   262

14   Observing Festivals in Schools   266
     Peter Woodward

     The British scene   266
     The practice of celebrating festivals in schools   269
     Assembly and worship   275

     Bibliography   277

     Notes on the Contributors   278

     Index   283

Acknowledgements

We are indebted to Baha'i World Centre for permission to reproduce tables from *The Baha'i World* vol. XVII 1976–79.

We are grateful to the following for permission to reproduce photographs:

Anglo Chinese Educational Institute, page 14; Aramco World Magazine, page 225; Baha'i World Centre, page 25; Rashid D Bamanbehrain, page 15; Barnaby's Picture Library (photo Marie J Mattson), page 125; Tony Benjamin, page 177; Mary Boyce, page 247 (above); Noshir M Desai, page 250; Douglas Dickins, page 241; Format Photographers (photo Jenny Matthews), page 89; Richard & Sally Greenhill, page 67; Hong Kong Tourist Association, page 71; Michael Houser, pages 155, 157; Geoff Howard, page 16; Jewish Chronicle, page 11; Keystone/Photosource, pages 44, 62; London Central Mosque Trust Ltd, page 217; Novosti Press APN, (photo V Kuzmin) page 91, (photo Viktor Budan) page 263; Christine Osborne, pages 144, 229, 238; Ann & Bury Peerless Slide Resources & Picture Library, pages 13, 51, 114, 131, 243, 247 (below); Picturepoint, page 260; Popperfoto, page 165; Press Association, page 95; David Richardson, pages 85, 221; Brian Shuel, page 264; Juliette Soester, page 203; John Walmsley, pages 12, 135; Zefa (photo Werner Braun), page 181.

Cover: Picturepoint

Preface

The Shap Working Party on World Religions in Education

The Working Party takes its name from the location of its first conference in 1969 near the village of Shap in the Lake District in England. Its aim is to encourage the study and teaching of world religions by producing accurate information, material and resources as well as by organising in-service training for teachers. Since 1972 the Working Party has produced a *Calendar of Religious Festivals* in co-operation with what is now called the Commission for Racial Equality. It is the success of this calendar that has provided the necessity for a book that could look at the festivals in much greater detail. The calendar will continue to be published annually providing the dates of festivals for the year ahead and this, with the book, will be an important aid to teachers, industrialists, welfare agencies and all others who regularly meet the diversity of religious practice and belief.

The book

Each chapter in the book retains its characteristic style and individuality while remaining a part of the unified whole. The Shap Working Party is a collection of individuals and it was considered important not to impose too uniform a structure on a book which by its very nature has to recognise and acknowledge diversity. Each author is an expert in their field and provides an introduction to the particular religion so that the role of the festival may be more clearly understood. In addition Geoffrey Parrinder has provided an introductory chapter which surveys the field of religious festivals and celebrations, Ninian Smart has contributed a chapter on the increasingly significant secular festivals and Peter Woodward, mindful of Shap's concern with teachers and school, has written of his personal experiences in observing festivals as celebrated in schools.

To read through the book is to recognise one of the many para-
doxes in the study and teaching of religion, for while all the religions included in the book celebrate festivals, they do so in different
ways and the role of the festival plays a distinctly different part in
the religion. It is a salutary lesson to all who study religion that
apparent uniformity masks subtle distinctions; questions that are
appropriate within one religious tradition are inappropriate within
another. This abundance of richness married to the idiosyncratic
makes festivals an exciting area of study, as well as providing
generous material for the classroom. They are another piece of the
infinite jigsaw which is the study of religion.

The text

Even the most cursory glance through the book will indicate the
variety of calendars that exist and, of course, many others are in use
which are not referred to here. Religions use different measures of
time to provide the means of establishing the calendrical cyclic:
some use a lunar calendar, some use a solar calendar, some use both
at the same time. For the sake of clarity and uniformity, and to avoid
giving offence to any religious communities, this book adopts a
system of chronology based upon the Gregorian calendar (see Introduction). The abbreviations BCE (Before the Common Era) and CE
(Common Era) correspond to BC and AD respectively. Dates
appearing in the text without any qualifying calendrical indication
refer to CE.

The different spellings in different chapters of festivals common
to two or more religions (notably those of Hinduism, Buddhism and
Sikhism) reflect usage among the religious communities involved,
which Shap considers important to recognise. The use of diacriticals
has been minimised as far as possible, though some authors have
retained their use where clarity is absolutely vital. Consequently the
book offers little guidance on exact pronounciation, but in recognition of the importance of correct pronounciation future editions of
the *Calendar of Religious Festivals* will give a transliteration of the
festival names in English.

The bibliography mainly reflects the work of the Shap Working
Party rather than provide further references related to the festivals.
Rather than include a large and somewhat unbalanced bibliography
it was decided to refer the reader to the *Calendar of Religious Festivals*
and *World Religions: A Handbook for Teachers*, already published on
behalf of Shap. The latter contains a considerable number of names
and addresses of various religious bodies to whom approaches may
be made for more detail. In addition, all the authors have written

widely on their subject and these and other books are increasingly available in libraries.

As editor it remains only to thank all the contributors who gave so freely and willingly of their precious time to help the Working Party. Not all the contributors are members of Shap, yet everyone felt able to lend their considerable scholarship to support the publication of the book. Whatever flaws the book may have must lie with the editor rather than with the individual contributors. I should also mention my family, which has borne with an occasionally absent-minded member, and my secretary, Judy Thursby, who has dealt with an enormous amount of work with efficiency and patience.

Alan Brown, Chichester 1986

1 Introduction

GEOFFREY PARRINDER

Religious believers may be expected to pray, meditate or perform some pious act each day in all the major historical and literary religions, and probably most others. Certain times and places are designated as being of particular significance, calling for devotion to a deity or holy being. Special days are prescribed for feasting or penitence. The observance of these occasions is important to the devout worshipper, and his or her participation may require absence from work or school, for a whole day or part of a day.

Absence from work for a religious festival is a holiday in the original sense of 'holy day', and indeed, normal work may be forbidden at such times. Such absence is, however, difficult to understand unless the employer or teacher has some knowledge of the religious requirement, and some idea of how important or obligatory the festival may be. In a multi-racial and multi-religious society, therefore, religious festivals and calendars are also of importance to all those who need to be aware of the customs of employees and pupils.

In many parts of the world, notably Asia, diverse religious communities have lived side by side for centuries, influencing each other's beliefs and practices, and often sharing festivals. This sharing continues today so that, for example, many non-Christians send Christmas cards, often with motifs from their own religion. In India cards showing Krishna and the milkmaids present a sort of 'Happy Krishnas'; in Japan mechanical dolls beat out *Jingle Bells* or *Silent Night*, but change to Chinese music for the New Year. In the West, on the other hand, there has not until recently been such religious diversity apart from the presence of small communities of Jews. The situation is now changing and increasing numbers of different religious communities have developed. In Britain alone there are more than two hundred mosques, more than fifty Sikh temples, and one hundred and fifty Buddhist societies have been listed, though they are mostly small study groups.

1

Religious festivals have widely differing characteristics: a Christian holy day may be observed from dawn to dusk, only in the morning or evening, or at a church service; Jewish holy days start at dusk and continue until dusk the next day. The Muslim fast of Ramadan need not involve absence from work, but it demands abstinence from all food and drink during the hours of daylight for a whole lunar month, and this may seriously affect work. In northern countries this requirement implies great self-discipline if Ramadan falls during the long days of summer in the solar calendar.

Feasts and festivals

In early English the word 'festival' was often used as an adjective, as in 'festival high day', but now it seems to have taken over noun usage, as in 'harvest festival'. But the word 'feast' is useful to show that an occasion is one for rejoicing, as opposed to a fast. After the fast of Lent, an annual observance and traditionally penitential, came the feast of Easter. In both the Jewish and Christian Bibles the Passover, like other celebrations, is called a feast. The feast was a time of celebration, even merry-making, but perhaps nowadays we tend to think of a feast as solely concerned with eating and drinking in large quantities, so it may be more helpful to use the term festival, which suggests more spiritual occupations.

Festivals are of different kinds, the most frequent being weekly celebrations for communal worship. The Christian Sunday has been observed on the first day of the week, in the Hebrew and Gregorian calendars, as a regular commemoration of the Resurrection of Christ which was held to have occurred on 'the first day of the week'. It seems that the first Christians (as Jews) kept Saturday Sabbath and also the Sunday, but in 321 the emperor Constantine made Sunday into a general holiday. A few Christian sects, such as the Seventh Day Adventists and some early Puritans, have observed the Saturday Sabbath, and Victorian Christians often spoke of Sunday as the Sabbath. It is curious that western European languages generally retain ancient pagan names for the days of the week: Sunday is the 'day of the Sun' worship, interpreted by Christians as dedicated to the 'Sun of Righteousness'.

The Jewish Sabbath, from Friday sunset to Saturday sunset, is the seventh day, 'the Sabbath of the Lord'. Sabbath means 'cessation' or 'rest', recalling the cessation of the work of the Creator on the seventh day, which God 'blessed and hallowed'. The Jewish Sabbath, like the Christian Sunday, is the chief festival and the Ten Commandments decree that no work should be done on that day, an injunction which has been observed by Jews, with different interpretations of the kind or time of work. The Muslim Friday, Jum'ah, is the 'day of assembly' on which males gather for worship at midday in the chief mosque. It is not mentioned as such in the Qur'an, but according to Traditions, the Prophet was said to have established this day by divine command. Legend has it that on this day Adam entered and left Paradise, and that it will be the day of resurrection. But Friday is not a whole day of obligatory abstention from work for Muslims, provided they have time to recite the prescribed prayers.

In other religions there may be less general regular worship in weekly periods, or little widespread obligation to observe such festivals. In parts of West Africa there is a seven-day week, as among the Akan of Ghana, or a four-day week, as among the Yoruba of Nigeria. Each day may be named after a particular deity, but worship is imposed only upon the special worshippers of that divinity. However in Ghana there was a general taboo against working on the land on Thursday, the day of the Earth Mother, which caused conflict for Christian converts who were also supposed to abstain from work on Sunday and so suffered a double economic deprivation.

The Buddhist Uposatha seems to have originated as a fortnightly fast day on the days of the new and full moons, when monks recited the rules of their order. This became extended to weekly meetings at four phases of the moon, with attendance of the laity also. There were expositions of teachings in monasteries and pagodas, and in modern times 'Sunday' or Dharma schools teach Buddhist children and adults, and there may be congregational worship.

Weekly worship may be a 'day of obligation', in Christian parlance, or a 'Red Letter Day', meaning one that was indicated in red ink in church calendars, like other important feasts. Similar obligation applies to the Jewish Sabbath and the Muslim Friday worship, and in varying degrees in other religions. Although the obligation may involve attending a place of worship and abstaining from ordinary work, the day is still a feast. It is an occasion for joy in creation, resurrection or worship, and therefore a sad or negative Sabbath negates its purpose.

The growing worldwide adoption of the Gregorian calendar, together with the English tradition of the weekend, extends the worship or rest day and provides a longer holiday for celebrating other religious events. Sikhs, Hindus and Buddhists living in the West often defer the celebration of their feasts to the nearest weekend, when they can be sure of free time and communal meeting.

Natural cycles and festivals

Cycles of months and seasons provided the basis for the earliest calendars and religious celebrations were fixed accordingly. The phases of the moon were calculated as four seven-day periods or weeks in a month (a word cognate with 'moon'). Where the moon was deified (in the West 'Moon-day' follows 'Sun-day') chronology was linked to religion. In ancient Sumeria the moon god, Sin, was called Lord of the Month.

The cycle of the sun, or rather the earth's movements round the sun, causes the seasons of spring, summer, autumn and winter in the northern hemisphere where all the great religions arose. The solar year was of great importance for the development of agriculture and in Egypt, where a solar calendar was used at least as early as 2776 BCE, this was connected with the annual flooding of the river Nile on which agriculture depended.

Various systems of chronology came into use: in Judaism time is reckoned from creation, in Christianity from the calculated date of the birth of Christ, and in Islam from the Hijra or Hegira, Muhammad's migration from Mecca to Medina (622 CE). Such chronologies are often called Linear systems: time is measured from a fixed point and progresses in a line to a climax, the end of the era or of the world. Indian chronologies, on the other hand, are based on a Cyclic view of time, in which there is a rise, maturation and decline, followed by a rebirth in another cycle. Eschatology, the 'doctrine of the last things', was fitted on to the linear system as a climax, and also to the cyclic with the end of each period.

Various calendars are discussed in connection with the different religions discussed in the following chapters of this book; here it suffices to note the lunar or solar calculations. In both calendrical systems, the beginning of the year is often marked with festivals of supplication or thanksgiving. The New Year is still celebrated in China and Japan as a time of cleansing and prayer for the future. Traditionally in China this occurs at the beginning of the first lunar month of the year, but in Japan, where the Gregorian calendar is in widespread use, it occurs at the beginning of January. In India, Divali, the Festival of Lights, is a new year festival addressed to Lakshmi, the goddess of wealth and prosperity. Houses are spring-cleaned, presents are sent to friends, and businessmen open new account books with prayers for success in the coming year. The Jewish New Year in the month of Tishri (September-October) is followed by the Day of Atonement, with penitence for the past and prayers for the future. On the other hand most Christians and Muslims, apart from the Shi'a, have made little of the New Year, concentrating their celebrations on their own particular festivals.

Christmas is one of the clearest examples of the adaptation of a festival from one religion into another. Since the Bible gave Christians no indication of the date of birth of Jesus, it was not celebrated till the third century. The Philocalian calendar, a list of Roman bishops named after an artist of that name, mentioned the observance in Rome in 336 of Christ's birth on 25 December. This coincided with the winter solstice, celebrated by the pagan festival Natalis Solis Invicti (Birthday of the Unconquered Sun), and Christ was now regarded in this light. The winter solstice, the darkest and coldest time in northern latitudes, was the natural new year, as it would give way to longer days and warmer weather. Thus Christmas was a new year festival and in recent times in the West the period of festivity has extended, merging with the calendrical new year to make a long holiday of ten days or so. In Eastern Orthodox Churches the birth of Christ was celebrated on 6 January, but it was still a new year festival.

After the New Year other festivals were celebrated in accordance with the pattern of nature, especially at springtime and harvest. Rituals were performed, and still are in Africa and the West Indies, asking permission of the spirit of the earth for digging the ground and for blessing on the seed. Then thanks were offered when the seeds produced fruit, and the firstfruits were offered to the appropriate divinities. The Jewish Passover perhaps incorporated a sacrifice of the first lambs in spring, which was said to be a substitute for the firstborn male child. The Christian Lent was calculated back from Easter, but its very name in English was probably related to the 'lengthening' of the days in spring. The date of Easter varies, falling on the Sunday after the first full moon after the spring equinox, in keeping with the biblical account of the time of the Crucifixion. According to the Venerable Bede the name of Easter was derived from Eostre, an Anglo-Saxon spring goddess.

The Jewish Shavuot, the Feast of Weeks, called Pentecost in Greek as the 'fiftieth' day after Passover, was the time when the firstfruits of the wheat harvest were presented to God. The Christian Lammas, still observed as a quarter-day in Scotland, was the Loaf Mass on 1 August, when bread made from the first ripe corn in these colder latitudes was consecrated at Mass. Harvest festivals have remained popular even in urban societies where there is little contact with seedtime and harvest. Rather mechanically, harvest festivals in September or October have spread to tropical Africa where the firstfruits and harvest have occurred in other months.

The worship of the sun seems to have been chiefly the concern of the cold northern regions, since in the tropics the sun is ever oppressively present and does not need to be implored to return north after a winter. There were sun festivals in ancient Europe, such as the Celti Samhain, (Summer End), when fires were lit to strengthen the ailing sun. Bonfires in November and December may perpetuate this custom. In Japan, another northern country, the greatest deity is Amaterasu, the sun goddess from whom came the imperial line. Mythology tells of her struggles in eclipse, darkness and winter; her shrine at Isé is the greatest of all for Shinto Japan.

Sacred history

The Semitic religions (Judaism, Christianity and Islam) are often called historical but their history is sacred, imposing a religious meaning upon events as upon the natural year. Other Asian religions such as Hinduism, Buddhism and Taoism may appear to be less factual, but they also have sacred history which mediates salvation. Mircea Eliade, who has written extensively on the subject calls a 'hierophany' a manifestation of the sacred.

'Every manifestation of the sacred takes place in some historical situation. Every hierophany we look at is also an historical fact.'

M. Eliade, *Patterns in Comparative Religion*, 1958, p 2

The Jewish Passover (*Pesah*) is primarily associated with the deliverance of the Hebrew people from captivity in Egypt at the Exodus led by Moses. Eating the sacrificial lamb united families and larger groups, and bound them to God whose angel had 'passed over' the Israelites when the first-born of the Egyptians were slain. At communal gatherings the sacred history is regularly recounted and confirmed.

Easter had as background the Passover, as well as Eostre, but its Christian significance lies in the Resurrection of Christ, leading on to Pentecost when the Holy Spirit descended on the apostles. The latter was called White Sunday in England, as a time of baptism of white-robed candidates, though it also suggests another link with spring in the new birth of baptism.

The new year festival Muharram is not a great festival for Sunni Muslims, who form the great majority of the religion, except for the fast on the tenth and final day, which is given some historical association as the day when Noah left the ark. But for Shi'a Islam this period is pre-eminent, both historical and salvation-history. It celebrates the martyrdom of Husain, son of Ali and grandson of Muhammad. At the end of ten days of celebration, passion plays enact the sufferings and death of Husain and his intercession for the salvation of believers. The two major Islamic festivals come at the end of the fast of Ramadan and in the month of pilgrimage, with sacrifices and confessions which are observed all over the Islamic world.

Buddhism would seem to be more historical than Hinduism, though the Buddhist scriptures which record the teachings of the Buddha and the events in his life were not recorded until some centuries after his death, and were often altered or enlarged. The life of Gautama, the Buddha of this present long era, is especially revered. The full moon of Wesak or Vaisakha, in April/May, is widely celebrated for the birth, renunciation, enlightenment and *parinirvana* of the Buddha. Mahayana Buddhism also reveres other holy beings, and in Japan the native reformer Nichiren is honoured and his life commemorated by powerful modern sects.

In Hinduism not only is Divali a new year festival, but the Holi festival in spring links up with ancient growing and fertility ceremonies. Yet it is connected with the loves of Krishna and Radha, and the salvation-history of the victory of Krishna over demons. Dashera in September/October recalls both the victory of the Mother Goddess, Durga, over evil and the fight of the avatar Rama with the demon Ravana. Pasteboard effigies of Ravana are packed with fire-works and exploded with fiery arrows from Rama to demonstrate the triumph of good.

Sacred history is re-enacted in rituals, and because the festival is a feast and a sharing, it requires participants, and so absence from daily work. The action of the liturgy illustrates the distinctive character of sacred history, the difference of the religious calendar from the secular, and the move from the secular into the sacred sphere. The ritual is not a mere repetition of a past event, but a living experience on a higher plane than everyday life.

'Every ritual has the character of happening *now*, at this very moment. The time of the event that the ritual commemorates or re-enacts is made *present*, "re-presented" so to speak, however far back it may have been in ordinary reckoning.'

M. Eliade, *Patterns in Comparative Religion*, 1958, p 392

This interpretation may be illustrated from the various names given to the distinctive Christian liturgy. It is called Eucharist (Thanks-giving) from the Greek, or Mass from the Latin words of 'dismissal' at the end, though the words may suggest the eternal nature of the rite. Protestants who speak of the Last Supper stress the memorial aspect of the ceremony, but it is significant that the only New Testament term is the Lord's Supper (I Corinthians 11:20), which indicates the constant presence of the Lord among his followers, a feeling that is preserved also in the term Holy Communion.

So Eliade continues,

'Christ's passion, death and resurrection are not simply *remembered* during the services of Holy Week; they really happen *then* before the eyes of the faithful. And a convinced Christian must feel that he is *contemporary* with these trans-historic events, for, by being re-enacted, the time of the theophany becomes actual.'

The purpose of religious worship is not simply to remember the past, but to experience the presence of God here and now.

Similarly during Muharram, Shi'ite Muslims identify themselves with the suffering Husain and vilify his persecutors. It was no sinecure to act the villainous parts in these passion plays, for at times the audience tried to lynch the actors. But the purpose of the play, its salvation value, was declared in the closing words with which the archangel Gabriel delivered the key of intercession with God to Husain.

'Go thou and deliver from the flames every one who has in his life-time shed but a single tear for thee. Bear each and all with thee to Paradise.'

E. G. Parrinder, *Worship in the World's Religions*, 1961, p 198

Sacred times

Religious rituals are necessary to the existence of any faith, expressing its doctrines in action. Therefore believers are justified in claiming absence from work to take part in sacred life.

A change from work is a human necessity: 'The Sabbath was made for man.' Even on the trade-union level the need for a break in toil is recognised. Arguments about Sunday closing are complicated because of the many interests involved. One need not share the sabbatarianism of the Lord's Day Observance Society to see the dangers to workers in having no fixed time of rest from toil. Even a secular society needs its celebrations, although a 'bank holiday' must be one of the most profane terms for a time of refreshment and renewal. The disagreement of the Church and State in England as to whether a service after the Falklands war was to be a triumphal celebration or a search for reconciliation, illustrates the clash of traditional religion with resurgent patriotism. But both testified to the need for holiday and representational ritual.

The problems of employers and teachers facing demands for religious holidays are especially difficult in view of the many different religions in our society but, as has been suggested, there is often a willingness to defer celebrations to the weekend, and this is a further reason for safeguarding the rights of workers to a Sunday holiday.

There are also longer holidays, and fortunately the automation of industry helps to allow extended summer holidays for many workers. But holidays have always been part of religious life, and in many religions pilgrimages have formed an important element in occasional or annual celebrations. Six hundred years ago Chaucer began the *Canterbury Tales* with a description of this custom:

> 'Whan that Aprille with his shoures sote
> The droghte of Marche hath perced to the rote . . .
> Than longen folk to goon on pilgrimages . . .
> And specially, from every shires end
> Of Engelond to Caunterbury they wende,
> The holy blisful martir for to seke,
> That hem hath holpen, whan that they were seke.'

In England they waited for fine weather, the rising sap of spring inciting to ritual pilgrimage to the shrine of Thomas Becket, and they must have saved up money like modern people stinting themselves for a summer holiday.

Modern European holidays may seem to have little that is holy about them. They simply show a need for change, if not rest. There may be residual or burgeoning faith in many who visit cathedrals or tramp the moors and hills, but there are secular pilgrimages which border on the religious. The multitudes that queue to revere charismatic leaders at the tombs of Lenin or Mao illustrate something of the religious trappings of Communism. And many traditionally religious pilgrimages hold their own or are even more popular owing to the ease of modern travel. Pilgrimages to Lourdes, Fatima or Israel have more participants than ever. About a million pilgrims go annually to Mecca, to make the visit which is a religious duty for all Muslims at least once in a lifetime, and they travel not only on foot or camel as in the past, but by lorry or ship or aeroplane. Over two million go every year to Vrindaban to feel the 'everlasting bodily presence of Krishna', making the round of sacred sites dedicated to his life and actions. Ten million, aided by all the machinery of modern transport, are said to visit the grounds and shrines at Isé in Japan dedicated to the goddess Amaterasu.

Pilgrimages are communal and often jolly, as the *Canterbury Tales* demonstrate, even if their climax is solemn or their purpose penitential. Their popularity, past and present, may be partly the result of the restless nomadic nature of mankind. But there is also a deeper feeling, an attempt to transcend the limitations of time and space and enter the eternal sphere, re-enacting the pilgrimage and triumph of the deity.

Sacred places

Not only are certain times sacred, but so also are certain places and they need to be preserved.

'Surely the Lord is in this place; and I knew it not. How dreadful is this place! This is none other but the house of God, and this is the gate of heaven.'

Genesis 28: 16–17

In these verses Jacob refers to Beth-el, 'the house of God', a famous sanctuary down the ages. It was at this royal shrine that Jeroboam erected a golden calf and Amos prophesied against injustice.

Eliade writes also of 'kratophany', meaning a 'manifestation of power'. He says that

'Every kratophany and hierophany whatsoever transforms the sacred place where it occurs; hitherto profane, it is thenceforward a sacred area.'

'In actual fact, the place is never "chosen" by man; it is merely discovered by him; in other words, the sacred place in some way or another reveals itself to him.'

M. Eliade, *Patterns in Comparative Religion*, 1958, pp 367, 369

The subject of sacred places, whether they be churches, synagogues, mosques or temples, is too vast to explore here, the present concern being with festivals and sacred times. But it may be noted in passing that sacred places have always been necessary to religion, and that new religious communities may manage for a time with a private room or secular hall, but will eventually want their own building, consecrated formally and hallowed by worship. Time, work and money will be needed for the erection of such a holy building, and absence from work or school may be requested.

Problems may arise in the registration of a building as a place of religious worship, which allows for solemnisation of marriages and exemption from rates. Organisations such as Scientology have been unsuccessful in obtaining registration, on the grounds that they are not a religion, while the Unification Church (Moonies) has faced demands for its removal from registration. Other problems have faced more established churches. Whether it is desirable or permissible for a church to loan or sell its own buildings to the adherents of another religion is a matter for debate. Permission is sometimes refused, or allowed grudgingly by leasing an 'ancillary' building rather than the church. It has been suggested that Hindus, for example, might be allowed the use of a church hall for weddings provided no religious words are used – an impossible condition.

There is in the East End of London a religious building first erected by Huguenot refugees from France. They worked hard,

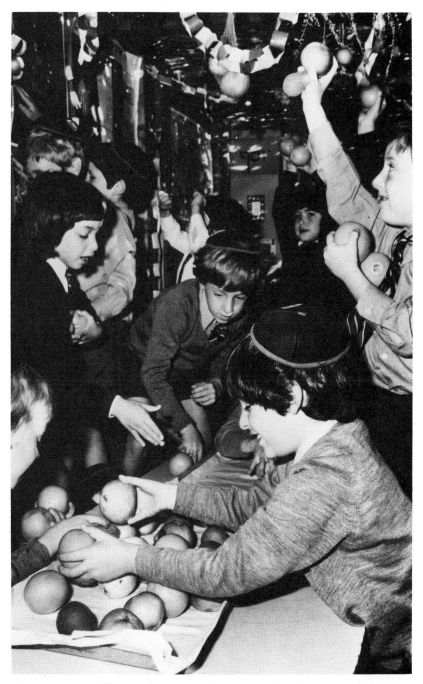

Tabernacles (Succoth) is a joyous and exciting time in the Jewish calendar. The succah (booth) is like a hut with no roof and is decorated with foliage and fruit.

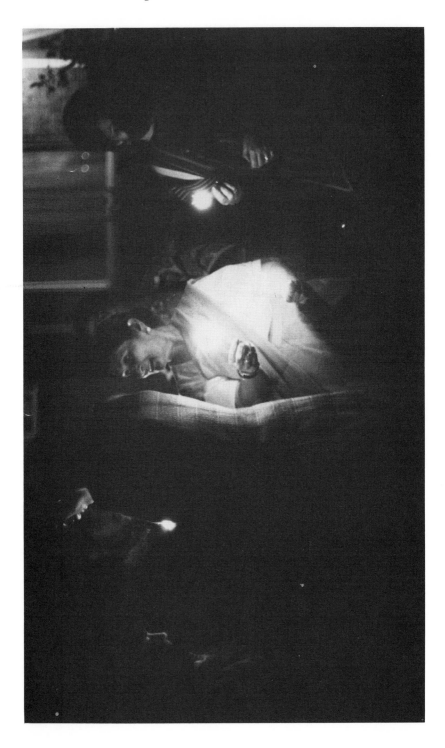

The Hindu festival of Durga Puja, in eastern India, marks the victory of the goddess Durga over the Buffalo Demon; in other parts it marks the victory of Rama over the demon Ravana.

Opposite: *Lakshmi, goddess of wealth, is worshipped by Hindus at Divali. The festival marks the return home of Rama, people light oil lamps and place them along their balconies and windows.*

Brightly coloured and gaily decorated kites provide a traditional way of celebrating festivals in China.

Opposite: *The celebration at a Zoroastrian gahambar involves the sacred flame and the blessing of food. This rare picture captures the intensity of the occasion.*

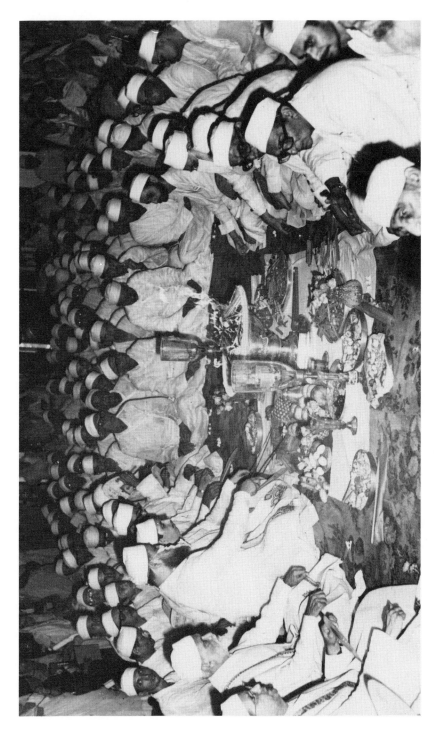

prospered, and moved away to more prosperous areas. The building was sold to poor Methodists, who also worked hard, prospered and moved away. It was then taken over by Jewish refugees from eastern Europe, and became a synagogue whose members again worked hard, prospered and moved away. The latest sale is to Muslims from Bengal, and it has become a mosque. No doubt they will work hard and migrate to more prosperous areas. But since the building is listed as a historic monument, dedicated to religious purposes, it may be wondered who will be the next occupants to call upon the name of their God there.

There are economic as well as religious considerations connected with sacred buildings, and within a religious community itself there may be tensions over the proper purposes of the building. There may be struggles between the concepts of the place of worship as a house of God and as a house of the people, between adoration and fellowship; but these are matters which the community has to resolve.

The Gregorian Calendar

Reference has been made to cycles of months, seasons, years and ages, and it remains to consider the different calendars in use. The chapters on the different religions discuss the calendars used in each faith, but most refer to the Gregorian or New Style Calendar; this has been adopted worldwide, but in varying degrees.

The word 'calendar' comes from the Latin *kalendae*, from a root meaning 'call' or 'proclaim': in ancient Rome the first day of the new month was proclaimed on the appearance of the new moon. Like nearly all other calendars, except for the Egyptian, it was a lunar calculation. The ancient Roman year of 355 days was shorter than the solar year which depended upon the seasons, and additional days had to be intercalated between lunar and solar.

In 46 BCE Julius Caesar introduced a year of 365 days, with an extra day every fourth or leap year. The length of the year was then reckoned according to the sun and seasons. In the first half of the sixth century CE the monk Dionysius Exiguus adapted this calendar to Christian usage by dating it from Anno Domini, the 'year of our Lord', that is the year after the birth of Christ. The abbreviations AD for the Christian era, and BC for Before Christ, remain in use, but in inter-religious and many international publications they tend to be replaced by CE for the Common Era, and BCE, Before the Common Era. Similarly in the Islamic world the initials AH have

Opposite: *The White Heron Dance Procession takes place each November in Tokyo. The heron is a symbol of beauty and good fortune in Japan.*

been used of their era, the Anno Hegirae or Hijrae, the year of the migration (Hegira, Hijra) from Mecca to Medina.

The Julian Calendar was not quite accurately calculated and there was a discrepancy with the solar year, which amounted to ten days by 1582 when Pope Gregory XIII proclaimed his New Style or Gregorian Calendar which has continued in use to this day. At first only Roman Catholic states accepted the new dating, but Protestant countries gradually fell into line, Britain accepting the continental custom in 1752. France abandoned it for twelve years in favour of a revolutionary calendar but then reverted to Gregorian usage. Turkey and Russia adopted the Gregorian Calendar in 1917, but most Orthodox churches in Russia and the Balkans did not conform till 1923.

Proposals for a World Calendar have been presented to the League of Nations and the United Nations Assembly, which would give equal quarters, an extra day at the end of the year, and another extra day in summer every leap year, but these have not been adopted. The use of the New Style or Gregorian Calendar has spread universally along with western imperialism and commerce, but there have been many variations in its adoption or part-adoption.

Religious festivals in many lands are still often based on ancient lunar calendars, but in the Islamic world and the Indian sub-continent official and commercial publications often print the date in both lunar and Gregorian systems. In China three calendrical systems are in use: the lunar, the Chinese solar, and the Gregorian solar. Urban society in Japan has adopted western usage more thoroughly, for example observing the new year at the beginning of the Gregorian Calendar, as opposed to China and much of rural Japan, which retain the old systems.

Religious festivals are important, but the times of their occurrence are complicated. In the Christian West most major festivals are celebrated on Sundays or public holidays. But the adoption of Sunday as a day of rest from work was a Christian regulation, and does not fit in with Jewish, Islamic or other systems. Easter and Whitsun fell on Sundays and helped to determine these days as public holidays. Other festivals, such as Christmas, were also introduced from the Christian tradition and, although the dates varied, these became Days of Obligation for both church and state in the West.

Nowadays the diverse religious scene, in both the West and the East, requires more understanding of various religious customs and adjustments in school and work accordingly. As Jews observed their Sabbath on the seventh day in western countries, but worked on Sunday, so other religious communities may do the same and they will expect to be treated with tolerance and respect.

2 Baha'i Festivals

PHILIP HAINSWORTH

Introduction

As the principle of the Oneness of Mankind is the pivot around which all the teachings of the Baha'i Faith revolve, Baha'is feel that it is essential to have one Calendar which could be recognised and accepted the world over. Such a Calendar, with its Festivals and Holy Days, is found in Baha'i Scripture.

While generally observing the calendars of the countries in which the believers live, the expanding Baha'i world community uses internally, and seeks to encourage the use of, this new Calendar. Baha'is not only observe their own Holy Days and Festivals as widely as the laws of the countries in which they reside will permit, but they actively work for the statutory recognition of those Holy Days. Today the Baha'i Holy Days are recognised officially in well over sixty countries.

In order to appreciate fully the Festivals in the Baha'i Faith it is necessary to examine in depth the Baha'i Calendar, to look at the eleven Holy Days and describe the background to the holiest and most significant of all Baha'i Festivals, the Feast of Ridvan. Other Festivals in the Baha'i year and the nineteen day feasts will also be described, as will the Baha'i month of fasting and the Intercalary days.

As any form of ritual is forbidden in the Baha'i Faith, there are no photographs to illustrate how a particular Feast or Anniversary is commemorated. All are planned by the local or national Baha'i administrative bodies (there being no clergy nor priesthood in the Baha'i Faith) in a manner most suitable to the time, place and environment where the occasion is to be celebrated. The variety of methods is almost infinite but the unity in spirit and dedication is worldwide. Some Holy Days may feature a gathering of Baha'is in a Baha'i house of worship (in the few countries where presently they exist), or in a home, hired hall, tent, igloo or, as frequently happens in tropical countries, under a shady tree.

The Baha'i Calendar

This was inaugurated by the Bab, the Prophet Herald of the Baha'i Faith, and it was then known as the Badi Calendar. Baha'u'llah (pronounced with the emphasis on the second *a*, *Bahaa ulla*), the Founder of the Baha'i Faith, ratified it and stated that it should commence with the year of the Declaration of the Bab (1844). The major features are:

1 It follows the solar year and there are no moveable feasts.
2 The Baha'i day starts and ends at sunset.
3 In the Baha'i year there are nineteen months each of nineteen days.
4 There being a total of 361 days in the nineteen Baha'i months, four intercalary days in ordinary years and five in leap years remain; these lie between the eighteenth and nineteenth Baha'i months.
5 The year begins with the vernal equinox, so that New Year's Day is the first day of Spring, which normally falls on 21 March.
6 The days of the month have the same names as the months themselves, and all are names of the attributes of God. (This effectively establishes a new approach to the names of the days and months now most commonly used, which in older calendars have associations preventing them from being universally acceptable.) Where a further division into seven-day weeks is considered essential, even these days are named in like manner.
7 The years following the date of the Bab's revelation are divided into cycles of nineteen years each, and each such cycle is called a *Vahid*. Nineteen cycles constitute a period called *kull-i-shay*. The numerical value of the word *Vahid* is 19, that of *kull-i-shay* 361. *Vahid* signifies unity, and is symbolic of the unity of God.

The names of the months

Month	Arabic name	Translation	First days
1st	Baha	Splendour	March 21
2nd	Jalal	Glory	April 9
3rd	Jamal	Beauty	April 28
4th	'Azamat	Grandeur	May 17
5th	Nur	Light	June 5
6th	Rahmat	Mercy	June 24
7th	Kalimat	Words	July 13
8th	Kamal	Perfection	August 1
9th	Asma	Names	August 20
10th	'Izzat	Might	September 8

The names of the months (continued)

Month	Arabic name	Translation	First days
11th	Mashiyyat	Will	September 27
12th	'Ilm	Knowledge	October 16
13th	Qudrat	Power	November 4
14th	Qawl	Speech	November 23
15th	Masá'il	Questions	December 12
16th	Sharaf	Honour	December 31
17th	Sultan	Sovereignty	January 19
18th	Mulk	Dominion	February 7
19th	'Ala'	Loftiness	March 2

Ayyam-i-Ha (Intercalary Days) 26 February to 1 March inclusive
– four in ordinary and five in leap years.

Source: *Baha'i World*, Baha'i World Centre, vol XVII, p 388

The names of the days of the week

Days	Arabic name	English name	Translation
1st	Jalal	Saturday	Glory
2nd	Jamal	Sunday	Beauty
3rd	Kamal	Monday	Perfection
4th	Fidal	Tuesday	Grace
5th	'Idal	Wednesday	Justice
6th	Istijlal	Thursday	Majesty
7th	Istiqlal	Friday	Independence

Source: *Baha'i World*, Baha'i World Centre, vol XVII, p 388

The names of the year in each cycle

1 Alif	A		11 Bahhaj	Delightful
2 Ba'	B		12 Javab	Answer
3 Ab	Father		13 Ahad	Single
4 Dal	D		14 Vahhab	Bountiful
5 Bab	Gate		15 Vidad	Affection
6 Vav	V		16 Badi'	Beginning
7 Abad	Eternity		17 Bahi	Luminous
8 Jad	Generosity		18 Abha	Most Luminous
9 Baha	Splendour			
10 Hubb	Love		19 Vahid	Unity

Source: *Baha'i World*, Baha'i World Centre, vol XVII, p 389

Holy Days

There are eleven Holy Days and it is obligatory for Baha'is to commemorate them. On nine of these days work should be suspended. 'Abdu'l-Baha (1844–1921), the eldest son of Baha'u'llah and his appointed successor, wrote:

'These nine days are the only ones on which work connected with trade, commerce, industry and agriculture is not allowed. In like manner, work connected with any form of employment, whether Government or other-wise, should be suspended.'

Baha'i World, Baha'i World Centre, vol XVII, p 387

Shoghi Effendi, Guardian of the Baha'i Faith (1897–1957), through his secretary, wrote:

'Believers who have independent businesses or shops should refrain from working on these days. Those who are in government employ should, on religious grounds, make an effort to be excused from work; all believers, whoever their employers, should do likewise. If a government, or other employers, refuse to grant them these days off, they are not required to forfeit their employment, but they should make every effort to have the independent status of their Faith recognised and their right to hold their own religious Holy Days acknowledged.'

Principles of Baha'i Administration, Baha'i Publishing Trust, 1976, p 55

The Baha'i Holy Days

Days on which work is suspended

1 Naw-Ruz – New Year's Day; first day of Spring; the vernal equinox:	21/22 March
2 First day of the Festival of Ridvan:	21 April
3 Ninth day of the Festival of Ridvan:	29 April
4 Twelth (and last) day of the Festival of Ridvan:	2 May
5 The Anniversary of the Declaration of the Bab:	23 May
6 The Anniversary of the Ascension of Baha'u'llah:	29 May
7 The Anniversary of the Martyrdom of the Bab:	9 July
8 The Anniversary of the Birth of the Bab:	20 October
9 The Anniversary of the Birth of Baha'u'llah:	12 November

The Baha'i Holy Days (continued)

Days on which work is not prohibited

10 The Day of the Covenant (Fête Day of
'Abdu'l-Baha):   26 November
11 The Anniversary of the Passing of
'Abdu'l-Baha: 28 November

Source: Baha'i World, Baha'i World Centre, vol XVII, p 387

The festivals

The Feast of Ridvan (21 April–2 May)

The Feast of Ridvan (pronounced *Rizwan*) is the most sacred and important of Baha'i Festivals. In the authentic history of the first Baha'i Century Shoghi Effendi opens his chapter on the Declaration of Baha'u'llah's Mission with this sentence:

'The arrival of Baha'u'llah in the Najibiyyih Garden, subsequently designated by His followers the Garden of Ridvan, signalises the commencement of what has come to be recognised as the holiest and most significant of all Baha'i festivals, the festival commemorating the Declaration of His Mission to His companions.'

Shoghi Effendi, *God Passes By*, 1945, p 151

Baha'u'llah, an exile from His native land, Iran, arrived in Baghdad, Iraq then a Turkish province – on 8 April, 1853. Gradually His fame spread and those among the Muslim clergy and the Turkish and Iranian Governments conspired to have Him exiled again. While still commemorating Naw-Ruz (New Year), 1863 in the outskirts of Baghdad, Baha'u'llah was 'invited' to Constantinople. On the thirty-second day after Naw-Ruz He moved to the Garden of Ridvan to prepare for the first stage of His long journey on horseback to the Turkish capital.

In another paragraph Shoghi Effendi commented:

'That historic day, forever after designated as the first day of the Ridvan Festival, the culmination of innumerable farewell visits which friends and acquaintances, of every class and denomination, had been paying Him, was one the like of which the inhabitants of Baghdad had rarely beheld . . . . The muezzin had just raised the afternoon call to prayer when Baha'u'llah entered the Najibiyyih Garden, where He tarried twelve days before His final departure from the city. There His friends and companions, arriving in successive waves, attained His presence and bade Him, with feelings of profound sorrow, their last farewell.'

Shoghi Effendi, *God Passes By*, 1945, pp 148–9

It was during the twelve days He spent in the Ridvan Garden that He announced to His followers that He was not only the One promised by the Bab, but the 'Promised One' of all religions.

'The nineteen years, constituting the first *Vahid*, preordained in the Persian Bayan by the pen of the Bab, had been completed . . .

'The Bab's own prophecy regarding the *Ridvan* (literally the "region or state of supreme bliss, paradise"), the scene of the unveiling of Baha'u'llah's transcendent glory, had been literally fulfilled . . .

'As to the significance of that declaration let Baha'u'llah Himself reveal to us its import. Acclaiming that historic occasion as the "most great festival", the "King of Festivals", the "Festival of God", He has, in His *Kitab-i-Aqdas*, characterised it as the Day whereon "all created things were immersed in the sea of purification", whilst in one of His specific Tablets, He has referred to it as the Day whereon "the breezes of forgiveness were wafted over the entire creation". "Rejoice, with exceeding gladness, O people of Baha!" He, in another Tablet, has written, "as ye call to remembrance the Day of supreme felicity, the Day whereon the Tongue of the Ancient of Days hath spoken, as He departed from His House proceeding to the Spot from which He shed up the whole of creation the splendours of His Name, the All-Merciful . . . The Divine Springtime is come, O Most Exalted Pen, for the Festival of the All-Merciful is fast approaching . . ."'

Shoghi Effendi, *God Passes By*, 1945, pp 151, 153–4

So important then is this twelve-day Festival that not only do the First, Ninth and Twelfth days form three out of the nine Holy Days on which work is suspended, but the First Day of Ridvan was selected by the Guardian as the day on which all local spiritual assemblies throughtout the Baha'i world were to be elected. The National Spiritual Assemblies, presently 143 in number and jointly constituting the Baha'i International Community, are also elected annually during this same Ridvan Festival. The Universal House of Justice, the supreme body of the Baha'i world, is also elected every five years during the Ridvan period.

New Year's Day, the birthday anniversaries of the Bab and Baha'u'llah, the Declaration of the Bab and the Day of the Covenant are all opportunities for demonstrating the essential joyousness of the Baha'i Faith. According to the needs of the community, their resources, the time of year and the local climate, there are happy gatherings of the believers, hospitality is extended, picnics are held and music and entertainment are enjoyed by the believers and the non-Baha'is who are invited to participate.

Opposite: *Worshippers attend the Shrine of the Bab at Haifa, Israel on Ridvan Holy Day (Ninth Day)*

New Year's Day (21 or 22 March)
Naw-Ruz (pronounced *Nawrooz*) or New Year's Day is the first Holy Day in the Baha'i calendar and is celebrated as such. It is also the first day of the first Baha'i month and therefore the day on which a Nineteen Day Feast (see below) is held. There are, therefore, two distinct activities carried out on this day.

Shoghi Effendi wrote through his secretary:

'Regarding Naw-Ruz: if the vernal equinox falls on 21 March before sunset, it is celebrated on that day. If at any time after sunset, Naw-Ruz will then, as stated by Baha'u'llah, fall on the twenty-second.'

Principles of Baha'i Administration, Baha'i Publishing Trust, 1976, p 57

The Anniversary of the Declaration of the Bab (23 May)
This Festival commemorates the Bab's revelation of His mission to His first disciple, Mulla Hussayn, in His home in Shiraz, Iran, about two hours after sunset on the night of 22/23 May, 1844. The Declaration of the Bab is of great historical significance to the Baha'is and the subject is dealt with in depth by many authors. (For the full authentic treatment, reference should be made to Shoghi Effendi, *God Passes By,*) 1945, chapter I.

The Anniversary of The Birth of the Bab (20 October)
This festival celebrates the Birth of the Bab in Shiraz, Iran in 1819.

The Anniversary of the Birth of Baha'u'llah (12 November)
This Festival celebrates the Birth of Baha'u'llah, the eldest son of Mirza Buzurg, a Persian nobleman, in Tehran in 1817. He was therefore two years older than the Bab, His Herald or Forerunner.

The Day of the Covenant (26 November)
This Festival is also known as the Fête Day of 'Abdu'l-Baha. He was born on 23 May 1844, and His birthday is celebrated as a Holy Day – the Declaration of the Bab.

The three other Holy Days are occasions when, with great dignity and feeling, believers remember the significance of the events in Baha'i history. This is enhanced by observing the anniversary at the exact hour of the occurrence of the event it commemorates.

The Anniversary of the Martyrdom of the Bab (9 July)
The Bab was executed at noon on 9 July 1850 in Tabriz, Iran. The Martyrdom of the Bab has unique value in the 'miracle' associated with it, witnessed by about ten thousand people. The Bab and one of His companions were strung up on the wall of the barracks in Tabriz, facing the square, and three ranks of soldiers, 750 in all,

fired at the two prisoners. When the dust cleared, the Bab had disappeared and His companion was standing by the wall unscathed. The bullets had merely severed the ropes. The Bab was found in the room He had occupied previously, completing the conversation with His amanuensis which had been interrupted when He had been taken for execution. 'Not until I have said to him all those things that I wish to say can any earthly power silence Me. Though all the world be armed against Me, yet shall it be powerless to deter Me from fulfilling, to the last word, My intention,' the Bab had stated when so interrupted. The colonel of the soldiers, a Christian, when he feared that carrying out his duty would provoke the wrath of God, had been assured by the Bab that if his intention be sincere, the Almighty would be able to relieve him of his perplexity. Remembering this assurance, the colonel was filled with awe and wonder and ordered his men to leave the barracks immediately. Another regiment under a different officer then carried out the execution. A detailed account of this event can be found in Shoghi Effendi, *God Passes By*, 1945.

The Anniversary of the Ascension of Baha'u'llah (29 May)
This occurred at Bahji, near Akka, in the Holy Land eight hours after sunset (3 a.m.) in 1892.

The Passing of 'Abdu'l-Baha (28 November)
This occurred an hour after midnight in 1921.

Fasting (2–20 March)
The Baha'i month of 'Ala' immediately precedes Naw-Ruz. For nineteen days during this nineteenth month of the year, the Baha'is abstain from all food and drink from sunrise to sunset each day. Shoghi Effendi, through his secretary, wrote:

'As regards fasting, it constitutes, together with the obligatory prayers, the two pillars that sustain the revealed Law of God. They act as stimulants to the soul, strengthen, revive, and purify it, and thus ensure its steady development.

'The ordinance of fasting is, as is the case with these three prayers, a spiritual and vital obligation enjoined by Baha'u'llah upon every believer who has attained the age of fifteen . . . .. It is essentially a period of meditation and prayer, of spiritual recuperation, during which the believer must strive to make the necessary readjustments in his inner life, and to refresh and reinvigorate the spiritual forces latent in his soul. Its significance and purposes are, therefore, fundamentally spiritual in character. Fasting is symbolic, and a reminder of abstinence from selfish and carnal desires.'

Principles of Baha'i Administration, Baha'i Publishing Trust, 1976, pp 8–9

Exemption from fasting is granted to those who are ill, over 70 years of age, pregnant and nursing women, and a few other categories of people such as those who are travelling or engaged in heavy labour. As the verb 'to drink' applies equally to 'smoking' in Arabic, those who do smoke must abstain during the same fasting period.

Intercalary Days (26 February–1 March)
The intercalary days (*ayyam-i-ha*) occur immediately before the Fast and follow the last day of the eighteenth month. They are days given to festivities, special hospitality, the giving of presents and the like.

THE NINETEEN DAY FEASTS (First day of each Baha'i month)
On the first day of each Baha'i month all members of the Baha'i community and any visiting Baha'is meet for prayers, consultation and social activity. The day has an important administrative function when the local administrative body reports on its work and consults on the progress of the Faith in the area, but it is also a deeply spiritual and joyous occasion and Baha'i children and youth participate. It is an occasion for Baha'is only.

A devotional period is followed by consultation with representatives of the local Spiritual Assembly. Decisions are taken to be passed for consideration by the Assembly, reports are made on the outcome of earlier recommendations, the Treasurer makes a report and the community's financial situation is discussed.

The consultation period is followed by some form of refreshment which may range from a glass of water to a full meal, depending upon the resources of the community. The host or hostess usually welcomes all the participants, prepares the devotional and serves the refreshments. An officer of the Assembly usually conducts the consultation period. Messages are presented from the World Centre, from the National Spiritual Assembly and its committees, from other communities and from absent friends. The precise conduct of each Feast may be planned by the local Assembly so that the maximum amount of good work is done in joy and unity and no set service or ritual is allowed to develop.

The following quotations from a compilation further clarify the purpose and significance of the Nineteen Day Feast. They also illustrate the basic principles underlying all Baha'i Feasts and Festivals and summarise their real objectives.

'This Feast was established by His Highness the Bab, to occur once in nineteen days. Likewise, the Blessed Perfection (Baha'u'llah) hath commanded, encouraged and reiterated it. Therefore, it hath the utmost importance. Undoubtedly you must give the greatest attention to its establishment and raise it to the highest point of importance, so

it may become continual and constant. The believers of God must assemble and associate with each other in the utmost love, joy and fragrance . . .'

'This Feast is a divine Feast. It is a Lord's supper. It attracts confirmation of God like a magnet. It is the cause of the enlightenment of hearts.'

('Abdu'l-Baha)

'With regard to your question concerning the Nineteen Day Feasts. These gatherings are no doubt of a special importance to the friends, as they have both a social and an administrative significance, and as such should be regularly attended by all confirmed believers. They should also be observed according to the Baha'i calendar every nineteen days.'

(Shoghi Effendi through his secretary)

'Ye have written as to the meetings of the friends, and how filled they are with peace and joy. Of course this is so; for wherever the spiritually-minded are gathered together, there in His beauty reigneth Baha'u'llah. Thus it is certain that such reunions will yield boundless happiness and peace.'

('Abdu'l-Baha)

Seeking the Light of the Kingdom, Baha'i Publishing Trust, 1975, pp 8–10, 12, 27

Table of Baha'i festivals

19 January   Nineteen Day Feast
7 February   Nineteen Day Feast
26 February–1 March   Intercalary Days
2 March   Nineteen Day Feast
2–20 March   Fasting
21 March   Nineteen Day Feast
21/22 March   New Year's Day (Work suspended)
9 April   Nineteen Day Feast
21 April–2 May   Feast of Ridvan (Work suspended 21 April, 29 April, 2 May)
28 April   Nineteen Day Feast
17 May   Nineteen Day Feast
23 May   The Anniversary of the Declaration of the Bab (Work suspended)
29 May   The Anniversary of the Ascension of Baha'u'llah (Work suspended)
5 June   Nineteen Day Feast
24 June   Nineteen Day Feast
9 July   The Anniversary of the Martyrdom of the Bab (Work suspended)

13 July   Nineteen Day Feast
1 August   Nineteen Day Feast
20 August   Nineteen Day Feast
8 September   Nineteen Day Feast
27 September   Nineteen Day Feast
16 October   Nineteen Day Feast
20 October   The Anniversary of the Birth of the Bab
   (Work suspended)
4 November   Nineteen Day Feast
12 November   The Anniversary of the Birth of Baha'u'llah
   (Work suspended)
23 November   Nineteen Day Feast
26 November   The Day of the Covenant
28 November   The Passing of 'Abdu'l-Baha
12 December   Nineteen Day Feast
31 December   Nineteen Day Feast

3 Buddhist Festivals

RICHARD GOMBRICH

Buddhism

Buddhists consider their religion to consist of the Three Jewels: the Buddha, the Doctrine he preached, and the Order of monks and nuns he founded.

THE BUDDHA

Buddha is a title, meaning 'Enlightened'. The Buddha attained enlightenment by realising the Truth, the Doctrine which he then went on to preach. In one sense, therefore, Buddhism began at the moment of the Buddha's enlightenment. On the other hand, the True Doctrine is always there, equally true whether anybody realises it and preaches it or not. Buddhists believe that though it is forgotten for long periods, every now and again another person is born who becomes enlightened (a Buddha) and preaches. For the Buddhist, therefore, Buddhism has no beginning in time; the series of Buddhas has neither beginning (for the world itself has no beginning) nor end. This makes Buddhism quite different from a 'historical' religion like Christianity, which is based on historical events like the crucifixion. For Buddhists, no historical fact is relevant to the truth of the doctrine they hold; it would not even matter if Gautama Buddha, the Buddha whom outsiders consider the historical founder of Buddhism, could be shown not to have existed.

Of course, he did exist. We know exactly where he lived, but we cannot be sure exactly when. He was born at Kapilavastu, on what is now the Nepali side of the border between Nepal and India, into a noble family who were members of a tribe called *Shakya*, which is why he is very often called *Shakyamuni*, meaning 'the Shakya sage'. He married and had a son, but at the age of 29 was overcome with concern at the sorrows of human life, especially at the inevitability of disease, decay and death. He left home, and for six years led a wandering life, trying to find some solution to these problems by undergoing physical hardship and learning to meditate. He fasted till he nearly died, but saw that this was useless. Only when he returned to a normal diet was he able to think things through calmly until he found the answer and became enlightened. This happened when he was sitting under a tree, which ever since has been known as the *Bodhi* tree, the Enlightenment tree. Though the original tree is long dead, its successor and descendant still stands at the spot, in the village of Bodh Gaya, in the state of Bihar in north-east India. The Buddha spent the remaining forty-five years of his life in and near Bihar – the name of the state actually means 'Buddhist monastery'. He delivered his first sermon in Varanasi (Benares) and continued to preach till his death at the age of 80.

The Buddha taught that salvation depends on one's own efforts alone. No god, no being can save you. He did not deny the existence of gods (in the plural), but considered them as a kind of supermen, powerful and comparatively happy beings who lived on earth or in the heavens, but would themselves have to die one day. They did not create the world (even if they thought they did). They did not reward or punish good or evil; that happened by a kind of natural law. The Buddha did not invent this moral law, which we have come to refer to as the law of *karma*; it is common to all Indian religions (with minor variations) and he inherited it from his environment. The law of *karma* goes hand in hand with belief in rebirth. It is all too obvious that good is not always rewarded nor evil punished in this life; and then there is the problem why people, for example young children, often suffer when they cannot be at fault. These apparent injustices are resolved by belief in the law of *karma*; any suffering you now undergo must be a punishment for a wrong you did, if not in this life then in a former one. If you do not get your just deserts in this life time, you will in a future one. This spectacle of endless rebirth horrified the Buddha; what he stressed was not so much the rebirth as the inevitable death following each cycle of rebirth. There seemed to be no end to suffering.

He thus took the law of *karma* as part of the law of the universe, of the Truth; but it was not this that he discovered when he became enlightened. What he discovered or rediscovered under the Bodhi tree he taught in his first sermon in the deer park at Benares, the sermon which is known as the Turning of the Wheel of the Law. He taught the Middle Way between self-indulgence and self-torture, both of which he said got you nowhere, and he taught the Four Noble Truths.

THE DOCTRINE

The Four Noble Truths are (1) suffering, (2) the origin of suffering, (3) the elimination of suffering, (4) the path leading to the elimination of suffering. 'Suffering' does not mean that there is nothing in life but pain. However, even pleasures are 'suffering' because they never last. Everything in life as we normally live it is unsatisfactory because even the good bits do not last; and they do not last, according to the Buddha, because they have no unchanging essence. And so everything has three characteristics: it is *unsatisfactory*, it is *impermanent* and it is *without essence*. These three features are all interconnected.

'The origin of suffering' is desire. Suffering is frustration of desire: if we did not want anything, we would not be disappointed. 'The elimination of suffering' is thus the elimination of desire. We are ablaze with the fires of the three roots of evil: greed, hatred and delusion. Greed and hatred are positive and negative desires, while delusion is our failure to understand the way things are, that is, unsatisfactory, impermanent and without essence. So our trouble is at the same time emotional (desire) and intellectual (delusion). The main thing we get wrong, and the most difficult to get right, is the understanding that we ourselves have no essence, no eternal or even unchanging core, nothing like what people call a 'soul'. If we examine ourselves we can find bodies and minds (which the Buddha analysed into perceptions, feelings of pleasure and pain, volitions and consciousness), but all of these change all the time. Nothing in us endures unchanged; our identity is just an idea, useful for practical life but a hindrance to salvation. We are selfish because we think 'that is mine', so desire, which is selfishness, also arises from the wrong notion of self. If only we can get rid of that wrong idea, we can blow out the fires of greed, hatred and delusion and attain that state of blissful calm which is called *nirvana*. We shall live calm and happy as long as our bodies keep going; then when they die we shall no longer be reborn, because rebirth is due to desire, which we have eliminated. *Nirvana* is *not* eliminating the self. It is eliminating the wrong idea that you ever had a self. If a madman has some notion, for instance that he is Napoleon, and he is cured, he has not abolished Napoleon, just his wrong idea that he was Napoleon.

'The path to eliminating suffering' consists of morality, meditation and wisdom. For Buddhists the foundation of all morality is generosity – the simple opposite to selfishness. In particular, every Buddhist layman is supposed to help maintain the monks and nuns, who do not work for themselves but depend upon such generosity. Buddhists do not consider that the monks are therefore parasites;

33

on the contrary, it is they who are doing the laity a favour by giving them this excellent chance to earn merit by being generous. All Buddhists also undertake to keep at least five moral rules: not to kill, steal, be unchaste, lie or take intoxicants (because intoxicants lead to breaking the other four rules).

The Buddha said that it is the intention that counts: if you kill or lie unintentionally you are not morally responsible for murder or lying, though you may have committed the lesser moral fault of carelessness. There are two reasons for trying to keep these moral rules. Firstly, though there is no god to punish the guilty, the law of *karma* will catch up with them and they will suffer for their sins, whereas the good will get a good reputation, prosper in life and be reborn as a god in heaven or as a rich and handsome person on earth. But that, of course, is a low motive for good behaviour, the motive of desire. If you really understand, you will be good because your unselfishness is the outcome of mental training, a psychological habit leading you towards the calm of *nirvana*.

Meditation has the same purpose. It is a training in calming the mind by concentrating on a single object. It gets you closer to *nirvana* both by further calming desires and by giving the training to obtain wisdom. The full attainment of wisdom is the same as attaining *nirvana*. Wisdom consists in fully realising, in a more than merely academic way, the truth expressed by the Four Noble Truths and so seeing everything (except of course the state of *nirvana*, which is not a 'thing') as unsatisfactory, impermanent and devoid of essence. In some religions the word 'gnosis' is used to describe this deep understanding; Buddhists call it 'seeing things the way they are'. They consider Buddhism to be not mystical but utterly realistic.

THE ORDER OF MONKS AND NUNS

The early Buddhists (and this has been true until quite modern times) believed that it would not be practically possible for laymen to meditate and so attain *nirvana*. Ordinary people are too involved in family life and earning a living. The Buddha himself had left home to work full time, so to speak, for his salvation. Buddhists have traditionally held that such full-time dedication is necessary if one is to make much spiritual progress: one has to give up one's social ties and activities, and renounce economic and sexual activity for a life of poverty and chastity. Buddhists therefore venerate those who have made this extremely difficult renunciation. They are the beacons who are keeping alive the flame of true Buddhist practice – for Buddhism is above all a practice, a way to solve life's problems, rather than a theory or a way of feeling. This reason for venerating monks – that they are the truest Buddhists – will always be valid. But there has also been another reason, which depends more on historical circumstance. The Order has been the preserver of the Buddha's teaching. In the Buddha's day there were no books; his words were preserved by the memory of monks, who were the only preachers. Again it was the monks who later wrote down the scriptures, and kept the books in their monasteries. As Buddhism spread, they translated those scriptures from Indian languages into Chinese and Tibetan, the largest translation projects the world has known till very recently. In China printing was invented in order to multiply the Buddhist scriptures: the oldest surviving printed book, dated 868 CE, is a Buddhist text. In most Buddhist countries – Sri Lanka, Burma, Thailand, Laos and Cambodia on the one hand, Tibet and several of its neighbours on the other – monasteries were centres of literacy and indeed until modern times the only schools. Monks were teachers not only of Buddhism, but of every aspect of learning. To Japan, Buddhism brought in its train virtually the whole of Chinese culture, beginning with writing; again, the bearers of this culture were monks. The Order, the Buddhist clergy, plays a more central and more dominant part in Buddhism than does the clergy in any other religion, so it should not surprise us that most Buddhist festivals are centred on monks and monasteries (often also called temples).

When they actively do good Buddhists are sometimes said to 'make merit'. They believe that men have more opportunities than gods to do good, as there is not much Buddhist activity in heaven. So when they have done a good act, such as offering flowers before the Buddha or feeding monks, they offer the merit earned to the gods. That means that they invite the gods to empathise and be happy at the good deed. However, since merit resides in intention, the god who feels as if he had offered the monk food may achieve the same state of mind as the man who actually has, and so make as much merit or spiritual progress. Men hope that in return for this consideration the gods will look after them here on earth. Buddhist festivals are occasions not only for having a good time but for making merit – usually at the monastery – and so improving one's prospects both in this life and hereafter.

THE OBJECTS OF VENERATION

The main objects of Buddhist veneration are monks, but Buddhists are also great worshippers of relics. Relics are classified into (1) physical parts (of the Buddha or saints), (2) objects used, (3) reminders. The Bodhi tree is worshipped as something the Buddha used. When he died his remains (after cremation) were put under large burial mounds). The shape of these mounds has been variously conventionalised in different countries; they are called stupas or pagodas. A stupa is itself a 'reminder' relic but, at least in theory, contains a physical relic. A Buddha image is also a 'reminder' relic. No relic works miracles; the benefit of worshipping them comes from the pure thoughts they arouse.

The development and spread of Buddhism

Buddhism did not spread beyond northern India till the time of the great Emperor Asoka (*c.*269–233 BCE), who was converted early in his reign. He organised missions to neighbouring countries and during his reign, or very soon after, Buddhism took root in central Nepal, in the areas now called Pakistan and Afghanistan, and in Sri Lanka. In central Nepal it has survived (among a people called the Newars) to this day. But it is only about Asoka's mission to Sri Lanka that we have much historical information. That mission, in 250 BCE, was headed by his son Mahinda, who was a monk. When Mahinda had converted the court, his sister, the nun Sanghamitta, brought to Sri Lanka a sapling of the Bodhi tree. Buddhists see the establishment of Buddhism in a country as being the establishment of the Order, and that was done by Mahinda. By allowing the Bodhi tree to be planted in Sri Lanka, however, Sanghamitta repeated the implanting of Buddhism on Ceylonese soil on a symbolic level. Sanghamitta also established ordination for women, which Mahinda had already done for men.

In talking of the Order so far, we have sometimes referred only to monks. This has been deliberate: as monks can only be ordained by other monks, likewise nuns can only be ordained by other nuns. There were nuns in Sri Lanka till about the eleventh century. At that time, the period when the local form of Buddism was first taken from Sri Lanka to continental South East Asia, the ordination tradition of nuns was lost, that is to say, there were no more nuns, so no new ones could be created. So in Theravada Buddhism, the form of Buddhism which exists in that part of the world, there are no nuns, even though there are some ladies who take vows and lead religious lives very *like* nuns. In other Buddhist countries there have always been nuns, but by Buddhist monastic rules they are subordinate to monks, and the social customs of most countries have made them generally less prominent than monks. In the early days of Buddhism many nuns, we know, attained *nirvana* and so became Buddhist saints; no doubt many have done so since, but they have not been allowed to play as important a social or historical role as monks.

Between the reign of Asoka and the first century CE Buddhism spread through Afghanistan into central Asia (later called southern Russia), and by that route into China. The first evidence for Buddhism in China is dated 65 CE, but it was not important there until the third century. It was also in that century that it reached Vietnam, the northern part of which was for about a thousand years the southernmost province of China. In the late fourth century Buddhism reached Korea, where one king made it the official religion of his kingdom in 392 CE, and via Korea it reached Japan, the official date being given as 538 CE.

In a separate development, Buddhism went direct from India to Tibet in the seventh century. From then on until the Chinese invasion of 1950 CE, Tibet was one of the most thoroughly Buddhist countries in the world. Tibetans have long lived outside the present political frontiers of Tibet, in the far north of India (Ladakh), Nepal, Sikkim and Bhutan. Sikkim was annexed by India in 1975 CE but Bhutan is still an independent and officially Buddhist country. The Mongols were converted to Tibetan Buddhism in the sixteenth century. A Mongol people, the Kalmuks, then moved west to the Volga region, so that for about three centuries there has been a Buddhist nation on European soil.

Another separate development took Buddhism direct from India around the middle of the first millennium CE to Indonesia. At that time there were also Buddhist contacts between India and continental South East Asia. Burma, however, acquired its present form of Buddhism, Theravada, mainly from Sri Lanka, beginning late in the eleventh century. This form of Buddhism spread into Thailand in the thirteenth century and into Laos and Cambodia in the fourteenth century.

By that time, Buddhism was virtually extinct in India. The decisive moment in a long decline was a Muslim invasion at the end of the twelfth century in which the great monasteries of Bihar and Bengal (including what is now Bangladesh) were sacked, the monks killed and manuscripts burned, very much as happened recently in the Chinese invasion of Tibet. Buddhism has, however, revived in India, the land of its birth, in recent years: India plays host to many Tibetan Buddhist refugees, who have even re-established a few of their monasteries on Indian soil, and some Indians have converted to Buddhism.

We have seen that Buddhism has at one time or other been strong in almost every country north, south or east of India, and even in a few countries further west. In many of these countries it has now become weak or died out altogether, having fallen mainly to Islam and, more recently, to Communism; Christianity made little impact on it. The fall to Islam was not always sudden or bloody, however, as was the case with the fall to Communism.

Today Buddhism is the dominant religion (and in some cases the official state religion) in Sri Lanka, Burma, Thailand and Bhutan. It is also extremely important, though not singled out for state recognition, in Japan, Taiwan, Hong Kong, South Korea, Singapore and Nepal. It is reviving, though still on a comparatively small scale, in India and Indonesia, and remains a religion of the large Chinese minority in Malaysia. It seems to be tolerated to varying degrees by the governments (all communist) of Mongolia, Vietnam, Laos and China. The attitude of the Chinese rulers under Mao was, however, extremely hostile to Buddhism, but since his death the government, which now also controls Tibet, has become milder. Physical destruction of Buddhism in Cambodia (Kampuchea) is still too recent for any such mildness to have become noticeable. There are also, of course, Buddhists in western countries, notably in the United States.

Different forms of Buddhism

In the first few centuries of its history in India, Buddhism split up into various schools; the differences between them now seem comparatively unimportant. However there arose a great movement, probably around the turn of the Christian era, which called itself the *Mahayana*, usually translated 'the Great Vehicle' but perhaps better translated 'the Great Career'. The allusion is to the career of a Bodhisattva, a 'future Buddha'. The aim of a religious person in earlier Buddhism, which the Mahayanists called *Hinayana* (the Lesser Career), was to attain one's own enlightenment, nirvana; and for an enlightened person nothing remains after the death of the body. The Mahayanists found this aim too negative, and said it was better to aim to be a Buddha in the distant future but in the meanwhile to become as perfect as possible by helping all living beings. They said that even the Buddhas did not cease to exist after their careers on earth; those earthly lives were just illusions created to help people. Really there are an infinite number of Buddhas, infinitely wise and kind, and also innumerable Bodhisattvas of the same character. All these great beings are there to help you, and you should have faith in them and pray to them for aid and protection. It remains true that only you yourself can attain *nirvana* – but that is not the best thing to aim for. It is finer to take the Bodhisattva vow.

The only surviving school or sect of the earlier Buddhism is the *Theravada*. To refer to it as the Hinayana is neither quite polite nor quite accurate. All the Buddhism surviving in the countries outside

Theravada territory (Sri Lanka and South East Asia) can be called Mahayana. However a further distinction is often made. Around the middle of the first millennium CE there arose a general religious movement in India called *tantra*. In *tantra*, meditation is always accompanied by complicated rituals. The Buddha was against rituals, which he said were useless for salvation. Nevertheless, a highly ritualised form of Mahayana arose, usually known as Tantric Buddhism, but calling itself *Vajrayana* (the Diamond Vehicle). It followed the earlier forms of Mahayana to most Buddhist countries, and is still the form of Buddhism found in Nepal and among Tibetans. The Tibetan form of Buddhism is also sometimes called *Lamaism* by westerners. Westerners sometimes refer to Mahayana as 'northern Buddhism' and Theravada as 'southern Buddhism' because the countries where they are now found lie respectively north and south of India. But that has not always been so; we must remember that all the main forms of Buddhist belief and practice began in India.

The festivals

This section will deal directly only with the festivals of the main Theravadin countries (Sri Lanka, Burma and Thailand) and of Tibet and China. Tibet and China are here shorthand terms which refer not to what goes on in those countries today, but to the practices of Tibetan and Chinese Buddhists anywhere. What is said of Tibet will also largely apply to countries bordering Tibet (though not to the Newars of central Nepal); what is said of China will largely apply not only to Taiwan, Hong Kong and Singapore, but also to South Korea; what is said of Thailand will largely apply to Laos and Cambodia. Japan is covered in the chapter on Japanese Festivals.

Chronology

Buddhist chronology varies from country to country. This is not surprising: unlike Christianity, Islam or Communism, Buddhism does not claim to be concerned with the things of this world. It is happy to coexist with other ideas and practices, even with cults of gods, so long only as they do not dispute the validity of the Buddha's path to ultimate salvation. So Buddhists are quite happy to accept any secular culture which does not go against their principles (for example by encouraging alcohol or sexual promiscuity). They are even happy to celebrate the festivals of other religions, such as Christmas.

For most purposes Buddhists now use the western (Christian) era and begin the year on 1 January. There is also a Buddhist era, which starts at the death of Gautama Buddha. But there is no general agreement as to when that occurred. Theravada Buddhists now put it at 543 BCE, but we know that this date arose from some misunderstanding in mediaeval times. Before this some Buddhists started their era in 486 BCE, others in 368 BCE. Most modern historians have chosen 486 or thereabouts, but we may never know the truth.

The only modern Buddhists to make much use of the Buddhist era (BE) are the Theravadins. The BE year begins in April (see below). The Theravada countries celebrated the 2500th anniversary of the Buddha's death in May 1956 and the anniversary year from April 1956 to April 1957 CE.

Tibetan and Chinese Buddhists do not use a 'Buddhist era'. Both use a hexagenary (sixty-year) cycle; each year is named by combining the name of an element (for example fire or earth) with the name of an animal, and after sixty years the pattern is repeated. The systems of the Tibetans and the Chinese are much alike but not identical.

Buddhist calendars all combine solar and lunar elements. The year is solar, so that festivals fall at the same season every year. There are normally twelve months to a year, but all the calendars sometimes have to intercalate an extra month. Sri Lanka, continental South East Asia and Nepal have adopted one of the Indian calendars with the year beginning on a fixed date in April. For Chinese and Tibetan Buddhists the New Year's Day is not fixed in the solar calendar but falls at a new moon – for the Chinese in the second half of January or the first half of February, for the Tibetans in February.

Days do not run from midnight to midnight in all Buddhist calendars. In Sri Lanka, for example, they run from dawn to dawn (which is always close to 6 a.m. in the tropics). The lunar month in Sri Lanka, however, is divided not into days but into thirty-two segments of the moon's course, called *tithi*. A *tithi* is thus rather less than a day.

The timing of festivals

All Buddhist religious festivals follow the lunar calendar, and most of the big ones (except the New Year) are celebrated on full moon days. But since all Buddhist calendars combine solar and lunar elements, working out the dates on which festivals will fall is a matter for specialists. Just as westerners find out the date of Easter by looking at calendars or diaries, Buddhists rely for such information on printed calendars and almanacs.

If one has no direct access to the Buddhists concerned or to their calendar, the only practicable way of finding out when a Buddhist festival will occur in a given year is probably to contact the Embassy or High Commission of that country. Tibetans throughout the world now depend on a calendar which is computed and published by the Tibetan Medical Centre at Dharamsala. (Dharamsala, in the north of Bengal, is the centre of Tibetan refugees in India and the normal home of their spiritual leader, the Dalai Lama.)

Buddhist festivals: general remarks

Except in modern Japan, Buddhism centres on its clergy far more than does any other world religion, and this applies to its festivals too. Some of the major festivals celebrate events which primarily concern monks, and almost all of them take place entirely or mainly at the monastery. The monastic calendar has two principal features, *uposatha* days and the Rains Retreat, both of which are relevant to also to lay observance.

Uposatha Days (weekly)

Originally all monks in a given area were supposed to assemble once a fortnight – every full moon and every new moon – to confess to one another in private any failures to keep to the monastic code of discipline. This rule is now much neglected. But these days are also days for more intense religious observance by lay people. The same applies, but much less so, to the other two quarter days of the month, the days half way through the lunar fortnight. All these days are called *uposatha* days in Pali, the language in which the Theravada Buddhist scriptures were written. An *uposatha* day is thus somewhat analogous to the Christian Sunday or Jewish Sabbath. But the *uposatha* days at full and new moon are far more important than the other two, and of them the full moon day is the more important.

What the more intense religious observance consists of varies from country to country, except that everywhere it is likely to include a visit to a monastery. It is popularly considered even worse to take life on an *uposatha* day than at other times: one is supposed to do no agricultural work on these days, and people also tend to abstain from eating meat or fish, especially in the Mahayana countries (Tibet, China). Religious observance is also likely to include making offerings to monks, especially of food, and paying one's respects to Buddha images and Buddhist shrines, most of which are at monasteries. In Theravada Buddhist countries a pious lay person may wear white and go and stay at a monastery for a large part of the day, or even till the following dawn. During that time they devote themselves to religious thoughts and exercises: they participate in the regular daily offerings before the Buddha image, listen to a sermon or two, recite religious verses and probably undertake some fairly simple form of meditation. The most important and regular feature of their practice, however, is that for that day they undertake eight observances ('Eight Precepts'): besides undertaking, as usual, not to kill, steal, be unchaste (which in this case means to have sex at all), lie or take intoxicants, they further vow not to eat after noon, use adornments, look at entertainments, or use grand beds. By these latter observances they temporarily behave rather like members of the Order, for monks and nuns undertake these same abstentions permanently, along with a further one not to accept gold or silver, which in effect means not to use money.

Rains Retreat
This is an important annual feature of the monastic calendar, which monks and nuns have to observe for three months. In northern India, where the Buddha preached, the monsoon normally starts at the end of June or the beginning of July. Few roads outside the cities were paved, and travel during the rainy season was difficult and uncomfortable. Thus the early monks, who led a wandering existence for most of the year, were supposed to settle down in one sheltered place for the rainy season. This developed into a strict monastic rule: every monk must formally take up residence in one place for the rains and not leave except in an emergency, in which case he may be away for up to seven days only. Nowadays monks mostly reside in the monastery where they live for the rest of the year too, but in the Theravada countries, where the Rains Retreat is still strictly observed, a pious person may offer a monk a special place to stay in for the retreat, such as a house he has just built and furnished but not yet moved into himself. In such a case the monk will probably be conducted to the house in a noisy procession and then he will preach a sermon.

At the end of the retreat, monks who have passed it together hold a special ceremony in which they ask the forgiveness of their fellows if they have offended them. Like the fortnightly confession, this is an event private to the monks, but is also the occasion for public religious activity. In the seventh year after his enlightenment the Buddha spent the Rains Retreat in one of the lower heavens, where his mother had been reborn, preaching to her. On the last day of the retreat he again came down to earth, attended with great pomp by the kings of the gods. This event is especially celebrated in Burma, Thailand and Tibet. In China the retreat comes earlier in the year and is less important, but nevertheless the main Buddhist festival falls on its final day and commemorates piety towards one's mother.

Kathina Ceremony

On the final day of the Rains Retreat or within the following month (there is local variation) the laity present monks with robes. The robe thus ceremoniously presented is called (in Pali) the *kathina* robe. This is the only calendrical ceremony involving laity for which there is authority in the earliest Buddhist scriptures. One monk in each monastery – in theory the most virtuous, but in practice whoever is chosen by the abbot – is presented with the robe, which is made according to canonical prescription by sewing patches together. Although the Rains Retreat is no longer observed in the Mahayana countries – where of course it corresponds to nothing in the climate or seasons – most of them seem to preserve some relic of the Kathina Ceremony. In the Theravada countries, the end of the Rains Retreat and the Kathina Ceremony are important occasions.

Unlike the *kathina* ceremony, commemorating events in the Buddha's life has no canonical authority and we do not know when it began. His Enlightenment is commemorated everywhere, but countries disagree about its date and in China his birth is more important. In the Theravada countries and Tibet the Buddha's birth, enlightenment and death are believed to have occurred on the same day.

New Year

The New Year is a major festival for all Buddhists, but is not really a religious festival and does not centre on the monastery. At the one extreme, the Chinese New Year has nothing to do with Buddhism at all; at the other, the Tibetan New Year, Losar, though largely secular, includes the rededication of the country to Buddhism. In Theravada countries the New Year is considered secular, but Buddhists tend, perhaps increasingly, to incorporate some Buddhist element into almost any public celebration. This tendency affects even the western New Year: on the first of January in Thailand monks are publicly fed on a vast scale, while in Sri Lanka at dawn crowds can be seen converging on the Temple of the Buddha's Tooth at Kandy, bringing flower offerings, in the belief that that is an auspicious way to start the year.

At the end of the monastic Rains Retreat, in or around October, Buddhist laity present monks with new robes. This is the only calendrical festival involving laity which goes back to the early scriptures. In Songkhla, in southern Thailand, a procession of decorated floats celebrates the occasion.

Festival of Lights
Western sources sometimes speak of a Buddhist Festival of Lights. Every Buddhist country has a festival – indeed, some have more than one – which is celebrated by lighting many lamps or candles and which could therefore earn this name. But in each country the festival takes a different form and celebrates a different occasion. There is no single such festival common to the Buddhist world.

Festivals in Sri Lanka

Some of its Buddhist festivals Sri Lanka shares with the Theravadin countries of the South East Asian mainland – which is only natural, since their Buddhism came to them from Sri Lanka. The remaining Sri Lankan festivals share a common theme: they celebrate the particular connections between Buddhism and the Sinhalese people. The Sinhalese are the majority community on the island; they are almost all Buddhists and have always strongly identified their nation with Buddhism.

New Year (13 April)
The celebration of New Year concerns one's worldly welfare and has no direct relevance to Buddhism. It is, however, the festival most like the modern western Christmas: everyone has leave to go home and spend a couple of days with their family; people give each other presents, especially cloth, and pay courtesy calls on all their neighbours; young people let off fire crackers and have a good time.

The Buddha's Birth, Enlightenment and Death (late May/early June)
This is the most important religious festival, occurring on the full moon day of the second month. The Indian name for this month is *Vaishakha* and the Sinhalese name derived from it is *Wesak*, which is used to denote both the festival and the month. Wesak commemorates the Buddha's birth, enlightenment and death, all of which are supposed to have occurred on the same day of the year. The accent in the festival is on the enlightenment, more important to Buddhism than a merely physical event. It is customary to put up decorations at the local temple and in particular to light lamps, a symbol of illumination in the metaphorical sense, after dark. Wesak lanterns are made of thin paper pasted over a light wooden frame. At temples the Bodhi tree, stupa and other features are often ringed with little oil lamps, consisting of a simple cloth or cotton wick in a small clay vessel of oil. People may send 'Wesak cards' to their friends, a custom modelled on Christmas cards, and there was even an attempt to popularise Wesak 'carols' on the Christian model, but

A selection of Wesak cards from Sri Lanka

a) The Buddha spent a whole Rains Retreat in a heaven preaching to his late mother. His return to earth is celebrated in Burma, Thailand and Tibet. Here it is shown on a Sinhalese Wesak card. Modern Buddhists in Sri Lanka send each other these cards as western Christians send Christmas cards.

b) Most Buddhists commemorate the Buddha's birth, Enlightenment and death on the same day, the full moon in May. In Theravada countries it is called Wesak/Visakha, in Tibet Saga dawa. Chinese Buddhists celebrate the birth at about the same time. His mother clung to a tree as she gave birth; then the king of the gods took up the baby.

c) The Buddha's Enlightenment. Having broken his fast with a meal of milk rice, the Buddha dropped his bowl in a stream, wishing that if his quest for Enlightenment was to succeed, the bowl should travel against the current. It did. He then sat down under a tree, the Bodhi tree, and meditated till, the same night, he realised the Truth.

that seems to have foundered. The main substance of celebrating Wesak is, however, the same as that of any Buddhist festival: abstaining from agriculture or other occupations which may harm living creatures; visiting the temple; feeding monks; listening to sermons (nowadays often on the radio, or even television) and, if possible, taking the Eight Precepts.

The Establishment of Buddhism in Sri Lanka (June/July)
The next full moon day, *Poson* (again the name of both month and festival), is also a major festival. It is on that day (in 250 BCE) that Emperor Asoka's son Mahinda, a monk, is supposed to have arrived in Ceylon to convert the island to Buddhism. Some temples, especially in towns, organise religious processions of the kind called *perahära*, in which some venerated person or object is conducted with a good deal of pomp and noise, especially drumming. (Enthusiastic small boys tend to let off fire crackers on any such occasion.) The Poson *perahära* conducts an image of Mahinda, which is usually made of cardboard and looks much like any idealised Buddhist monk. The image advances on a cart or other vehicle, much like a float in the West. At Poson there is always a large gathering at Mihintale, near the ancient capital of Anuradhapura, which is the place where Mahinda was supposed to have arrived and encountered the Sinhalese king, who was out hunting.

The Buddha's First Sermon (normally July)
The next full moon day is *Asala*. This is the anniversary of the Buddha's preaching his first sermon, the Turning of the Wheel of the Law. Monks preach sermons recalling this event, which began the Buddha's ministry. Asala is also the beginning of the Rains Retreat (in Sinhala called *vas*).

Procession of the Month of Asala (July/August)
In the latter half of the month of Asala occurs the *Asala Perahära* (Procession of the month of Asala), the most spectacular ceremony in the Sri Lankan calendar. It is hard to know whether to call it religious: though it is certainly performed by Buddhists, it is rather religio-national. Monks take no part in it, though they are allowed to watch. It consists of conducting the Buddha's tooth relic through the streets of Kandy. Kandy was the capital of the Sinhalese kingdom from the sixteenth to the early nineteenth century CE, and to be regarded as legitimate a Sinhalese king had to control the tooth relic. The purpose of the procession was thus mainly to display the king's power and legitimacy (under a show of piety). It is really an

amalgamation of five processions, one for each of the four guardian deities of Ceylon, which precede – and thus conduct – the tooth relic itself. Caparisoned elephants, innumerable dancers, drummers and waving firebrands make this a world-famous tourist attraction, and local people too flock to see it.

The Buddha's First Visit to Sri Lanka (normally September)

Two full moons later is the anniversary of the Buddha's first visit to Sri Lanka. (He is supposed to have paid three visits, all of which modern historians consider mythical.) He flew in and landed at Mahiyangana, on the east side of the central highlands, where he preached to the Väddas, the aboriginal population. After dark at Mahiyangana there is an interesting pageant: Väddas run in with torches, looking as fierce as possible, and pretend to attack the Buddhist temple, only to be cowed into submission. They thus represent the conversion of an originally hostile population.

Kathina Ceremony (October/November)

The end of the Rains Retreat (normally the full moon in October) is not as much of a lay festival as in other countries, but during the following month, usually on an *uposatha* day (in Sinhala called *poya*), the laity present the *kathina* robe at their local temple. The first monks were supposed to dress in such cast-offs as rags and shrouds, which they were to wash, dye yellow or orange, and sew. Most robes these days are bought readymade at a shop for clerical requisites, but the *kathina* robe is more archaic in composition. The cloth is not found, but bought by laymen, and in some villages they retain the custom of buying white cloth which they dye themselves, traditionally using the wood of the jak tree, which dyes pale yellow. A monk then cuts the cloth into patches and stitches it together again in a set pattern. The robe is then brought to the temple in procession by lay donors. The actual ceremony of giving it to the virtuous monk, who puts it on, is carried out among the monks themselves, but the laity gain merit by watching.

Arrival of Sanghamitta (full moon, late December/early January)

The full moon of *Durutu* is the anniversary of the arrival in Ceylon of Sanghamitta, who brought a sapling of the Bodhi tree and founded the Order of nuns. This is thus the female counterpart to Poson and Sanghamitta's image is paraded, like Mahinda's at Poson. The festival is attended especially by pious women, including those who now dress and live like nuns – though the Order is extinct in Theravada countries.

Festivals in Burma

The Burmese religious calendar is much the same as the Sinhalese, except that the New Year falls three or four days later, on 16 April (or rarely 17 April). The New Year and the 'Festival of Lights' at the end of the Rains Retreat in October are easily the two most important festivals; for both there is a public holiday of three or four days.

New Year (16 or 17 April)

Although people buy and release fish at the New Year, thus saving life, this is mainly a secular festival. Its character suggests that the main purpose is to ensure rain and fertility: people throw water at each other and also hurl insults and play practical jokes, and it is bad form to get angry. This period of licence recalls the western carnival.

The Buddha's Birth, Enlightenment and Death (full moon, late May/early June)

On this day (= Sinhalese *Wesak*) it is customary to water the Bodhi tree – the tree under which the Buddha attained enlightenment. Unlike in Sri Lanka, this is not a special day for lights; those come later in the year. The Burmese believe that this is the day on which *all* Buddhas attain enlightenment.

The Buddha's First Sermon and Beginning of the Rains Retreat (July)

For the Burmese this day, two full moons after the Buddha's birth, is also the anniversary of the Buddha's conception (this would accord with the scriptures if he was born in May, but the Sinhalese do not stress it) and of his great renunciation, when he left his dear family and comfortable home to lead a wandering life and seek enlightenment. This day is also the beginning of the Rains Retreat, and in Burma it is the custom for some men to take ordination and live as monks for the next three months. Many of those who cannot go so far do at least take the Eight Precepts on this day. The Rains Retreat affects the life of the laity directly: for example, there are no weddings during this period.

End of the Rains Retreat (October)

The full moon which ends the Rains Retreat is known as *Thitingyut*, and is a huge festival, a time of rejoicing and a festival of lights. During this three-day festival everyone is supposed to visit all their elder relatives, friends and acquaintances to pay their respects, and the elders reciprocate with small gifts. Lamps, consisting of candles inside paper lanterns, are put almost everywhere: in every room in the house, on important objects like the family rice bin, on the shrines of the *nats* (local deities), in big trees, and round the stupas. The lights are to illuminate and welcome the Buddha's descent from heaven after preaching to his mother (see above).

Kathina Ceremony (October/November)
During the following month the *kathina* robe is offered at each monastery, as in Sri Lanka. The tradition in Burma is for girls to weave the monks' robes. Along with the robes are offered toy trees, representing the mythical wishing trees of heaven, from the branches of which are hung currency notes.

Festivals in Thailand

New Year (13–16 April)
The Thai religious calendar is the same as the Burmese, but here New Year is celebrated on 13 April, as in Sri Lanka, and celebrations continue until 16 April. As in Burma, it is a water-throwing festival: Buddha images, venerated abbots and respected grandfathers are bathed or sprinkled with water. As on all important public occasions, monks are fed. On 14 April the laity come to the temples and in the compounds make little stupas of sand. Later these are levelled and the sand scattered to give the compounds clean new surfaces. On 15 April yellow robes are put on the Buddha images and left there for some days; subsequently monks use them.

The Buddha's Birth, Enlightenment and Death (late May/early June)
This festival, known as *Visakha*, is a major festival at which lights celebrate the Buddha's enlightenment. At dusk the laity come to the monastery, carrying lighted candles, flowers and incense sticks. They circumambulate the compound, which contains an image house, a Bodhi tree and a stupa. They go around three times, clockwise: once for the Buddha, once for the Doctrine, once for the Order. They then listen to a sermon on the Buddha's life. The rite of circumambulation, circling a respected person or object keeping him or it on your right, is found all over the Indian world; such triple circumambulations are a common feature of Thai Buddhist holy days.

Opposite: In Sri Lanka, the full moon of Asala is celebrated with processions. Elephants, drummers, and dances make it a popular and colourful occasion.

The Buddha's Cremation (May/June)

Wan Atthami, eight days later, commemorates the Buddha's cremation. Again there is a candle-lit circumambulation of the temple after dark. Some monasteries erect a catafalque with flowers, lights and parasols (emblems of royalty), and on it put a coffin with a representation of feet at one end. In the scriptural account of the Buddha's death it says that he is given an emperor's funeral (hence the parasols); but he died during the absence of the senior monk alive, Maha Kassapa, and when Kassapa returned to worship the coffin, by a miracle the Buddha's feet appeared so that he could put his head to them in homage.

Rains Retreat (July–October)

As in Sri Lanka and Burma, the Rains Retreat starts at the full moon in July and, as in Burma, some men get ordained to spend the retreat in the Order. In Thailand they usually do so between ten days and a week before the retreat begins, that is between the fifth and the eighth days of the lunar month. On the morning of the eighth the laity present monks with cloths for bathing in the rain, which they use during the retreat. The laity also bring candles and from them light lamps which are to burn in the monastery for the three months of the retreat.

End of the Rains Retreat (October)

As in Burma, there is a festival of lights at the end of the Rains Retreat, on the full moon of October; but here the major lights festival is the one which comes a month later. People illuminate their houses and stupas, and there are local festivals in which images are paraded to temples in decorated carts. Monks preach by reading out the scripture which tells how the Buddha preached to his mother in heaven.

Kathina Ceremony (October/November)

The month is full of *kathina* ceremonies. In Thailand the king and other members of the royal family offer robes; the king for this purpose visits nine temples each year, travelling by state barge or by car. All kinds of organisations have excursions to monasteries to offer *kathina* robes, after making arrangements in advance with the abbot. As elsewhere, only one *kathina* can be offered per year to a monastery.

Festival of Lights (November)

The full moon in November, *Loi Kratong*, is the main Thai Festival of Lights. The festival is not centred on the temple and may not be of Buddhist origin, though it now has Buddhist features. People decorate the gates and doors of their houses with palm leaves, banana stalks, coloured lanterns, lamps and candles, and the monastery compounds with all kinds of lights, paper flags, and sets representing scenes from the *Vessantara Jataka*. This ancient text tells how, in a former birth, the future Buddha was so selfless that when asked he even gave away his wife and children. (The story ends happily with their return.) This affecting story of superhuman generosity is perhaps the most popular one in the Buddhist world. In the early evening there are fireworks and later readings from the *Vessantara Jataka*. But the centrepiece of the festival is the taking of all kinds of floating trays, made especially for the occasion, down to rivers and streams to be let go on the water, each bearing lighted candles, coins and food. These are offerings for the river spirits, who in return will rid people of misfortune. The processions are noisy with cheering, firecrackers, drums and gongs; the craft vary from big floats built by organisations to little trays of plaited banana leaves. The thousands of candles reflected on the water produce an effect of magical beauty.

All Saints' Day (February)
More important, however, from the religious point of view, is the full moon in February. This festival, called *Magha Puja*, is referred to in English as All Saints' Day or Dharma Day. It commemorates the occasion when, three months before the Buddha's death, 1,250 of his enlightened disciples met spontaneously where he was staying. The Buddha predicted his death and gave his disciples the code of discipline which all monks ever since are supposed to recite every fortnight (see above).

In northern Thailand and Laos the main festival of lights occurs not in November but on this day in February. Since there are few streams there, the lights are not put to float on water. There the centrepiece of the festival becomes the reading of the *Vessantara Jataka*, which is supposed to be read through in one day. In addition to the illuminations there is a great fair.

Festivals in Tibet

Since 1027 CE, the Tibetans have been reckoning their years in a sixty-year cycle, much like the Chinese. They have five elements (wood, fire, earth, iron and water) and twelve animals, and each year is named by combining an element with an animal. However, they now also use an absolute chronology based on an era starting in 27 BCE, so that, for example, 1983 CE is for them 2110. Their new year starts with the new moon in February.

Their calendar is lunar, and nominally there are 360 days in the year, divided into twelve months. To keep in phase with the moon, some months are less than thirty days (twenty-nine, or even twenty-eight days); they always omit days which are considered unlucky. To keep in phase with the sun they have to add a month in some years. Though the months have names, they are normally known just by their number – 'first month' and so on. The fifteenth day will always be the full moon day. Days are reckoned from midnight, as in the West; festivals tend to start well before dawn, at about 3 a.m., and to end in the evening around sundown.

There are many regional and sectarian festivals, but we can list seven observed by the whole population. Since virtually all Tibetans are Buddhists, they do not think of any festival (such as the various New Year celebrations) as non-religious or non-Buddhist.

New Year (February)
The first fifteen days of the year are devoted to commemorating the Buddha's early life, his struggle for recognition after enlightenment, and his contests (all peaceful, of course) against rivals and disbelievers. Before the Chinese occupation, the capital, Lhasa, and its surroundings were given over for this fortnight to clerical administration – Buddhism literally ruled. It is considered a period of trial, and on the fourth day, which is called The Great Prayer (*Mönlam Chenmo*), monks sit their examinations for higher degrees. The fifteenth day, the full moon, is *Chönga Chöpa*. That night there is a spectacular display of sculpted scenes from the Buddha's life, all made out of butter, coloured with various dyes, and some scenes are enacted in puppet shows. Both shows are put on by the monks of two famous monasteries called the Upper Tantric School (*Gyütö*) and the Lower Tantric School (*Gyümé*). Both Schools, and the displays, used to be in Lhasa. The two monasteries have now been reconstituted in India (in Arunachal Pradesh and Karnataka respectively) and the monks come to Dharamsala to put on the displays.

The Buddha's Birth, Enlightenment and Death (May)
Saga dawa, the fifteenth day of the fourth month, normally the full moon day in May, commemorates the Buddha's birth, enlightenment and death. As in Sri Lanka, this is a festival of lights, and lamps are lit everywhere. This is the day of strictest Buddhist observance, and absolutely no meat is eaten. Some people undertake what in other religions might be considered penances: they go all the way round Buddhist monuments (always keeping them to their right) measuring out the distance with their bodies, that is, by prostrating themselves, then standing where their head was, and

repeating the process. Some take a vow to fast and keep silent for seven days. The last practice, in particular, shows that the festival contains an element of mourning the Buddha's death.

Dzamling Chisang (June)

The next full moon day, that of the fifth month, is a day of purification, on which fire offerings are made to guardian spirits for the common good. Tibetans believe in all kinds of guardian spirits; they protect individuals, families, places, the whole country. Shrines to them are put up, usually next to Buddhist temples, and renewed on the third day of the first month. Having been converted to Buddhism and become its protectors, the spirits are vegetarian and accept burnt offerings of vegetarian food such as the roast barley mixed with butter, which Tibetans love to eat, and various sweets. Before making these offerings one should abstain from meat oneself for three days. The making of these offerings is obligatory for laity but not for monks. Monks, however, officiate at the ritual.

The Buddha's First Sermon (June/July)

The fourth day of the sixth month is *Chökhor*, it commemorates the Buddha's first sermon, the Turning of the Wheel of the Law, just like the Sinhalese and Burmese festival eleven days later. In Tibet it was a particularly colourful and happy occasion, occurring in the middle of summer when the weather was always fine. Every district had its local monastery and every monastery had its Buddha statues and its xylographs, scriptures engraved on wooden blocks of long, narrow rectangular shape. The entire community, male and female, clerical and lay, would carry these xylographs and statues all round the district in a great procession, with much music and jollity. This of course symbolised the promulgation of the Buddha's teaching. After the procession there was a huge picnic.

The Buddha's Descent from Tushita (October)

The twenty-second day of the ninth month is *Lhabap*, the Descent from Tushita. This festival coincides with the end of the monastic Rains Retreat in Theravada countries. As in Burma and Thailand, the festival celebrates the Buddha's triumphal return to earth after spending the Rains Retreat preaching to his mother in the Tushita heaven. People go to temples on this day and also feast.

Death of Tsongkhapa (November)

The twenty-fifth day of the tenth month is *Ngachö Chenmo*, the anniversary of the death of Tsongkhapa in 1419. Tsongkhapa is maybe the greatest figure in the history of Tibetan Buddhism, a monk famous for his learning and his strict monastic discipline, qualities he passed on to the 'Yellow Hat' sect which he founded. (This sect includes the Upper and Lower Tantric Schools.) Tsongkhapa is believed now to be in the Tushita heaven. His death is mourned by adherents of all schools of Tibetan Buddhism, who that day eat a special food of mourning – a porridge containing lumps of dough. This, too, is a festival of lights: lamps are lit in Tsongkhapa's memory. In Lhasa his image used to be carried in a torchlight procession. This was also the day on which robes were offered to monks at the end of the Rains Retreat.

The Conjunction of Nine Evils and The Conjunction of Ten Virtues (January)
This two-day festival to mark the end of the year falls some time before the actual end of the year, perhaps corresponding to the time when the year changed on an older calendar. The first day is known as the Conjunction of Nine Evils and is very inauspicious: no one goes to work, sets out on a journey, or tries to undertake anything good or pleasant. The second day, the Conjunction of Ten Virtues, is very auspicious: in particular, there is much washing, and people completely clean out their houses.

Festivals in China

The great days of Buddhism in China ended about a thousand years ago, but only fifty years ago there were still about half a million Buddhist monks and many nuns. People combined Confucian, Taoist and Buddhist beliefs and practices, so that of most Buddhist festivals only the Order were normally aware. The most popular ones reflect two Chinese characteristics: intense concern for their dead ancestors, and the celebration of birthdays (which is not usual in the Indian world).

Like the Tibetans, whom they influenced, the Chinese use a sixty-year cycle of years, which they call 'the ten stems and twelve branches'. The only absolute era much used nowadays is the western one. Calendars used to be published under imperial auspices but are now privately produced. The months are lunar and New Year falls at the new moon in late January or early February.

On major Buddhist festivals the laity tended to abstain from meat and sex. They would buy living creatures, such as birds and fish, from pet shops and butchers, and release them; temples had fish ponds for this purpose. They visited the temples to worship at the shrines and to consult bamboo divination slips (especially at the New Year), but by the temples there were also fairs. The day would culminate in a vegetarian feast organised by the monastery.

Summer Retreat (June–August)
The monastic Rains Retreat in China somehow moved forward in
the year and became the Summer Retreat, from the fifteenth (full
moon) of the fourth month to the fifteenth of the seventh month.
It lost its character as a period for staying in one place, but remained
a time of more intensive study for monks. It is interesting that the
biggest Buddhist festival coincides (as it does, for instance, in
Burma) with the end of this retreat, even though it has nothing to
do with the retreat. There is also, however, a thematic connection
with the Buddhist festivals held in other countries at this time:
caring for one's mother.

Festival of Hungry Ghosts (August)
The Festival of Hungry Ghosts, which is also known as All Souls'
Day, lasts for seven days, ending on the fifteenth day of the seventh
month. Mu-lien, one of the Buddha's chief disciples, visited his
mother in the lowest hell and saved her by offering a feast to all
Buddhas and monks. (In other versions she was a hungry ghost
with a tiny mouth.) On the full moon day monks performed the
'release of the burning mouths' *(fang yen-k'ou)*.

'This was a Tantric ritual lasting about five hours and always held in the
evening when it was easier for hungry ghosts to go abroad. The presiding
monks wore red and golden hats in the shape of a five-pointed crown.
Before them was a collection of magical instruments – mirrors, scepters,
spoons, and so on. The monks assisting them – usually six to eighteen –
were equipped with . . . bells (which sounded, when rung together, rather
like a team of reindeer). In the first half of the ceremony the celebrants
invoked the help of the Three Jewels. In the second half they broke through
the gates of hell, where, with their instruments and magic gestures, they
opened the throats of the sufferers and fed them sweet dew, that is, water
made holy by reciting a [prayer] over it. They purged away their sins,
administered the Three Refuges [declaring one's trust in the Three Jewels],
and caused them to take the Bodhisattva resolve. Finally they preached the
dharma [the Buddha's teachings] to them. If all this was properly done, the
ghosts could be immediately reborn as men or even in the Western Paradise.'
Holmes Welch, The Practice of Chinese Buddhism, pp 185, 187

Gautama Buddha's Birth
The eighth day of the fourth month is the anniversary of Gautama
Buddha's birth. When he was born the gods bathed him in scented
water, so in the morning an image of the baby is ritually bathed in
the temple.

'After hymns and offerings the monks poured spoonfuls of water
over a tiny image of the infant Sakyamuni, standing in a low basin

of water. Sometimes each of the [lay] visitors was allowed to pour a spoonful too.'

Holmes Welch, The Practice of Chinese Buddhism, p 109

Kuan-Yin
Chinese Buddhists worship a female Bodhisattva called Kuan-yin who embodies compassion. Her birth, enlightenment and death are commemorated on the nineteenth day of the second, sixth and ninth months respectively.

Table of Buddhist festivals

Weekly   Uposatha Days

Sri Lanka

13 April   New Year
May/June   The Buddha's Birth, Enlightenment and Death
June/July   Establishment of Buddhism in Sri Lanka
July   The Buddha's First Sermon
July/August   Procession of the Month of Asala
September   The Buddha's First Visit to Sri Lanka
December/January   Arrival of Sanghamitta

Burma

16/17 April   New Year
May/June   The Buddha's Birth, Enlightenment and Death
July   The Buddha's First Sermon/Beginning of the Rains Retreat
October   End of the Rains Retreat
November   Kathina Ceremony

Thailand

13–16 April   New Year
May   The Buddha's Enlightenment
May/June   The Buddha's Cremation
July–October   Rains Retreat
October   End of the Rains Retreat
November   Kathina Ceremony
November   Festival of Lights
February   All Saints' Day

Tibet

February New Year
May The Buddha's Birth, Enlightenment and Death
June Dzamling Chisang
June/July The Buddha's First Sermon
October The Buddha's Descent from Tushita
November Death of Tsongkhapa
January The Conjunction of Nine Evils and the Conjunction of Ten
  Virtues

China

June/August Summer Retreat
August Festival of Hungry Ghosts
      Gautama Buddha's Birth
      Kuan-Yin

4 *Chinese Festivals*

DOUGLAS JONES

Religion in China

It is usual to recognise three religions in China: Confucianism, Taoism and Buddhism. Islam can also claim about twenty million adherents and there is a large Christian community comprising various denominations. Confucianism, Taoism and Buddhism all have long histories of development and are not so much religions as philosophical systems with religious dimensions. Confucians in particular have been more interested in ethics than metaphysics, and in the art of government and social reform than in the fate of the soul after death. Nevertheless, each of these systems has made its contribution to the sum of beliefs, rites and customs of the Chinese people and each has its festivals.

Beyond these great philosophical systems however, lies a set of beliefs older and even more deep-rooted in the culture of the Chinese people. These beliefs centre on Ancestor-worship. It is commonly held that overseeing and constantly interacting with the everyday world of the living is another world of gods, spirits, ghosts and demons, both benevolent and malevolent, and the myriad souls of the dead. Spirits inhabit mountains and rivers; gods and goddesses guard houses, protect localities, raise winds, bring rain and direct the movement of insects. Shang Ti is the spirit emperor of this unseen world, with his hosts of officials, courts, prisons, tortures and innumerable spirit people.

It is to this world that the dead soul goes, and where he must be remembered and sustained by his sons and grandsons in perpetuity. On entering it at death, souls become an active force for good or ill. Thus the need for ancestors to be worshipped for they exercise a potent influence on the fortunes of the family, the household and the environment they have left behind them. There are two points of contact between the living and the dead: the grave and the ancestral tablets set up in the home or family ancestral-hall to commemorate the dead ancestors. Sacrifices to ancestors are carried out at the grave or before the ancestral tablets. Without some understanding of Ancestor worship, it is impossible to appreciate the significance of some festival activities.

Before the great traditional Chinese festivals can be described, it is important to bear in mind the influences on Chinese religious and secular life resulting from the western domination of the country in the nineteenth century and the subsequent Chinese revolution. Sun Yat-sen, father of the revolution, was greatly influenced by western ideas as were many Chinese intellectuals of his time. Sun was a Christian as was his successor Chiang Kai-shek, and both married girls from the Methodist Soong family. Under Chiang's Nationalist (Kuomintang) government, traditional Chinese festivals became interspersed with western, so that bank holidays in China included not only celebrations like the Chinese New Year, the Dragon Boat Festival and the Birthday of Confucius, but also the western New Year (a three-day holiday), Easter and Christmas. The Nationalists also introduced a National Day celebration, usually referred to as Double Tenth because it fell on the 10 October, to commemorate the revolution of 1911 (HGW Woodhead, 1939, p 591; see Bibliography, p 277). The bureaucracy may have enjoyed all these holidays, but there is no reason to suppose that the masses of the people did also. Undoubtedly the peasantry, armed with their old-style lunar calendars, carried on much as before, though the effect on them of secularisation can be shown by the fall in the number of village temples used for purely religious functions (Sidney D Gamble, 1963, p 125; see Bibliography, p 277).

With the overthrow and expulsion of Chiang Kai-shek's Nationalist government in 1949 by the Communists, old Chinese traditions came under more severe attack. The new People's Republic of China adopted a constitution embracing a provision allowing freedom to hold religious beliefs or not to hold religious beliefs. Religious practice could henceforth only take place inside temples and churches. The freedom not to believe was given much publicity and the people were encouraged to equate religion with superstition. At the same time, religious movements with well established institutional bases (Christianity, Buddhism, Taoism and Islam) were subsumed under new associations which claimed to represent them, but which were effectively agents of government control. Buddhists probably suffered most under this reorganisation. Their lands were confiscated, temples converted to other uses and monks and nuns denounced as parasites. Confucius and Confucian philosophy also came under attack, culminating in the 'Criticise Confucius and Lin Piao' campaign of 1974 (Lin Piao, once regarded

as Mao's successor, is alleged to have died in an air crash while fleeing the country, having failed in an attempt to assassinate Mao.) Most difficult to suppress however, particularly in the countryside, was Folk-religion because, apart from its association with Taoism, it was not centred on any recognisable institution. Folk-religion embraces Ancestor-worship and the veneration of many gods, goddesses, deified heroes and spiritual powers. Nevertheless, practices associated with it became confined to the home. Similarly, many practices associated with the traditional festivals considered to have religious significance, like sending the kitchen god to heaven at New Year or making offerings to ancestors at Ch'ing Ming, came in for severe criticism. By and large, the festivals were secularised and shorn of any religious content. The Chinese New Year for example, has been redesignated 'The Spring Festival'.

The condemnation of religious institutions, practices and beliefs reached a climax during the Cultural Revolution. Throughout this struggle between contending political factions, Folk-religion again came under attack. Temples, shrines and images were destroyed and many people removed ancestral tablets from their homes replacing them with pictures of Marx, Lenin and Mao Tse-tung. Following Mao's death in 1976 however, and the subsequent trial of the 'Gang of Four', there has been a noticeable softening of official attitudes towards religion: some selected places of worship have been given permission to reopen; the training of small numbers of Buddhist monks and Christian clergy has recommenced and increased church attendance has been reported in Peking. Even Confucius has been recently reinstated as a great thinker, teacher and politician. The extermination of Folk-religion however, continues unabated.

The Communist takeover in China in 1949 bifurcated the Chinese world between 800 million inhabitants of the People's Republic of China and some 20 million overseas Chinese spread throughout south-east Asia (residing mainly in Taiwan, Hong Kong, Thailand, Indonesia, Malaya, Singapore and Vietnam). Doubtless old cultural traditions die hard and sometimes even survive revolutionary change, but it is among the overseas Chinese communities that the great traditional festivals continue to be celebrated rather than on the Chinese mainland where, despite recent slackening of the pressure to change old ways, the festivals have been largely secularised and politicised.

Opposite: *Chinese burial rite in Hong Kong, with posters mounted on a push cart.*

The Chinese calendar

The old-style Chinese calendar is a lunar one comprising twelve lunar months of twenty-nine or thirty days each. The first calendar is said to have been devised by the legendary Yellow Emperor, Huang Ti, conqueror, legislator and regulator of sacrifices and religious ceremonies. He is also credited with inventing metallurgy, writing and the chariot. The earliest Chinese calendars, dating back to the Shang Dynasty, probably 1765–1123 BCE, were inscribed on bone. These calendar-tablets bore the name of sixty consecutive days – roughly two months. Each date-name in the sixty-day cycle was arrived at by combining one character from a list of ten 'Heavenly Stem' characters with one character from a list of twelve 'Earthly Branch' characters in such a way as to produce sixty combinations. The first characters from each list, combined to form the name *Chia-tzü*, name of the first day of the cycle. Once the cycle of sixty combinations was completed, it would immediately start again with the first name. (The complete combination can be found in *Archaeology in China* (Cheng Te-k'uu, 1960, vol II, p 135). This series of names was later used to date sixty consecutive years. The passage of years was then calculated by a regular succession of repetitions of the sixty-year cycle. Thus Tennyson's remark 'Better fifty years of Europe than a cycle of Cathay.'

Each day commenced at dawn and was divided into seven, or sometimes ten 'hours' depending on which school of astronomers was in control of the calendar. 'Large' (thirty-day) and 'small' (twenty-nine day) months alternated throughout the twelve-month year. Nevertheless, the Shang calendar makers understood the solar year. It was known that their lunar year, amounting to only 354 days, would gradually throw the calendar out of step with the seasons if uncorrected. To redress the shortfall of days in each lunar year, an intercalary month was added to the calendar roughly once every three years. (The exact addition necessary is seven intercalary months every nineteen years.)

The Shang calendar established the model for all subsequent Chinese calendars and the system has continued since the first sixty-year cycle set by Huang Ti. The present cycle, beginning in 1924, is the seventy-eighth since his inception of the system. Each year is dominated by one of twelve animals of the zodiac, these being: rat, ox, tiger, hare, dragon, snake, horse, sheep, monkey, fowl, dog and pig. The animals rotate in a given order so that, for example, 1935, 1947, 1959, 1971 and 1983 are years of the pig. They are deemed to possess individual characteristics which influence the course of events. The year of the horse is likely to prove unlucky for those born under pig but good for those born under dragon. The Shang calendar was reformed during the Han Dynasty so that New Year's Day, which ushers in the most important of Chinese festivals, always falls on the day of the first new moon after the sun enters Aquarius. This determines the Chinese New Year to begin on some date falling between 21 January and 20 February by western reckoning.

With the sweeping away of the Ch'ing Dynasty and the founding of the Chinese Republic in 1912, the Gregorian calendar was introduced. The old lunar calendar, however, still continued in use. But the seasonal cycle of the peasants' world of crop rotation is determined more by the influence of the sun than the moon. Although the two systems are adjusted in the long run by the periodic insertion into the lunar calendar of intercalary months, the dates of one system can never regularly correspond with the other and the lunar calendar alone can never be an accurate guide for agricultural activity. So an underlying solar system has been built into the Chinese lunar calendar. This consists of a series of twenty-four sections or joints which occur every fifteen days throughout the year and are based on solar reckoning. The periods covered by these sections are designated by names which guide activity, for example Beginning of Spring, Waking of Insects, Grain in the Ear and Summer Solstice. Two sections – Pure Brightness and Winter Solstice – also indicate the occasion of festivals. Thus some festival dates are determined by the solar rather than the lunar calendar. Waking of Insects also symbolises first stirrings of nature in the spring, and is an occasion for women to pray for fertility before the altar of the God of Soil and Grain. (A full account of the sections and their relation to the lunar calendar is given in Hsiao-tung Fei, *Peasant Life in China*, Routledge and Kegan Paul 1939, pp 146–8.) Peasants follow the twenty-four sections closely as a guide to the correct times for initiating their various agricultural activities.

The introduction of the Gregorian calendar has not led to the abandonment of the traditional Chinese system of time reckoning. The Chinese now use all three systems: the lunar, the Chinese solar (the sections) and the western solar. The lunar is still the most popular calendar since it governs the timing of traditional social and religious activities and most festivals. The Chinese solar acts as a guide to climatic change and agricultural work, while the western solar governs the activities of the administrators and institutions of the state. Many Chinese calendars incorporate all three systems, showing the Gregorian in Roman numerals and the lunar together with the sections in Chinese characters.

The festivals

Chinese New Year (January/February)
Yüan Tan, the Chinese New Year, is the first, and the most important of the traditional Chinese festivals. New Year's Day falls on the first day of the first lunar month of the year. Preparations for the festival begin on the twenty-third of the twelfth month, one week before New Year's Day. Each family gathers in the kitchen to worship the kitchen god, or god of the furnace (Tsao-shen), whose picture is pasted on the chimney above the stove. The stove symbolises the unity of the family and the kitchen god who resides there oversees all members of the household. He decides how long each member shall live and reports annually to the Emperor of Heaven on each person's conduct during the past year. On this night, he returns to heaven to make his report.

On the occasion of the kitchen god's departure, it is customary to smear his lips with honey so that he reports only good or, some-times, with wine so that, drunk, he is not permitted to report at all on his arrival in heaven. The paper on which his image (or the character representing his name) is printed is then burned in a paper palanquin thus symbolising his ascension. A sweetmeat of sticky rice is sold around this time of year and sometimes a portion of this is also thrown into the fire with the god to ensure that he only reports in sweet words.

Other gods are also worshipped before the New Year and thanked for the blessings they have conferred on the family during the past year. This is usually a duty of the housewife who chooses lucky days indicated on the calendar (the first and fifteenth days of each month are particularly auspicious days for worship) for making appropriate offerings to these gods. One week after the departure of the kitchen god, that is, on New Year's Eve, the last day of the dying year, he is welcomed back by the family. His return is regis-tered by the pasting of a new picture on the chimney and the family express their joy at his presiding over a happy New Year by exploding fire crackers.

New Year's Eve is a busy time, for it is also one of the three accounting days in the Chinese year. Shopkeepers make up their books and all debts must be paid before New Year dawns, even if it means borrowing money from new sources in order to settle old accounts. Failure to do so means loss of face. Also, families are

Opposite: The Lion Dance, part of the Chinese New Year celebrations in London's Chinatown. The lion dispels evil spirits and brings good luck.

laying in last-minute provisions for the festival and buying new clothes for the occasion. The holiday will last for at least three days and shops will be closed. Those who can afford it will prolong the vacation beyond this time.

The streets are deserted on New Year's Day and everyone is at home. The day is devoted to the family and the enjoyment of family reunion. Parents and grandparents are worshipped and incense is burned to deceased ancestors. Food and drink may also be offered them and paper money burned for their sustenance in the spirit world. Sacrifice is also made to heaven and earth and the idols of the house. Though there is much to eat and drink, meat and fish are avoided on this day and no sharp implements used or brooms wielded about the house so that the New Year will start with no accident either to members of the family or unseen spirits.

On the third day, friends visit each other with presents and gifts of food and drink including special New Year biscuits. Large red cards bearing New Year congratulations are exchanged and mottos and prayers inscribed on red paper – the lucky colour – are affixed to doorposts of houses. Children expect gifts of money – usually only small amounts – wrapped in lucky red paper. After the holiday is over, it is usual for a representative of the family to visit local gods again with offerings of food, drink, candles and incense to ensure their protection from ghosts and malevolent spirits during the coming year.

Lantern Festival (February/March)
Teng Chieh, the Lantern Festival, falls on the fifteenth day of the first lunar month. This is the day of the first full moon of the new year. Traditionally, it occasioned the reopening of courts of law and public offices after the New Year Festival. The Lantern Festival also celebrates the lengthening of the day, the increasing light and the warmth of the sun after the winter's cold. City shops and market stalls display lanterns in various traditional designs; homes, restaurants and temples are also similarly decorated. Villagers erect tent-shaped strings of lanterns draped from a central pole. Lanterns are also carried in procession, some representing animals, birds and mythical creatures of which the most striking is the dragon.

Festival of Pure Brightness (March/April)
Ch'ing Ming, the Festival of Pure Brightness, is an important festival, and one of those the occasion of which is not determined by the lunar calendar but by solar observation. It falls on the 106th day after the winter solstice, about 5 April by our reckoning. This is a family festival and the first occasion in the year when families visit

the graves of their ancestors. Burial customs vary in different parts of China, but usually the family buries its dead in its own family graveyard. These are often established in the village fields or on hillsides amid groves of trees. Individual grave sites are very carefully selected in accordance with the geomantic principles of *fung-shui* (wind and water; that which cannot be seen and cannot be grasped) so that each grave is sited in the most propitious possible spot for the contentment of the dead soul. Failure in the matter of correct grave-siting is thought to bring the dead soul's avenging wrath down upon the whole family. In the Crown Colony of Hong Kong, the Kowloon Peninsular, the New Territories and 235 outlying islands, it is customary to deposit a dead person's remains in a large, sealed, earthenware jar as a temporary measure while the geomancer is searching for a good grave site. This may take some years. These jars, which are laid up on hillsides, are also visited by their respective families during Ch'ing Ming.

Ch'ing Ming is the occasion for sweeping and tidying up the graves and sacrificing to the ancestors. Offerings of food and wine are made to the spirits of the dead and the quality and variety of these can vary depending on the resources of the family. Following the sacrifices, each family usually enjoys a picnic by the graveside as though sharing the enjoyment of a feast with the dead.

Since this festival is an occasion for families to come together, there is much travelling about and in Hong Kong, considerable congestion of the railway which links Kowloon with the many villages in the New Territories. Family members in distant places also try to make the journey home but if they cannot, they prepare a small sacrifice wherever they are, in the hope that the 'spirit' of the offering they burn will reach their ancestors. Among the Chinese in Britain, many of whom come from the Crown Colony of Hong Kong, it is now becoming customary to return to the home village once every three or four years for an extended holiday which embraces both the New Year Festival and Ch'ing Ming.

Dragon Boat Festival (May/June)
Tuan Yang Chien, the Dragon Boat Festival, is a major one which takes place on the fifth day of the fifth lunar month. It celebrates the death by drowning of Ch'u Yuan (*c.*343–279 BCE), celebrated poet and high ranking official in the feudal state of Ch'u. Ch'u Yuan lived during the turbulent 'Warring States' period of Chinese history. Depressed by the political events of the time and dismissed by the king who, influenced by slander, turned against him, he renounced the world and, in despair, committed suicide. Legend has it that a kind of dumpling was thrown into the sea to

feed the fish who would otherwise have eaten his body. These dumplings, containing rice, meat and other ingredients, are still made and eaten during the festival.

It was the custom to suspend aromatic herbs from doorways at this time, to ward off evil spirits. In south China particularly, people made for the nearest shore or riverside where they hired boats and drifted about eating, drinking and making music. They also watched the dragon-boat races which are still a feature of this festival. These dragon boats are very narrow and up to one hundred feet in length, with the body of the boat shaped like a dragon and culminating in a dragon's head at the prow. Crews consist of rowers squeezed in two abreast and men waving flags and beating gongs. These crews, having raced during the day, parade the river at night with colourful lanterns. In Hong Kong an impressive international dragon-boat race is held with overseas teams participating.

Herd Boy and Weaving Maid (July/August)
Ch'i Hou Chieh, the Herd Boy and the Weaving Maid, falls on the seventh day of the seventh month. The celebration of this festival is not an important occasion but is worth including because it perpetuates an ancient folk tale. Two stars, one on either side of the Milky Way which the Chinese call the Heavenly River, are said to be a herd boy and a weaving maid. The weaving maid was banished from heaven to earth for a certain time, where she married the herd boy with whom she lived happily. When her time came to return to heaven, the herd boy tried to follow her but was prevented by the Heavenly River. Since then, the lovers have only been allowed a reunion on the seventh day of the seventh lunar month when a bridge across the Heavenly River is formed by magpies so that the two may meet. But should it rain on that day, the Heavenly River will overflow and sweep away the bridge. In that event the lovers have to wait another full year before they can meet again. Women therefore pray for clear skies on the night of the seventh day of the seventh moon. They also pray for skill in needlework at this time.

All Souls' Festival (August)
Chung Yüan, the Festival of All Souls, sometimes also called the Festival of Hungry Ghosts, falls on the fifteenth day of the seventh lunar month. It is primarily a Buddhist festival. From this day until the end of the month, the unhappy dead – those spirits who are homeless, have no descendants to sacrifice to them, or having been drowned have no resting place – have offerings made to them. The offerings, which are intended to appease these ghosts, include paper money, paper houses and clothes, fruit and other useful

Hong Kong's Dragon Boat Festival is held on the fifth moon each year. The festival commemorates a statesman who drowned himself in the hope of bringing reforms to ancient China in the third century BCE.

articles needed in the spirit world. The paper objects are burned and in some cases floated down rivers to propitiate the drowned souls. In and around Hong Kong one sees small roadside fires at this time where these offerings can be despatched.

In Buddhist temples, masses are said for these 'hungry ghosts' and large paper boats are made. These boats – so called 'boats of the Buddhist law' – are also burned on the evening of the fifteenth day of the month. The boats are intended to help tormented souls cross the sea of suffering to which their past lives have doomed them and thus to enable them to reach *nirvana*.

Mid-Autumn Festival (September)

Chung Ch'iu, the Mid-Autumn Festival, celebrates the moon's birthday and falls on the day of the full moon, the fifteenth day of the eighth lunar month. This is a major festival in the Chinese calendar similar to the western Harvest Festival. Traditionally, offerings of moon cakes are made to the goddess of the moon by the women folk. Offerings are also made to the rabbit in the moon, the Chinese asserting that what we see in the moon is not a man's face but a rabbit pounding the elixir of life with a pestle. Many fairs are held at which sacrificial objects like 'spirit money' may be purchased. These are offered to the moon while incence is burned and obeisance made by the womenfolk. Since the moon is, according to Chinese thinking, female, the proverb has it that 'Men do not bow to the moon, women do not sacrifice to the god of the kitchen.'

The moon cakes themselves are special cakes made of a pastry crust filled with a mixture of ground lotus and sesame seeds or dates. They also contain duck eggs. They commemorate an uprising against the Mongols in the fourteenth century when the call to revolt was written on paper embedded in the cakes. The cakes usually exhibit a crescent moon or an image of the rabbit in the moon on their surface.

This is primarily a family festival. In Hong Kong, streets and shops are decorated, and moon cakes sold before the festival begins together with many brightly coloured lanterns. Children are allowed to stay up late and go to some high place with their parents where they can light their lanterns, eat their cakes and watch the full moon rise.

Double Ninth Festival (September/October)

Ch'ung Yang, the Double Ninth Festival, falls on the ninth day of the ninth lunar month and is the day for hill climbing or 'going up on a high place'. The festival is based on an old story which goes back to the Han Dynasty (206 BCE – 202 CE). The story has it that an imminent natural calamity was foreknown to an ancient seer who warned of it in advance. Having done so he went up into the hills and escaped. On returning, he found that all other living things had been destroyed. On this day, people betake themselves to some high place where they picnic and enjoy themselves, though symbolically, by going up a hill or city wall they are avoiding a possible calamity. People often fly kites on this day, and it is also a time for visiting family graves again as at Ch'ing Ming. This is also a chosen time for large clans to sacrifice to ancestors in the clan ancestral hall. Whole roast pig, known as 'golden pig', is offered together with fruit, wine, tea and rice. When the ancestors have taken their fill, of course, these offerings are enjoyed by all those who attend the ceremony.

Winter Solstice (November/December)
Tung Chih, which falls in the eleventh lunar month, is the Festival of the Winter Solstice and is held on the longest night of the year. It is a time for family reunion and feasting and also a time when all gods and shrines are worshipped. Ancestors are also worshipped, not at the graveside, but in the principal temple or in the place – either the house or the ancestral hall – where the ancestral tablets are lodged. Chairs are also provided for them at the feast, these being placed on the north side of the table. The position is determined by the belief that the spirits of the dead dwell in the dark northern hemisphere.

Table of Chinese festivals

January/February   Chinese New Year
February/March   Lantern Festival
March/April   Festival of Pure Brightness
May/June   Dragon Boat Festival
July/August   Herd Boy and Weaving Maid
August   All Souls' Festival
September   Mid-Autumn Festival
September/October   Double Ninth Festival
November/December   Winter Solstice

5 *Christian Festivals*

JOHN RANKIN

Christianity

Christianity appears in many different forms in the world and it is by no means easy to represent it briefly and succintly. However, the majority of Christians would subscribe to the following:

1 There is one God, creator and sustainer of the cosmos.
2 God is personal in the sense that he can both speak to people and can be addressed by them.
3 Jesus, called the Christ, born as man in Bethlehem approximately 6 BCE was also God in human flesh. He died by crucifixion during the Roman occupation of Palestine about 30 CE. He rose from the dead on the third day. By that death and resurrection those who believe in him are on earth made righteous in God's sight and will, after a final judgment, enjoy a blessed rest in heaven.
4 The power of God by which this 'salvation' is accomplished is known as the Holy Spirit. This power was felt especially by the assembled disciples of Jesus, fifty days after his resurrection. The Holy Spirit now guides and strengthens believers.
5 God as Creator, as Redeemer in Christ and as Power in the Spirit, has shown God's nature as dynamic, that there is a divine activity within the one God which involves a continuing saving activity in the world. This belief is expressed in the doctrine of the Trinity. This is not understood as making God more than one, but simply as recognising that the mystery of God's oneness is more complex than can be expressed in one 'person'.
6 The activity by which God redeems mankind is known as 'grace', a word which emphasises the sense of the need for God's loving help.
7 Christ caused a continuing life to be fostered among his disciples which has been called the Church.
8 The sacred books known as the Old Testament, being the auth-

oritative scriptures of the Jews, together with the collection known as the New Testament are called the Bible, and thus form the authoritative scripture for Christians. For many Christians this is not understood in a direct or uncritical sense, that is, the words are not seen simply as direct messages from God.

9 The Christian salvation lays particular stress on 'community'.

Most Christians lay stress on the experience of God's power in some degree and the history of Christianity shows it to be a religion characterised by energetic action. On occasions this has been misguided and there has arisen the paradoxical situation of recognisably evil deeds being performed in the name of Christ. However there is also much evidence of good deeds. Christian Churches have been pioneers in the establishment of hospitals and schools and of self-sacrificing works of mercy throughout the last two millenia.

The most characteristic act of worship is the sacred meal known variously as the Lord's Supper, the Holy Communion, the Eucharist, the Mass or the Holy Liturgy. The faithful receive token amounts of bread and wine set apart and consecrated, as a sacramental means of 'communion' with Christ and with one another. However a few groups, such as the Society of Friends and the Salvation Army, do not use this sacrament and where it is used, interpretation varies considerably between Churches.

Christian denominations

The interpretation of Christian truths takes several directions. There are those, for example, who consider that Christ's authority continues to be exercised in the Roman Catholic Church and that the Pope is the spiritual inheritor of St Peter, the leader of the apostolic band to whom Jesus entrusted his Church. There are others who consider that there can be no such earthly authority and that Christ alone must be head of his Church. There are also divergencies concerning the position of Mary, the mother of Jesus, within Christian devotion. This has some bearing on the observance of festivals related to Mary.

In the 1980s Christianity is the religion professed by about one third of the world's population. It is not, however, a unified body. There are about 20,000 separate denominations and groupings of Christians throughout the world. Of course they are not all of equal size. Roman Catholics account for more than half of the world's Christians. Many Protestant denominations share a common starting point and make a useful second classification. 'Protestant' is the name given to those Christians whose distinctive position historically derives from the division of the Church in the sixteenth and seventeenth centuries CE, the time often referred to as the Reformation. A further main grouping is represented by the Eastern Orthodox Churches whose separation from the Roman Catholic Church dates effectively from the eleventh century CE. Yet another smaller classification is the Anglican Church representing those autonomous Churches which owe their origin to the Church in England. It requires a separate classification since the changes in England at the time of the Reformation do not exactly parallel the changes in other countries on the European continent. Outside of these there are numerous other Christian groups and also what are sometimes called 'marginal' Christian bodies. These are so called because in many respects their doctrines vary radically from the mainstream Protestant Churches and they usually include a separate authoritative revelation – and an additional authoritative scripture. These include such bodies as The Church of Jesus Christ of the Latter Day Saints and Jehovah's Witnesses. No attempt has been made to include these in the consideration of Christian festivals.

Recent development has seen vigorous efforts at growing towards the reunion of Christian Churches exemplified by the firm progress of the World Council of Churches. At the same time there has been a steady growth in smaller autonomous (particularly in Africa) indigenous Churches. However this is not the place to provide an historical analysis of the divisions within Christendom. For the purposes of this book the major groupings are as follows.

THE ROMAN CATHOLIC CHURCH
This is the largest single grouping in terms of numbers of adherents. Roman Catholics look to the Pope in Rome as their spiritual leader and the observances of this Church are more centrally regulated than the others.

THE EASTERN ORTHODOX CHURCH
The customs of this Church have been assiduously preserved over many centuries. Orthodox Churches do not have one central authority but they are an association of self-governing Churches each with its own 'Patriarch', and form of government. Liturgical practice (including observance of the Church's Year) tends to be very conservative.

THE REFORMED CHURCHES
This title is used to include all those Churches whose separate exist-

ence derives from the radical changes in relation to the doctrines and government of the Church which took place at the Reformation in Europe in the sixteenth century CE. Many of these Churches have, of course, a major continuation in the USA (such as the Baptists).

THE ANGLICAN CHURCH AND THE LUTHERAN CHURCH
These two Churches, both related to the Reformation, need special mention. They are singled out because in varying degrees they have preserved and continued elements of practice which other Reformed Churches have not. The Anglican Church is the title used to describe all those Churches which have their derivation in the Church of England. The Anglican Church generally observes the Church's Year in its entirety. Lutheran Churches are those Churches which owe their derivation to the particular reforms of Martin Luther in Germany. Lutherans observe the main festivals.

The Church's Year

For many Christians, particularly the faithful of the Eastern Orthodox Church, their religion is almost organically bound up with the observance of the Church's Year. In the sequence of ritual commemoration and celebration, the great truths of their theology are knit into their lives, so that to speak of their religion is to speak of this dynamic involvement in word and gesture and symbol. The Church's Year is also fundamentally built into the practice of the Roman Catholic Church, although the practice is not identified with theological thought in quite the same way. Anglicans and Lutherans follow the same sequence of seasons as the Roman tradition but the number of other holy days and saints' days observed are fewer (particularly in the Lutheran Church). Most Reformed Churches observe only those feasts which they feel are to be found in the New Testament, that is Sundays, Holy Week and Easter, Pentecost, and to some extent Christmas. This latter festival has come to be observed so widely that even Churches which originally had some theological objection have accepted it.

It is perhaps important to understand that the observance of the Christian Year is simply a matter of either Church regulation or custom. It is not a matter of divine revelation. In some sects religious festivals are considered to be irrelevant and even sinful. However most Christians will acknowledge the two major festivals of Easter and Christmas.

Origins of the Church's Year

Christianity inherited the seven-day week from Judaism and from earliest times (the first century CE), *Sunday*, the first day of the week, became the regular day when Christians assembled for worship. Sunday was observed because it was the day of the week when Jesus Christ rose from the dead. Thus for Christians every Sunday is a celebration of the Resurrection. The *first* day of the week began to symbolise the new beginning, the new life inaugurated by Jesus. The observance of Sunday has, however, assimilated some of the aspects of Sabbath observance in Judaism. Its observance varies widely among Christians. In countries with large Catholic populations, religious observance is usually confined to the eve (Saturday) and Sunday morning. The remainder of Sunday is the normal day of sports and recreation. In some Protestant Churches the observance of Sunday involves not only attendance at worship but abstention from work or any kind of secular recreation. In the past this has caused problems in relation to international sports encounters when Protestants of this kind of persuasion have been asked to compete on Sunday.

THE EASTER CYCLE
The main annual festival for the first Christians was also the commemoration of the Resurrection of Jesus Christ, that is, Easter. The first Jewish Christians simply added this celebration to the celebration of the Passover which took place at the first full moon of the first month of spring (the night of 14–15 Nisan in the Jewish calendar). Since it was known that Jesus rose on the first day of the week the feast was eventually transferred to the first Sunday *after* Passover.

Christians also adopted the fifty days from Easter to Pentecost. Pentecost is the Jewish harvest festival which is also the commemoration of the revelation of the *Torah* (Law) to Moses. In the New Testament Book of the Acts of the Apostles it is recorded that it was on the day of Pentecost that the followers of the risen Christ received the Holy Spirit (Acts 2:1). In English-speaking countries Pentecost is sometimes called Whitsunday (White-Sunday). Thus the most ancient Christian Year focussed on the celebration of Easter through to the feast of Pentecost.

COMMEMORATION OF SAINTS AND MARTYRS
Of course, in the early centuries of the Church's life, there was much persecution and local churches would adopt the custom of commemorating annually the deaths of their own martyrs and

saints. The intensity of their faith is shown in that those commemorative days were sometimes referred to as the saint's 'birthday'. They meant their birth into a new risen life beyond the grave.

Later developments in the Church's Year

In the Roman Empire at the time of Emperor Constantine, Christianity became tolerated and two early developments resulted for the calendar. Firstly a longer time of preparation for Easter was established (called Lent in English). Originally this period was to prepare candidates for baptism at the Easter festival. It gradually became a general period of discipline and penance for all members of the Church. Secondly, a new feast was introduced to celebrate the birthday of Christ.

THE CHRISTMAS CYCLE

No one knows the date on which Christ was born, but the Church fixed the celebration on 25 December. In the Roman world the Saturnalia was celebrated on 17 December and 25 December was kept as the birthday of the Iranian god Mithras, sometimes also called *Sol Invictus* (the Unconquerable Sun). The choice of date around the winter solstice and associated with the unconquerable sun seems to have been deliberate, and some would say well-chosen since from that time the light grows steadily longer each day.

The Church in the eastern part of the Roman Empire originally commemorated both the birth and baptism of Jesus on 7 January . However, under the influence of Rome, 25 December was gradually adopted by most Churches, although some still hold to 7 January. The Armenian Church, for example, still celebrates the nativity on that date. In the West the Epiphany is kept on 6 January and it celebrates the coming of the Magi to the Christ child. The twelfth night after Christmas is taken as the end of the Christmas festival and has acquired its own aura in western culture. The Eastern Church still celebrates the baptism of Jesus at Epiphany. Later, the Church in the West added a preparatory season before the Christmas festival, known as Advent.

Three bases of the Church's Year

The Christian Year is an amalgam of three cycles. The most ancient is the Easter cycle, the date of which varies because it depends on the phases of the moon, while the accepted calendar year is based on the solar seasons. Next there is the Christmas cycle which has a fixed day related to the sun (the winter solstice). Lastly there are throughout the year a number of other festivals on fixed dates together with the commemorations of saints and martyrs.

While having the same basic structure the Eastern Byzantine tradition and the Roman Catholic tradition show a slight difference.

THE EASTERN ORTHODOX TRADITION

The Easter and Christmas cycles produce the following pattern. In addition to Easter, which the Orthodox call the 'Feast of Feasts' there are twelve major feasts, indicated below in bold letters. (Certain Orthodox Churches follow the Julian calendar, which in the present century is thirteen days behind the current Gregorian use; for example, 6 August Julian = 19 August Gregorian.)

September	*March*
1 New Year	
8 **Nativity of Blessed Virgin Mary**	
14 **Exaltation of the Holy Cross**	25 **Annunciation**
October	*April*
	Orthodox Sunday
	The Great Fast (Lent)
	Palm Sunday
	Easter (movable)
November	*May*
21 **Presentation of Blessed Virgin Mary in the Temple**	**Ascension** The Fathers of the First Ecumenical Council
December	*June*
25 **Christmas**	**Pentecost** The Feast of All Saints
January	*July*
6 **Epiphany**	
February	*August*
2 **Hypapante** ('Meeting' of Christ with Simeon)	6 **Transfiguration**
	15 **Falling Asleep of Blessed Virgin Mary**

The Easter cycle includes a period of ten weeks before the feast and eight weeks after it. The first four Sundays of the ten-week period prepare for the Great Fast (Lent). Many Sundays in the Orthodox Church take their title from the Gospel lesson for the day. The first two of the four preparatory Sundays are called 'The Sunday of the Pharisee and the Publican' and 'The Sunday of the Prodigal Son'. The eight weeks following Easter include the feast of the Ascension and culminate in the Festival of All Saints on the Sunday after Pentecost.

THE ROMAN CATHOLIC TRADITION
The Christmas and Easter cycles are shown below. Major festivals are indicated in bold letters.

November
     1st Sunday in Advent
 30 St Andrew (First of the
       fixed holy days)
	May
	
	 Ascension (40 days after
	     Easter

December
     2nd Sunday in Advent
     3rd Sunday in Advent
     4th Sunday in Advent
 25 **Christmas**
	June
	 Pentecost
	 Trinity Sunday
	 Corpus Christi

January 6 **Epiphany**	*July*

February
     Ash Wednesday (40 days
       before Easter excluding
       Sundays)
	August

March
     Palm Sunday
     Holy Week
     Easter (movable)
	September

April	*October*

The Roman Catholic Church devised rules for deciding on the canonisation of saints. This resulted in the steady addition of saints' commemorations to the calendar. The Church also prescribes certain days as 'holy days of obligation', when all the faithful are expected to attend Mass. *All* Sundays are holy days of obligation. These holy days usually include:
Christmas Day (*25 December*)
The Octave of Christmas Day (*1 January*)
Ascension Day

Assumption of the Blessed Virgin Mary (*15 August*)
All Saints' Day (*1 November*)
Immaculate Conception of the Blessed Virgin Mary (*8 December*)
St Joseph's Day (*19 March*)
Annunciation (*25 March*)
Sts Peter and Paul Day (*29 June*)
Corpus Christi (*Thursday after Trinity*)

THE YEAR IN OTHER CHURCHES

As already indicated, observance of the Church's Year is of most importance to members of the Orthodox and Roman Catholic Churches. One should also include here the Anglican and Lutheran Churches both of which are traditionally committed to the cycles of the Church's Year.

In many Reformed Churches, only Sunday observance is obligatory. This, of course, includes Easter and Pentecost. Nevertheless there is a revival of interest in the observance of the traditional seasons in spite of a tendency to proliferate special Sundays devoted to particular themes such as Education Sunday, Race Relations Sunday, and so on.

Harvest Festivals, although not assigned any particular date, are held in the autumn and have been common in the Christian Church since the Middle Ages.

A relatively recent development is the observance of an Octave or Week of Prayer for Christian Unity from 18 to 25 January – now jointly sponsored by the World Council of Churches and the Vatican Secretariat for Promoting Christian Unity.

The festivals

The Christmas cycle

Advent (November–December)

The Christian Year begins with the First Sunday in Advent which occurs on the fourth Sunday before Christmas. The season of Advent ('coming') as a preparation for Christmas seems to have originated in Gaul in the sixth century CE. To begin with the length of the period varied (in one ancient calendar this was as much as six Sundays before Christmas). The four Sundays now observed in the West date from the time of Pope Gregory the Great (died 604 CE).

Advent is a sombre but hopeful season. The first Sunday is often observed with a solemn procession in a darkened church, illuminated only by the candles carried by the acolytes. There are readings from the Old Testament which are interpreted by Christians as foretelling the coming of a saviour, and hymns and carols are sung appropriate to the season, such as the well known *O Come, O Come, Emmanuel*.

In some Reformed Churches in Europe there is the custom of the 'Advent crown' which has four candles on it. On each of the Advent Sundays another candle is lit and the light increases as the great festival approaches.

The season is one full of expectation, but sometimes overwhelmed with anticipations of Christmas, as many people celebrate with Christmas carol services before the actual day has come.

Christmas (25 December)
From the religious point of view, the most important Christian festival is undoubtedly Easter, but the most widely celebrated is Christmas. Christmas is celebrated in both secular and religious fashion. The English name derives from the Old English *Cristes maesse*, Christ's Mass. (Mass is the name of the liturgical meal, sometimes called the Eucharist or Lord's Supper.)

Christmas commemorates the birthday of Jesus Christ. For Christians it marks the coming of God the Son to the earth, becoming incarnate in the womb of Mary and being born as a man. This is seen as the greatest gift of God to man and the surest reason for thanksgiving and celebration. In many countries the name of the feast refers more directly to the birth such as the Spanish *Natividad* or the Italian *Natale*.

The religious celebrations include the lavish decoration of churches and attendance at the liturgy. The custom of the Midnight Mass, which originally was the custom for Easter Eve, has been widely adopted at Christmas also.

St Francis of Assisi in 1223 CE used a crib in celebrating the Christ Child at Greccio in Italy. The building of a crib at Christmas has become a universal custom since then, and most churches will have a blessing of the crib, which is set in a stable with the figure of Mary, the mother of Jesus, and Joseph her husband, together with animals, such as an ox and an ass. These images derive from the account in Luke's Gospel of the announcement by angels of the birth of Jesus to shepherds in the fields and the story of the birth at Bethlehem. In Luke's account Jesus was born in a stable or cattleshed because there was no room in the inn. His cradle was a manger (Luke 2: 1–18).

The account in Matthew's Gospel tells of the coming of wise men from the East, often referred to as Kings or Magi, who followed a star which stood over where the young child was. They brought the symbolic gifts of gold and frankincense and myrrh. Gold for a king, incense for God, and myrrh as a presage of suffering (Matthew 2).

Many of the customs associated with Christmas derive from its occurrence at the midwinter solstice. This has traditionally been a time of great merrymaking and of an exchange of presents. Some of the feeling of the feasting and celebrating seems to reflect the Roman festival of Saturnalia (17 December) and some from the proximity of the new year when the giving of presents was an attempt to influence the fortunes of the year to come. In the West other customs come from the Teutonic midwinter rituals such as the lighting of the Yule log and decorating homes with mistletoe and other evergreens. Two traditions seem to meet in the Christmas tree, which derives from the Tree of Paradise in mystery plays and is yet associated with the evergreen of Teutonic custom.

The music of Christmas is represented by carols which are an amalgamation of secular and religious practice. Carols were originally songs for dancing and that is why many of the older ones are so cheerful and rhythmic. Many carols are also in the style of madrigals and motets.

Another popular feast day in the Middle Ages was that of St Nicholas of Myra on 6 December. The saint was supposed to visit children with rewards and punishments according to their desserts. This behaviour is still acted out in several countries. In Britain and many other countries the St Nicholas tradition has been assimilated to the Christmas festival and in the form of Santa Claus (from the Dutch *Sinter Klaas*) he has become a legendary figure who is supposed to bring presents to children on Christmas Eve. Sometimes he is simply called Father Christmas and a whole folk tale has grown up around him attributing his home to the North Pole and giving him transport in a magical sledge drawn by magical reindeer.

The secular celebration calls for a great feast on Christmas Day and this has come to have a turkey as the most common dish. However in bygone times, it was a goose and even further back a swan. Britain has developed the custom of the Christmas pudding and its hidden coins or trinkets.

Many regret however the commercialisation of Christmas – with shops inviting excessive spending and excessive preoccupation with material goods from as early as October.

Opposite: *The building of a crib at Christmas has become a universal custom . . . with the figure of Mary, the mother of Jesus, and Joseph, her husband, together with animals, such as the ox and an ass.*

Feast of the Holy Innocents (28 December)
This festival commemorates the slaying of all the male children in Bethlehem under two years of age by Herod, the ruler, who, because of the message of the wise men, feared the birth of a rival.

This is a sad festival but it is a repeated reminder to Christians that the innocent suffer for the sins of men and the death of these children was a precurser of the innocent suffering of Jesus. It is also a reminder not to expect that there will be an equitable distribution of pain and joy in this life, that sometimes one has to trust God to make sense of the bitter suffering of the innocent.

Epiphany (6 January)
Epiphany means 'manifestation' and in Greek usually referred to the manifestation of some divine power. In early Christian use it refers to the manifestation of Jesus as the Son of God at his Baptism. In the fourth century CE the Epiphany appears in the Eastern Churches to commemorate three 'manifestations': Jesus' birth, his baptism and his first miracle at Cana (John 2: 1–11). Eventually virtually all Eastern and Western Churches adopted 25 December to celebrate the birth of Jesus and in the West the Epiphany was used primarily to commemorate the adoration of the magi or the 'manifestation of Christ to the Gentiles'. The interval between the festivals of Christmas and Epiphany established the twelve days of Christmas.

Epiphany is often celebrated by processions in which the Magi figure – traditionally considered to be three kings (legend even provides them with names) who brought the three gifts mentioned in St Matthew's Gospel: gold, frankincense and myrrh.

The Easter cycle

Shrove Tuesday (February)
The day before Lent begins has several traditional customs associated with it. The name derives from the practice of going to confession for absolution and penance before Lent begins (Middle English 'shriven'). The custom of making pancakes on Shrove Tuesday arose because of the need to get rid of the fat in the home before the fast of Lent. There also arose the secular custom of having a 'party' on Tuesday before facing the rigours of the Lenten fast. In many parts of the world (including the famous New Orleans) this became a carnival – the carnival of *Mardi Gras* (Fat Tuesday).

Lent (February–March/April)
Lent is the season of penitence and preparation which precedes Easter, lasting forty days. In the Eastern Church it is called the Great

Fast and is itself preceded by four weeks of preparation.

The Lenten period was originally a period of instruction for candidates for baptism. The baptisms would take place at Easter, the great feast of new life. Later it became a time of discipline for all the faithful.

Ash Wednesday (February)

Lent begins on Ash Wednesday, so called because of the custom in some churches of the imposition of ashes on that day. The priest marks the forehead of the faithful with a little ash as a sign of penitence and a recognition that the worshipper is no more than ashes in the sight of God and totally dependent on his grace.

Holy Week (March/April)

The last week of Lent, called Holy Week, is dedicated to a remembrance of the Lord's Passion, that is, the sufferings and death of Jesus.

On each day of Holy Week up to and including Friday, the Gospel reading is taken from the passion accounts found in all four Gospels, such that all four passion narratives are read in full. Sometimes these are solemnly sung with a narrator and other voices to represent Jesus and other occasional speakers. The congregation or choir takes the part of the crowd.

Palm Sunday (March/April)

Holy Week begins with Palm Sunday (now also referred to in the Anglican and Roman Catholic Church as Passion Sunday), so called because there was a blessing of palms and a procession with palm branches on that day reflecting the Gospel account of Jesus' entry into Jerusalem on the last week of his earthly life. This custom continues in various forms throughout the world. Sometimes the faithful receive pieces of palm leaf in the form of a cross or plaited into a decorated motif, or a small spray of boxwood. In England sometimes palm willow or rosemary is used.

Maundy Thursday (March/April)

Thursday in Holy Week is known as *Maundy Thursday*. The word 'maundy' is thought to come from the Latin *mandatum* (commandment), and this day is marked by a festal celebration of the Eucharist because it is the day on which Jesus commanded his disciples to perform this act in remembrance of him. Thus it commemorates the institution of the sacrament.

In Roman Catholic churches and others which follow the Easter customs, the altars are stripped of their decoration and washed on Maundy Thursday. Some follow the ritual of a symbolic washing of feet in imitation of the action of Jesus at the Last Supper, described in John's Gospel (John 13:34).

Good Friday (March/April)
On Friday of Holy Week, the day that commemorates the crucifixion of Jesus, some churches keep the Mass of the Presanctified. It is called 'presanctified' because on Good Friday there is no conse-cration of bread and wine, but communion is given from the reserved sacrament, the consecrated bread kept from a previous Mass. On this occasion the reserved sacrament will have been kept on a special altar surrounded by flowers and attended by one or two of the faithful all through the night of Thursday. This practice reflects a response to Jesus' rebuke to his disciples in the Garden of Geth-semane: 'Could you not watch with me one hour' (Mark 14:38 *et al*).

On Good Friday churches are cleared of all hangings and dec-oration so that the building will look plain and austere. A simple cross or crucifix occupies a central position. In many churches there is a three-hour meditation between twelve noon and three o'clock, representing the time that Jesus is believed to have hung on the cross. Some churches also have the ceremony of Veneration of the Cross, in which the faithful come to prostrate themselves in ador-ation before the cross. One of the most ancient and moving of Chris-tian hymns is sung on Good Friday, the *Pange lingua* (*Sing my tongue the glorious battle*), in which Christ's passion is seen as a victorious struggle against the forces of evil.

Of course, it must be recognised that not everyone in a Christian culture will make these observances. Good Friday has become a public holiday and many sporting fixtures are kept on that day, including horse-race meetings. A food associated with Good Friday is the hot cross bun – a small spiced sweet bread with currants, marked on top with a pastry cross.

Some places have dramatic local customs, such as the procession of penitents in Seville – all hooded so that their anonymity is preserved and they should gain no personal applause. Other places have set up pilgrimages in which a wooden cross is carried over a fairly long distance as a witness to their commitment to 'take up the Cross' of Jesus.

Holy Saturday (March/April)
No special ceremonies take place on the Saturday in Holy Week until the late evening. In the Gospel account Jesus lies dead in the tomb. The faithful in the Orthodox Churches of Romania will go to church, where an icon of the dead Jesus lies flat on a table. As part of the devotion they will pass under the table from one side to the

Good Friday in Guatemala. The act of penitence is accompanied by the statues of the Virgin Mary and other saints and the procession is led by a band.

other, symbolising the desire to die with Jesus (and so die to sin) and rise again, through his death, to a new (sinless) life.

Easter (March/April)

The name of this festival derives from the old English *easter* or *eastre*, a festival of spring. Most Romance languages, however, use a name derived from the Hebrew *Pesah* (Passover), for example the French *Pâques*. Easter commemorates the resurrection of Jesus Christ from the dead and it is observed on the first Sunday following the first new moon after the vernal equinox. The date, being based on a lunar calculation, varies therefore within the solar year adopted by western countries. The time of year, as with Christmas, symbolises something of the sense which the festival has for the believer. It is the time of the burgeoning of new life which reflects for the Christian the new life and promise of life in Christ's resurrection.

In the Orthodox Churches, Easter is awaited at midnight on Holy Saturday. The church is dark and on the stroke of the new day light is passed from one to another in kindling candles and lamps. A show is made of searching for the body of Jesus in an empty tomb and the cry goes up 'Christ is risen' with the response 'He is risen indeed'. This custom is also observed in some modern African churches.

There is a similar liturgy in Roman Catholic, and some Anglican, churches in the West: A new fire is struck to represent the light of Christ and a special large paschal candle is carried through the church representing the coming light of Christ in his resurrection, driving away the powers of darkness and death. There are readings from the Old Testament.

In the ancient Church, candidates for baptism would be taken to the baptistry at this point for their initiation. In the present time the baptismal waters are indeed blessed, using the paschal candle in the ceremony, but there may not be any candidates for baptism; instead of the Easter Eucharist or Mass beginning around dawn, it is begun much sooner. The church will have been decked with flowers and the best vestments and chalice which the church possesses will be used. Easter is the highest point of the Church Year and for the Christian it is the most important feast of the year.

Of course Easter also has many secular customs associated with it also. Many of them seem to be survivals of ancient spring fertility rites, such as the symbols of the Easter egg and the Easter hare or rabbit.

For the Church, the Easter celebration is intended to continue for fifty days to Pentecost and include the commemoration of the Ascension.

An Easter service in the Patriarchal Cathedral, Moscow.

Ascension (May)

Originally the ascension of Christ (see Luke 24:50–51) Acts 1:1–11) was simply included as part of the total victory of the risen Christ, and indeed theologically this is so. The concept of the resurrection of Christ includes the idea that he has totally overcome death and returned to the Father. By the end of the fourth century CE the ascension was, however, being universally observed in the Church on the fortieth day after Easter. But even today some Christians feel that the separate commemoration of the ascension is unwarranted.

Ascension always falls on a Thursday. There are no widespread special customs accompanying it other than the celebration of the appropriate Eucharist. In most countries, Ascension Day passes with very little notice and it is only public institutions with some Christian foundation which treat it as a holy day – or 'holiday'.

Pentecost (June)

The name Pentecost derives from Greek *pentecoste* (fiftieth day) and the festival is celebrated on the seventh Sunday after Easter.

Pentecost was, and is, a Jewish feast taken over and given another meaning by the Christian Church (see Leviticus 23: 15–26). It remains for Jews a harvest festival occurring on 'the day after the seventh sabbath', that is, after Passover, and is called the Feast of Weeks. It was at an early stage associated with the giving of the Law at Sinai.

The Christian festival celebrates the gift of the Holy Spirit to the disciples of Christ (Acts 2: 1–11) and also the beginning of the Church and its mission. Arrangements are made in church similar to those at Easter for candidates to be baptised. Indeed the Anglo-Saxon name for Pentecost is White Sunday (Whitsunday), said to have arisen from the white garments worn by the newly baptised.

Pentecost is an important festival completing the Easter cycle, but it is for the most part much less observed than Easter and its function appears to be less understood among the population of Britain than any of the other major Christian festivals. Some popular customs associated with Whitsunday persist in the North of England – such as the Whit Walk and Well-dressing – but these seem to have non-Christian origins.

Trinity Sunday and the Festival of All Saints (June)

Trinity Sunday is the Sunday following the Feast of Pentecost. It is a festival which developed relatively late (in the tenth century CE) and its connotations are more theological than rooted in popular devotion. It is the culminating Sunday of the whole Christian Year, celebrating the glory and majesty of God in all his fulness. Many powerful hymns are associated with this feast, such as the famous *Holy, Holy, Holy, Lord God Almighty*. It is one of the designated days in the western Church for the ordination of priests.

The Orthodox Church keeps the Festival of All Saints on this Sunday.

Corpus Christi (June)

Corpus Christi is a Latin name meaning 'the body of Christ'. However the new Roman Catholic calendar has adopted the title the Body and Blood of Christ with Corpus Christi as a subtitle. This feast was instituted in 1264 by Pope Urban IV and it is observed on the Thursday after Trinity Sunday. For the Roman Catholic Church this feast ranks with the other major feasts of the Church. In the Church of England the feast does not generally have the same prominence, but appears in the calendar as the Day of Thanksgiving for the Institution of Holy Communion.

The thanksgiving for the Holy Eucharist was originally kept on Maundy Thursday but in the Middle Ages it was felt that the festive element had to be muted because it fell in Holy Week. It was in 1215 that the doctrine of transubstantiation was officially proclaimed by Pope Innocent III. This is the doctrine that the bread and wine of the sacrament are transformed in essence into the body and blood of Christ, and it is in response to this renewal emphasis that the feast was instituted.

The principal way in which the feast is celebrated is by processions in which the host (consecrated bread) is carried in a monstrance (an ornate, usually silver, vessel with a small glass container at the centre of a circular shape in which the bread can be seen). Over the monstrance and the priest carrying it will be a canopy borne up by four poles carried by acolytes. The procession often passes through the town and is accompanied by all the banners which can be mustered. Sometimes the route of the procession is strewn with flowers (carefully laid in patterns). The faithful will kneel, as the host passes, to honour the presence of Christ in the sacrament. In medieval times the procession would be accompanied by representatives of the trade guilds each carrying their distinctive banners. As it was already a day of pageantry, it also became the traditional day for the performance of the miracle plays, many of which have been revived in recent times.

The feast was repressed by the Reformed Churches because of their rejection of the doctrine of transubstantiation. It is revived in the form of a thanksgiving in the Church of England and many Anglican churches do celebrate it as the Feast of Corpus Christi.

The Sacred Heart of Jesus (July)

This is another festival whose date depends ultimately on the date of Easter. It is celebrated on the Friday of the third week after Pentecost. This feast dates back to the late seventeenth century CE, but was only introduced into the Roman calendar by Pope Pius IX in 1856. It is therefore, a feast of the Roman Catholic Church only.

The use of the symbol of Jesus' heart to show his love for men is not found in the Bible, but it became much encouraged by Carthusians and Jesuits. St Francis de Sales made the heart the emblem of his order. It was perhaps a reaction to the over-intellectualism of late seventeenth- and eighteenth-century theology. Devotion to the sacred heart of Jesus is widespread and the image of Jesus with a superimposed heart in conventional shape is often displayed in the homes of the faithful. The great basilica of the Sacré-Coeur in Paris designed in the nineteenth century by Paul Abadie bears witness to the popularity of this devotion.

Feasts of the Blessed Virgin Mary

These are:

1 The Nativity of the Blessed Virgin Mary (*8 September*)
2 The Immaculate Conception of the Blessed Virgin Mary
   (*8 December*)
3 The Annunciation of the Lord (*25 March*)
4 The Visitation of the Blessed Virgin Mary (*31 May*)
5 The Assumption of the Blessed Virgin Mary (*15 August*)
6 The Solemnity of Mary, Mother of God (*1 January*)

These feasts are all observed in the Roman Catholic Church. The calendar makes a distinction in importance between numbers 2, 3, 4 and 6, which are all referred to as 'solemnities', ranking with the major feasts of the Church. The others are referred to simply as feasts.

The Blessed Virgin Mary is the mother of Jesus. She is the focus of especial devotion and worship because she is the point at which the Incarnation takes place, the meeting place between heaven and earth. Devotion to Mary is quite central in both the Orthodox

Opposite: *A crowd of 10,000 people take part in the annual pilgrimage to the Shrine of Our Lady at Walsingham, Norfolk. An Anglican pilgrimage, it is led by bishops from the Church with a service held in the grounds of the abbey, before proceeding to the shrine itself.*

Churches and the Roman Catholic Church. Some of her festivals are also kept in the Anglican Church (see below). In the Reformed Churches, the Blessed Virgin Mary does not figure in liturgical practice or any other observance other than in her New Testament historical role. Indeed, the veneration of the Virgin is one of the points of contention between the Reformed Churches and the Roman Catholic Church. The Reformed Church fears that the role given to Mary in the Roman Catholic and Orthodox Churches is a threat, theologically, to the unique mediation of Jesus Christ. This explains why these feasts are not observed by all Christians.

The Nativity of the Blessed Virgin Mary (8 September)
The celebration of the Virgin Mary's birthday is attested in the East from the eighth century but was not generally observed in the West until the eleventh century.

The Immaculate Conception of the Blessed Virgin Mary (8 December)
In Anglican calendars this appears simply as the Conception of the Blessed Virgin Mary. The date is deduced from having fixed the Nativity on 8 September. According to various sources the festival is thought to have originated in England before 1066. It was abolished at Canterbury by Lanfranc, (*c.*1010–89 CE), but was reintroduced in England in the twelfth century. Since 1854 it has been called the Immaculate Conception in the Roman Catholic Church.

Mary was declared Mother of God at the Council of Ephesus in 431. This gave rise to the conviction that one so close to God could not have committed any sins. It was therefore increasingly felt that she must have been free of any disposition to evil – or 'original sin', inherited from Adam. John Duns Scotus argued in the thirteenth century that Christ's redemptive grace was applied to Mary to prevent sin reaching her soul so that she was redeemed in a more perfect manner than anyone else. This 'advance redemption' means that Mary must have been conceived 'immaculate', since original sin is thought of as residing organically in the flesh of man. This was declared a doctrine of the Roman Catholic Church by Pius IX in 1854. The doctrine received considerable impetus from the reported visions of Bernadette Soubirous at Lourdes in 1858. There the Virgin Mary revealed herself as The Immaculate Conception.

The Annunciation of the Lord (25 March)
This festival celebrates the incident described in St Luke's Gospel (Luke 1: 26–38) when the angel Gabriel came to announce to Mary that she would conceive in her womb and bear a son whom she would call Jesus and that he would be the Son of God. She is

assured that this will come about by the power of the Holy Spirit. Mary's response is contained in the canticle which has become known as the *Magnificat* from the first word in the Latin translation. This day is often called Lady Day, from the custom of referring to Mary as Our Lady.

This is, of course, a festival observed by the Orthodox, Roman Catholic, Anglican and Lutheran Churches. It encapsulates the theology of the incarnation, with the heavenly messenger, the assurance of a miraculous birth by divine intervention and the acceptance by Mary of her vocation: 'Behold I am the handmaid of the Lord; let it be to me according to your word.'

The Visitation of the Blessed Virgin Mary (31 May)

In the Roman Catholic calendar this does not rank so importantly as the Annunciation. The Church of England Alternative Services Book 1980 lists the festival under the heading 'Lesser festivals and holy days'. Again it celebrates an event described in the Gospel of St Luke (Luke 1: 39–49) where Mary visits her cousin Elizabeth who is the mother-to-be of John the Baptist.

The Assumption of the Blessed Virgin Mary (15 August)

This festival is observed by the Orthodox and Anglican Churches as the Falling Asleep of the Blessed Virgin Mary. The doctrine that Mary was taken up (assumed) into heaven, body and soul, is not mentioned in the New Testament; the earliest mention is met in Coptic texts.

'Jesus took the soul of His mother to heaven on Tobi 20. On Mesore (August) 15 the Apostles assembled, and on the morrow saw Jesus with Mary in a chariot, the body being no longer in the tomb.'
WK Lowther Clarke, *Liturgy and Worship*, SPCK 1932, p 230
(quoting MR James, *The Apocryphal New Testament*)

The Assumption of the Blessed Virgin Mary became a frequent theme in religious painting in the West, for example Titian's *Santa Maria dei Frari* in Venice. The theme became even more popular in the Renaissance and Baroque periods. The Virgin is 'shown in an attitude of prayer, supported by angels, ascending above her open tomb, around which the Apostles stand in amazement'.

The festival is celebrated with great vigour in many parts of western Europe and is often kept as a public holiday in addition to religious observance. In many places in Brittany, where devotion to the Virgin Mary is particularly strong, it is celebrated with processions of a statue of the Virgin Mary and village fêtes: traditional dress is worn and the festival is a colourful event. However, celebration of this kind is not confined to Brittany, and in the Catholic world this festival is probably second only to Christmas in popular appeal.

The Solemnity of Mary, Mother of God (1 January)
This is an exclusively Roman Catholic festival. The first of January in the Anglican calendar is kept as the Circumcision of our Lord.

The doctrine of the Mother of God was made explicit at the Council of Ephesus in 431 CE (see The *Immaculate Conception*). The same Council thereby condemned Nestorius, the Bishop of Constantinople, who felt that the title Mother of God (the literal translation from the Greek is 'Bearer of God') did not do justice to the human nature of Christ. He preferred the title Bearer of Christ, or Mother of Christ. However the title Mother of God triumphed and became one of the tests of orthodoxy.

A further theme which has developed in Roman Catholic devotion to Mary is her coronation in heaven. As a theme in religious art it developed in France and Italy in the twelfth and thirteenth centuries CE and often appeared over a major portal of a church. Again, like the assumption, it was a favourite for altarpieces in the Renaissance and Baroque periods. The theology of this event has never been fully developed, but it represents the culmination of Christ's redemption where Mary is seen as being representative of all humanity whose ultimate destiny is to reign in heaven. She is celebrated on the first of January because it is the octave (eighth day) of Christmas and in the Roman Catholic cult Mary the Mother of God is the human partner of the act of incarnation.

Saints' Days

The origin of the practice of commemorating saints was connected with the outbreaks of persecution against Christians before the time of the Emperor Constantine and the custom was generally restricted to a memorial of those who suffered martyrdom. Church buildings were often later erected over the tombs of martyrs, and the anniversary of their deaths kept as a reminder of the communion of the saints. The observance of local saints still continues, together with particular national saints' observances.

Holy days set aside for the commemoration of saints vary widely in the Christian Church. As stated earlier, the Orthodox Church did not add any saints to its calendar after the tenth century CE. The Church of England did not add any saints after the Reformation, but has added commemorations of persons important in Christian history since the Reformation – such as Thomas Ken and William Law (eighteenth century), John Keble (nineteenth century) and

Josephine Butler (twentieth century).

The Roman Catholic Church has evolved an exhaustive system for nominating a person as a saint, and therefore saints have been identified at irregular intervals over the centuries. Some of these are martyrs persecuted by other Christians at the Reformation, such as St John Fisher and St Thomas More.

The Reformed Churches on the other hand wish to dispense with the title saint, in the sense of implying some higher status than other Christians. The objection to the term varies in its emphasis. Some would consider it blasphemous to presume to know the fate of any Christian and still more so for the Pope to presume to pronounce on the saintly status of a departed Christian. They would insist that we are all sinners saved by grace and the idea that some can acquire greater merit than others by their own efforts is particularly abhorrent. So the veneration of saints is primarily an Orthodox and Roman Catholic practice. The Orthodox in particular represent the saints by icons and feel that these icons are windows into heaven and that they bring the consciousness of the unity of the Church on earth with those who have triumphed in heaven.

St Joseph (19 March)
The Roman Catholic Church gives particular stress to this feast and it is included in the major feasts called solemnities. St Joseph was the husband of the Blessed Virgin Mary and acted as Christ's earthly father. He was a carpenter and is the patron of manual workers.

The Birth of John the Baptist (24 June)
The birth of John the Baptist also ranks as a solemnity in the Roman Catholic Church and is celebrated at the time of the longest day, in contrast to the birth of Jesus, celebrated on the shortest day of the year. John said, 'I must decrease, he must increase.' From 24 June onwards the light begins to decrease. John was the wandering prophet who announced the coming of the Christ before the latter began his preaching.

St Peter and St Paul (29 June)
In the Church of England this is the feast of St Peter alone. In the Roman Catholic Church the feast is a solemnity; these two saints are seen as the twin founders of the Church and Peter in particular is held to be the predecessor of all the Popes. He was appointed as leader of the apostolic band by Jesus shortly before his death.

All Saints (1 November)
This festival is kept in the Orthodox Church on the first Sunday

after Pentecost. It was possibly transferred to its present date in the West by Gregory VII (died 1085). It was originally called All Martyrs. It is an acknowledgement that the Church does not know *all* who are saints and also it expresses the conviction that the saints are many in number. The feast is a solemnity in the Roman Catholic Church.

The day before *All Saints* is the secular feast of *Hallowe'en* – from 'all hallows e'en' (the night before All Saints Day). It so happens that in ancient Britain the Celtic festival of Samhain was observed on 31 October as the end of the summer. It was also the eve of the new year in both Celtic and Anglo-Saxon times – a time of huge bonfires on hilltops to frighten away evil spirits. The souls of the dead were supposed to revisit their homes on this day and so the day acquired all its connections with ghosts, witches and black cats.

The Four Evangelists and the Twelve Apostles
Generally speaking, in addition to those mentioned above, Churches which celebrate saints' days will also include the following (dates given are those of the Roman Catholic Calendar) in their year:

1 The Four Evangelists
  St Mark (*25 April*)
  St Matthew (also an Apostle) (*21 September*)
  St Luke (*18 October*)
  St John (also an Apostle) (*27 December*)

2 The Twelve Apostles
  St Philip and St James (*1 May*)
  St Matthias (who replaced Judas Iscariot) (*14 May*)
  St Peter (and St Paul) (*29 June*)
  St Thomas (*3 July*)
  St James (*25 July*)
  St Bartholomew (*24 August*)
  St Matthew (also an Evangelist) (*21 September*)
  St Simon and St Jude (*28 October*)
  St Andrew (*30 November*)
  St John (also an Evangelist) (*27 December*)

3 Those given the rank of Apostle in the post-Resurrection period.
  Conversion of St Paul (*25 January*)
  St Barnabas (*11 June*)
  St Stephen (the first martyr) (*26 December*)

There are many more, but the reader is advised to consult the published calendars of the Churches.

Other Christian festivals

The Transfiguration (6 August)
This is a festival whose observance originates in the Eastern Church. It commemorates the incident described in the Gospel of St Luke (Luke 9: 28–36) when Jesus was seen transfigured and talking to Moses and Elijah. The theme is a popular one for icon-painting; the icon, so much a part of orthodox spirituality, 'hovers' between heaven and earth and in this story there are the signs of the encounter of this side with the 'other'.

St Michael and All Angels (29 September)
This feast appears as Sts Michael, Gabriel and Raphael, Archangels in the Roman Catholic calendar. The chief celebration of the angels in the Eastern Church is on 8 November.

Christianity, like Judaism and Islam and other western religions, has always included a belief in angels as celestial or spiritual beings. Archangels are chiefs, rulers or princes of angels. The number of archangels mentioned in texts varies from three to twelve, with the numbers four and seven being the most popular. The number seven seems to be related to the seven planetary spheres as defined in Greek and Persian astrology. Each sphere is ruled over by an archangel. The number four may be derived from the four shrine guardians of the diety in the sacred writing of Judaism, Christianity or Islam, or it may perhaps derive from the symbolism connected with the number four which signifies perfection. The four most frequently noted are Michael, Gabriel, Raphael and Uriel, although the last name scarcely appears in the Christian tradition:

Michael (the Hebrew means 'who is like God') is the warrior leader of the heavenly hosts against the forces of evil. He is seen as the main adversary of Satan, the angelic prince of evil (see Daniel 10, 12; Jude 1: 9; Revelation 12: 7–9)

Gabriel (the Hebrew means 'man of God') is God's messenger. He explains the prophet's visions (Daniel 8, 9) and announces the coming birth of Jesus and of John the Baptist (Luke 1). As Jibril in Islam he reveals the Qur'an to Muhammad.

Raphael (the Hebrew means 'God heals') is prominent in apocryphal Jewish books and in the Kabbalistic tradition of Judaism, but is of lesser importance in Christianity.

Uriel is one of the seven 'angels of presence' most closely associated with the person of God, but is little known in the Christian tradition.

Whatever view of angels may be taken by individuals, popular piety in medieval times was much oriented towards these celestial beings. For Christians they are a reminder that God's creation is not necessarily confined to human persons, and that the issues of good and evil are of cosmic significance.

Michaelmas as a popular abbreviation has come to give its name to a season in the year and in some ancient seats of learning it is the name given to the autumn term.

The Presentation of Christ in the Temple (2 February)
This feast was originally called the Purification of the Blessed Virgin Mary from the words in the story as recorded in St Luke's Gospel (Luke 2: 22–35). Modern calendars rightly emphasise the presentation of Christ since the feast is much more related to Jesus than to his mother.

The old English name for the festival is *Candlemas*. The name arises from the beautiful custom still observed in many churches of carrying lighted candles in procession. In the story Simeon meets Jesus with his parents in the temple and pronounces the words:

> 'Lord now you let your servant go in peace
> Your word has been fulfilled
> My own eyes have seen the salvation which you have
> prepared in the sight of every people
> A light to reveal you to the nations and the glory
> of your people Israel.'

Luke 2: 29–32

This is called the *Nunc Dimittis* (from the Latin translation of the first words) and was adopted as the canticle in the monastic service of compline and incorporated in the Church of England form for Evening Prayer.

The lighting of candles picks up the reference to the 'light to reveal you to the nations' and the procession commemorates the entrance of the infant Christ, the True Light, into the temple.

Table of Christian festivals

1 January   The Solemnity of Mary Mother of God
6 January   Epiphany
25 January   Conversion of St Paul
February   Shrove Tuesday; Ash Wednesday
2 February   Hypapante
            The Presentation of Christ in the Temple

February–March/April Lent (The Great Fast)
19 March St Joseph
25 March The Annunciation of the Lord
March/April Holy Week: Palm Sunday; Maundy Thursday; Good Friday; Holy Saturday; Easter
25 April St Mark
May Ascension
1 May St Philip and St James
14 May St Matthias
31 May The Visitation of the Blessed Virgin Mary
May/June The Fathers of the First Ecumenical Church Pentecost; Trinity Sunday; All Saints; Corpus Christi
11 June St Barnabus
29 June St Peter and St Paul
July The Sacred Heart of Jesus
3 July St Thomas
25 July St James
6 August The Transfiguration
24 August St Bartholomew
1 September New Year (Eastern Orthodox Church)
8 September The Nativity of the Blessed Virgin Mary
14 September The Exaltation of the Holy Cross
21 September St Matthew
29 September St Michael and All Angels (Michaelmas)
18 October St Luke
28 October St Simon and St Jude
1 November All Saints
21 November Presentation of the Blessed Virgin Mary in the Temple
30 November St Andrew
November–December Advent
7 December St John
8 December The Immaculate Conception of the Blessed Virgin Mary
25 December Christmas
26 December St Stephen
27 December St John
28 December Holy Innocents

6 *Hindu Festivals*

ROBERT JACKSON

Hinduism

Hinduism is better described as a tradition rather than a religion. Though its history ranges over about 5,000 years, it has no founder, no single idea of God, and no essential creeds or doctrines. Even the term 'Hinduism' is a western and modern attempt to encapsulate the complex and organic family of religious phenomena that are rooted in the Indian tradition and have made no conscious attempt to break from it. The variety of Hinduism includes many contrasting features: sophisticated philosophical and theological speculation alongside the propitiation of localised malevolent powers; individual asceticism as well as a close family life and the corporate religious solidarity of many of Hinduism's numerous sects.

There is, however, a thread linking Hinduism's loosely associated constituent parts. This is made up of various strands corresponding to the tradition's remarkable sense of self-identity and to certain central – though not universal – practices, institutions, concepts and beliefs.

The key institutions are caste (each person is born into a hierarchically ranked, hereditary and normally endogamous social grouping) and the joint or extended family. One of the principal concepts is *dharma*, a rich idea which can denote the religious and moral duty incumbent on a member of a family and caste; others include *karma*, the notion that every action reaps in inevitable consequence and *samsara*, the soul's cycle of birth and rebirth.

Particularly difficult to grasp are Hindu views of deity which, although hard to express in terms of specific beliefs, illustrate important tendencies in the tradition. There is, for example, the notion of *Brahman*, the impersonal Absolute or World Soul that pervades the universe. The fact that *Brahman* is considered to be immanent as well as transcendent gives rise to a pantheistic tendency in Hinduism – a belief that the divine principle is present in

104

everything. At the same time there is tendency to personalise the divine, perhaps as *bhagvan* or *ishvara* (the Lord) and in this sense the Hindu religion has a monotheistic current. Hinduism is not crudely polytheistic for the *devas* (gods) are usually regarded as different aspects of the same reality. A peasant farmer may make offerings to several *devas* and yet still affirm *'bhagvan ek hai'* – 'God is one'. Further there is the notion of the *ishtadeva*, the chosen deity who is worshipped by a person as the Supreme God, while that same individual denies neither the reality of other gods nor that other people will have different chosen deities.

The three main theistic aspects of Hinduism involve devotion to Vishnu (Vaishnavism), to Shiva (Shaivism), or to the Mother Goddess (Shaktism). Vishnu is regarded as a benevolent god, who in times of moral decline appears in the world in various forms (*avatars*, literally 'descents') to restore justice. Generally there are thought to be ten such *avatars* (animal, semi-human or human), the most important being Krishna and Rama. Krishna is worshipped as a divine child, a mischievous flute-playing young man and as a great hero. In the popular text known as the *Bhagavad Gita* Krishna appears as a divine charioteer who speaks of salvation through enlightenment, action and especially through *bhakti* (loving devotion to the Lord). In the *Ramayana* epic Rama is a god-prince who, by destroying Ravana, a demon who had abducted his wife Sita, restored righteousness to the world.

Shiva's complex character has various sides. To some he is loving and full of grace, but he is also the fearsome destroyer, a great ascetic god and a god of procreation. Iconographically he is generally pictured in an aggressive form, carrying a trident and wearing a necklace of cobras or as the *linga*, an ancient male fertility symbol.

The cult of the Mother Goddess had its origins in devotion to Shiva's wife – Durga in her fierce form, Parvati in her benevolent aspect. Its followers came to be called Shaktas, since they believed the goddess to be the *shakti* (the energy, immanent and active in the world) of the remote and transcendent Shiva.

In the villages – the home of about 80 per cent of the Indian population – devotion to one or more of the great *devas* is found alongside worship of the *gram devatas*, village deities or 'godlings'. While these lack the *devas*' great power, they are less remote and can affect a person's welfare, especially bringing disaster if they are not suitably propitiated. Many 'godlings' are conceived of in female form (*mata*) and occasionally one of these figures is identified with a major goddess. A villager who propitiates a local godling, it should be noted, may also venerate one or more of the *devas* and still affirm that God is one.

The final, and probably most important, strand consists of the main religious practices. These include devotional rituals (which vary from caste to caste, being particularly elaborate for devout brahmins), the *samskaras* or life-cycle rites (marking the main transitions of a Hindu's life such as initiation, marriage and death) and worship. Worship (*puja*) may take place in the home or in the temple, and in the *bhakti* tradition may be performed through the group-singing of devotional hymns. Another meritorious religious act is pilgrimage to local, regional or national sites such as Varanasi (Benares).

The most colourful feature of Hindu practice, however, is the annual cycle of festivals which again may be local, regional or all-Indian (for example Divali and Navaratri). The festivals bring gaiety and life to Hinduism, being occasions of celebration as well as a yearly reminder of religious values. Since they illustrate many of the features of Hinduism outlined above their study can provide an excellent introduction to the tradition.

The festivals

Introduction

Hinduism almost certainly has a longer list of festivals than any other religion. In a country of India's vastness, with its geographical, cultural and linguistic variety, it is hardly surprising that only a small number of festivals are universally observed. Many others are celebrated in a group of northern or southern states, in a single state or in a more restricted area. There are numerous festivals confined to a few villages or even to a single hamlet. It should also be remembered that in many places Muslim festivals and sometimes the celebrations of other religions take place alongside those of Hinduism.

A piece of research conducted between 1959 and 1961 by the Anthropological Survey of India gives us some idea of the large number of Hindu festivals that could be encountered throughout the country, listing fifteen festivals known in at least six states, about fifty regional festivals and nearly three hundred 'local' festivals. The research was carried out in a total of 290 districts in nineteen states so the figure for regional festivals is conservative while that for local festivals represents a fraction of the real national total.

More daunting than the number of festivals is the staggering diversity of religious practice and belief within Hinduism which is reflected in the festivals. The all-Indian festival of Divali, for example, takes place at the same time throughout India although its length varies from two to five days. According to where it is celebrated Divali may be associated with one or more myths concerning Lakshmi (the goddess of wealth), the defeat of King Mahabali by the dwarf *avatar* of Vishnu, the god Yama, the goddess Kali or the return of Rama and Sita to Ayodhya. In many villages, however, there is only a hazy connection between the festival and such all-Indian myths, if any association is made at all. In Adrian Mayer's account of Divali in a central Indian village, for example, the festival includes such activities as the singing of traditional songs by members of Rajput, Weaver and Farmer castes; various customs performed by men of the Weaver caste involving the skin of a young calf; cow-baiting (again by the Weavers); the visit by some villagers to the shrine of a local *gram devata* or godling and the possession by a medium (a member of the Carpenter caste) of another godling who was consulted by various villagers about such matters as a wife's desertion; the education of a son; and a man's eye complaint (Mayer, 1960). There is no lighting of lamps and the only feature recognisable as belonging more generally to the festival is the recognition that it marks the New Year according to the Vikram era.

This brief account of Divali confirms that a comprehensive account of even the best known festivals is out of the question and shows that local, popular religion is of much more importance than many textbooks on Hinduism would suggest. It also suggests that the full significance of a festival in religious and moral terms can only be properly assessed in the context of a more general account of the religious life of the people who live in the place where the festival is observed. In this connection, the work of scholars such as Dube (1955), Lewis (1958) and Babb (1975) who have studied the complete festival cycle in one location, is particularly valuable.

In spite of the difficulties imposed by their large number and their variety there is still some value in giving a selective account of festivals as they have been observed in different places. Most importantly, such an account can illustrate the variety which characterises Hinduism: its rich mythology, seen live, as it were, in the festivals; the multifarious local manifestations; its several calendars; the multiplicity of languages through which the religion is expressed, and so on.

It can also draw attention to some common if not universal themes: the importance of time and season; the attainment of merit (*punya*) and the removal of sin (*pap*); fasting (*upavas*) and the making of vows (*vrata*); the place of religion in the home as well as in the temple and at the pilgrimage site; the part played in festivals by different members of the community – women, for example, or different caste groupings. It can also show that the localised worship of godlings and local goddesses is connected in various ways with devotion to the major gods and goddesses of Hinduism.

In drawing on examples of festivals from different parts of India, however, there is a danger that the reader might be tempted to generalise from particular instances cited. It must be remembered that accounts of festivals in villages refer to one place (even neighbouring villages may observe a different list of festivals) and one time (even though, for convenience, they have been written in the present tense).

The selection of festivals given below includes all those celebrated widely in more than half a dozen states, some of the better known regional festivals from different parts of the country and a small number of local celebrations chosen because they illustrate themes or motifs to be found in many other local festivals – for example, the propitiation of a goddess of disease. Note that although alternative names are specified in some cases, there are likely to be other regional and local titles.

Finally it must be emphasised that the examples below are not intended to be a curriculum! Information can be extracted to meet the needs and interests of pupils whether they be six-year-olds exploring the theme of celebration, eleven-year-olds finding out about the place of myth in religious life or sixth-formers grappling with the relationship between Hinduism and another faith or studying the festival cycle observed by a migrant Hindu community.

The Hindu Calendar

Several calendars are currently in use in India, including the Indian National Calendar and the Gregorian Calendar, both of which are used for civil affairs. Religious events such as festivals (apart from modern celebrations such as Gandhi Jayanti) are calculated according to the ancient luni-solar calendars which have their roots in the Vedic literature.

Although there are a number of regional variations, two main luni-solar systems operate in India. These are the *purnimanta* system in which the moment of the full moon ends the lunar month, and the *amanta* system in which the end of the month is marked by the moment of the new moon. The *purnimanta* system is used in most of northern India, while the southern states use the *amanta* system. Both have lunar and solar features and these will be described separately.

LUNAR FEATURES

The two systems have a year consisting usually of twelve lunar months, with each month (*chandra mas*) representing the time taken for the moon to complete a phase. Every month is divided into two fortnights (*pakshas*). The waxing fortnight or 'bright half' (*shukla-paksha*, often abbreviated to *shudi*) lasts from the moment of the new moon to the moment of the full moon. From this time to the moment of the new moon is the waning fortnight or 'dark half' (*krishnapaksha* or *badi*). Each month consists of thirty lunar days (*tithis*) which are usually slightly shorter than solar days, so that a complete month is equivalent to approximately twenty-nine and a half solar days. The names of the lunar months are the same as twelve of the twenty-seven constellations (*nakshatras*). In the *amanta* system the lunar month in which the vernal equinox (*mesha sankranti*) occurs is given the name of the constellation Chaitra and becomes the first month of the year.

The *purnimanta* system derives the names of the months from the *amanta* system, but since *purnimanta* months begin and end with the full moon, the first (bright) fortnight of an *amanta* month becomes the second (bright) fortnight of the equivalent *purnimanta* month. Thus, according to the *amanta* system, the first day of the Hindu religious year is Chaitra, *shudi* 1, while the *purnimanta* new year is Chaitra, *shudi* 15. Note, however, that variations on these systems, as well as alternative calendars, place New Year at other times (see the entry on New Year).

It is important to remember that the second half of any *amanta* month. Chaitra, *badi* 1 on the *amanta* system, for example, is equivalent to the *purnimanta* system's Vaishakha, *badi* 1. Hence, although a festival celebrated all over India may take place on different dates according to the two systems, it may well occur at the same time.

Another point to remember is that the standard names for lunar months (Chaitra, Vaishakha, etc.) are in the Sanskrit language. The names vary in the north Indian vernacular languages, although they generally bear some resemblance to the Sanskrit original. The names in the four south Indian Dravidian languages are sometimes very different from the Sanskrit ones. The Tamil names are included in the table (below) since Tamil is an ancient language of considerable literary and symbolic importance to south Indians. Even in the case of languages as different as Sanskrit and Tamil there are some obvious equivalent names, such as Chaitra (Sanskrit) and Chittrai (Tamil).

Names of months on Indian Calendars

Gregorian months	Indian solar months: astrological names (rashis)	Indian solar months: Sanskrit lunar names (as used in the Indian National Calendar)	Purnimanta months: Sanskrit names (beginning with the dark fortnight)	Amanta months: Tamil names (beginning with the light fortnight)
January	Kumbha (Aquarius)	Magha	Magha (Jan/Feb)	Tai (Jan/Feb)
February	Mina (Pisces)	Phalguna	Phalguna (Feb/Mar)	Maci (Feb/Mar)
March	Mesha (Aries)	Chaitra	Chaitra (Mar/Apr)	Pancuni (Mar/Apr)
April	Vrishabha (Taurus)	Vaishakha	Vaishakha (Apr/May)	Chittrai (Apr/May)
May	Mithuna (Gemini)	Jyaishtha	Jyaishtha (May/June)	Vaikaci (May/June)
June	Karkata (Cancer)	Ashadha	Ashadha (June/July)	Ani (June/July)
July	Simha (Leo)	Shravana	Shravana (July/Aug)	Ati (July/Aug)
August	Kanya (Virgo)	Bhadrapada	Bhadrapada (Aug/Sep)	Avani (Aug/Sep)
September	Tula (Libra)	Ashvina	Ashvina (Sep/Oct)	Purattaci (Sep/Oct)
October	Vrishcika (Scorpio)	Karttika	Karttika (Oct/Nov)	Aippaci (Oct/Nov)
November	Dhanus (Saggitarius)	Margashirsha or Agrahayana	Margashirsha or Agrahayana (Nov/Dec)	Karttikai (Nov/Dec)
December	Makara (Capricorn)	Pausha or Taisha	Pausha or Taisha	Makali (Dec/Jan)

SOLAR FEATURES

The western solar calendar has been known in India since the fourth century CE and is of great importance in making astrological calculations. The names of the Indian solar months are in all but one case – Makara (crocodile) replaces Capricorn (goat) – Sanskrit equivalents of the Latin names of the signs of the zodiac (see table). Confusingly, the zodiacal names for the solar months tend to be used only by astrologers, while the names of the lunar months are commonly applied also to the nearest equivalent solar months (see table).

In addition to its use in astrology the solar calendar provides the dates for a number of important festivals associated with solstices and equinoxes (see, for example, Makar Sankranti and Vaisakhi), and various inauspicious days such as solar eclipses.

Note that the Indian solar day begins and ends at sunrise and not at midnight as in the West. Lunar days may begin at any point during the solar day. In order to correlate lunar and solar days, any solar day is given the same number as the lunar day that was current at sunrise, that is, the beginning of the solar day. Lunar days vary in length to some degree, and some of the shorter days begin after sunrise and end before the next sunrise. These days are deleted from the calendar. Should a festival or ceremony be scheduled for one of them it is generally celebrated or performed on the previous day. In like manner a lunar day is added whenever there are two sunrises on the same lunar day. Usually there are thirteen deleted lunar days and seven added ones during a year. Festivals are usually fixed to occur on lunar days but they are generally celebrated during the solar day which bears the same number as the correct lunar day.

The lunar year is brought into accord with the solar year by the addition, and very occasionally the deletion, of lunar months. The rules for adding and deleting months in both the *amanta* and *purnimanta* systems are complex. For present purposes it is necessary to know that a month is added every two and a half to three years, while months are deleted rarely. Added months are often placed after the month Ashadha (June/July) or Shravana (July/August) and are simply called 'second Ashadha' or 'second Shravana', though in 1982 a second month of Ashvina (September/October) was added. In Britain, Gujarati Hindu communities took account of the added month when arranging the dates of festivals, whereas many Punjabi Hindu and Sikh communities failed to do this. The result was that many Punjabis celebrated Divali on 15 October, while Gujarati Hindus held the festival on 15 and 16 November.

Needless to say the calculation of the correct Gregorian dates for

111

festivals in any particular year is difficult. Readers wishing to know the correct dates for Hindu festivals should consult the current *Calendar of Festivals* published by the Shap Working Party or an Indian Gregorian calendar which includes the dates of major festivals. Such calendars are often on sale in Asian general stores.

ERAS

In India before *c*.100 BCE there seems to have been no system of recording the year of an event by dating it in a definite era. Subsequently several different systems were adopted, of which the Vikram era (dated from 58 BCE) is the earliest, becoming widely used in north India. Originally its year began with the month of Karttika (and indeed it still does so in Gujarat state), and this is why Divali is regarded as a New Year festival. By medieval times, however, most states using the Vikram era had adopted the *amanta* method of reckoning New Year in the month of Chaitra.

The other commonly used era is the Shaka, begun in 78 CE. As well as being used by many states for the luni-solar calendar, the Shaka era was adopted for the solar Indian National Calendar when it was introduced in 1957–58. Other eras no longer in use are the Gupta era begun in 320 CE and the Harsha era started in 606 CE.

Of mythological and religious interest are the four *yugas*, eras of the world's existence. The three periods *krita* (or *satya*), *treta* and *dvarapa* have already elapsed and we are now in the most decadent age, the *kali* era which is reckoned to have started at dawn on 18 February 3102 BCE.

SEASONS

There are six seasons on the Indian calendar, each corresponding to two months. Phalguna and Chaitra comprise spring; Vaishakha and Jyaishtha, summer; Ashadha and Shravana, rainy; Bhadrapada and Ashvina, autumn; Karttika and Margashirsha, winter; and Pausha and Magha, dewy.

SPECIAL DAYS

Regardless of whether or not a festival is held, certain days of the month are widely regarded as being religiously significant. The most important days are *purnima* (full moon) and *amavasya* (new moon) on which many orthodox Hindus fast. *Purnima* is considered to be an especially auspicious day.

The fourth days (*chaturthi/cauth*) of both fortnights are frequently connected with Ganesha or Ganpati, the elephant-headed son of Shiva who is regarded as a remover of obstacles. The eighth days (*ashtamis*) are commonly associated with the goddess in one form or another, although the important festival of Krishna's birthday also occurs on an eighth day. The eleventh days (*ekadashis*) are very important, especially to Vaishnavas – devotees of Vishnu in one or other of his manifestations – and they are considered to be fasting days. Several of the more important *ekadashis* are regarded as festivals and these are mentioned below in the entry on Ashadhi Ekadashi.

FAIRS

In many places *melas* or religious fairs are held during the year, and they vary greatly in size and importance. The smallest and most local of these are known as *marhais*. For reasons of space, only the great Kumbha Mela has been included in the selection of festivals that follows.

The festival cycle

Makar Sankranti/Til Sankranti/Lohri (around 12 January)

The first day of each solar month corresponds to the sun's entry into a particular sign of the zodiac. All such days (*sankrantis*) are regarded as auspicious, especially those marking the winter and summer solstices and the vernal and autumnal equinoxes. Of these the most important is the winter solstice, marking the sun's entry into Makara (Capricorn). This was at one time regarded as New Year (see below) and in some areas of Gujarat is an important day for almsgiving. In some parts of north India it is customary to patch up quarrels, especially between a married girl and her in-laws. Other customs include the eating of rice pudding, pancakes, halva, ghee and brown sugar and the feeding of cattle.

In some regions, for example the Punjab, the festival is known as Lohri. Children collect money from neighbours, and bonfires are lit in the evening, attracting large numbers of people. Corn and sweets are thrown into the fires and popular folk songs are sung. In Tamil Nadu the festival is known as Pongal (see below) and in Andhra Pradesh it is called Til Sankranti. At certain winter solstices bathing fairs called Kumbha Melas (see p. 115) are held in north India.

Pongal (January)

This south Indian festival is both a 'rite of passage' of the sun marking its entry into Makara (Capricorn) and, with its emphasis on rice sheaves and sugar cane, a harvest festival. It begins on the winter solstice in the Tamil month Tai, and continues for the next two days. The word *pongal* means 'boiling' and refers to the fact that rice boiled with sugar is an essential item of diet at the festival.

Sweet rice pudding is offered to Surya, the sun god, during the Tamil festival of Pongal.

The day before the festival people buy lengths of sugar cane from market or roadside stalls. The cane is crushed and boiled to make jaggery, a sugary syrup. Milk is heated until it boils, and jaggery and rice are added. This sweet rice pudding, having been already offered to the deities, is eaten as the climax of a festive meal.

Traditionally, the second day is devoted to the worship of Surya, the sun god, and sweet rice pudding is offered to the sun. The third day (sometimes the second day), is called Cattle Pongal (*Mattu Pongal*). In each household a selected cow is worshipped, fed on boiled rice and then driven off! Cattle, including water buffaloes, are garlanded, their horns and sometimes their sides are painted, and they are bedecked with rice sheaves. The cattle are herded together and driven off by drumming and the playing of a large oboe-like instrument. Bullock fights are traditionally held in some villages at this time.

National cricket matches (for example the 1982 Test Match with England held in Madras) are often arranged to coincide with the festival.

Kumbha Mela (every twelve years, date varies)
The Kumbha Mela, a massive gathering of pilgrims, is held every twelve . years at four sacred places in north India: Prayag (Alla-habad), Hardwar, Nasik and Ujjain. The date of the festival varies according to place. At Prayag it is the occasion when the sun's entry into Makara (Capricorn) and Jupiter's entry into Vrishabha (Taurus) coincide, while at Hardwar it occurs when the sun's entry into Mesha (Aries) coincides with Jupiter's entry into Kumbha (Aquarius), a date which places the Kumbha Mela later in the year.

The festival is rooted in the myth of a battle between the gods and the demons in which neither could defeat the other. Both sides fought over a pitcher (*kumbha*) of immortality-giving nectar which had been acquired from the bed of the ocean by churning it up. Ultimately the gods won the battle and became immortal but in the course of the struggle drops of nectar fell at the four sites where Kumbha Melas are held.

In 1966 nearly fifteen million pilgrims went to Prayag in the period between 7 January and 18 February. On the great day of the Kumbha Mela (the new moon of Magha) nearly seven million pilgrims bathed at the confluence of the Ganges and the Yamuna, a stretch of water shorter than 2,500 metres! Between the Kumbha Melas held at Hardwar in 1962 and 1974 there was an increase in the number of pilgrims, due to better transport arrangements and the use of modern technology in making the festival safer.

Hindus from many different regions and backgrounds attend the Kumbha Melas, with members of the numerous sects and ascetic orders being prominent.

Vasanta Panchami/Shri Panchami/Saraswati Puja (January/February)

Vasanta Panchami is celebrated on Magha, *Shudi* 5. It marks the advent of spring and is widely celebrated in north India. Although not celebrated in south India as a public or household festival, Vasanta Panchami is celebrated in some temples. The name of the festival literally means 'yellow fifth' or 'spring fifth'. Many families wear yellow clothing on this day, a ceremonial bath is taken, and some women fast.

The festival is also known as Shri Panchami. Although in antiquity the celebration may have been associated with Shri, or Lakshmi, goddess of wealth, it is commonly linked with Saraswati, goddess of learning and the fine arts. Indeed in some places the festival is known as Saraswati Puja, although this name is more generally used of one of the days in the Navaratri festival (see below). In many places, since Saraswati is the goddess of learning, books and writing implements are not used on this day, but are set up near the domestic shrine, and a *puja* (worship) to Saraswati is performed. In some areas, especially west Bengal, clay images of Saraswati are processed through the streets and eventually immersed in a river or a pond. The BBC film *Three Hundred and Thirty Million Gods* in the series 'The Long Search' includes an excellent sequence on Saraswati Puja showing a school boy, assisted by his Sanskrit master, reciting verses and performing rituals intended to invoke the presence of Saraswati in an image of the goddess specially set up at the school for the duration of the festival.

Bhogali Bihu (January/February)

This harvest festival in the month of Magha is included as an example of a regional festival from the eastern state of Assam. After the winter paddy harvest, thatched pavilions are erected only to be burnt as part of the festivities.

There are two other Assamese Bihu festivals, Goru and Rongali Bihu, the latter being a spring festival of dance and music celebrated in Vaishakha (April/May).

Mahashivratri (January/February)

The eve of each new moon is a special night for Shiva (*shivratri* means Shiva's night), but the full moon night (*badi* 14) in the month of Magha (in some areas Phalguna) is known as Mahashivratri (Great Shiva Night), and some devotees spend the whole night singing the praises of Lord Shiva and sometimes reading the *Shiva Purana*. According to Hindu mythology Shiva performs the cosmic dance of creation, preservation and destruction on this night. Special celebrations are held the following day at the most important Shiva temples and centres all over India, for example at the temple of Lord Visvanatha at Varanasi (Benares) in the north and at the Brihadesvara temple at Tanjore in the south. The sculptures of Shiva cut out of the rock in the cave on the island of Elephanta near Bombay are among the many centres attracting a great number of pilgrims on this day.

An account of the festival in one village in Uttar Pradesh reports that villagers take an early morning bath and fast until afternoon and even then only eat a few berries and millet-seed sweets. At about one o'clock in the afternoon the women of the village, singing as they go, walk in family groups to a Shiva temple in a nearby village, each woman carrying a pot of water, some flour, a few berries and an earthenware *ghi* lamp, all on a metal tray. Each woman pours the water over the *linga* (a phallic stone representing Shiva) and places her offerings in front of it. A non-Brahmin priest employed at the temple later accepts the various offerings. The women then return to their village and end their fast. About three quarters of the women in the village – mainly from high and middle ranking castes – take part in the festival, though a small number of men visit the temple early in the morning. About twenty pilgrims from the village visit larger and more distant Shiva temples where there are entertainments such as fairs and wrestling matches. These larger temples offer overnight accommodation to pilgrims.

In the central Indian village of Chhattisgarh, Mahashivratri, like Teej (see below), is connected with the marital welfare of women. Married women who worship Shiva on this day pray for the welfare of their husbands, while unmarried women make offerings to Shiva in the hope of getting a good husband.

Among the various myths connected with Mahashivratri is the following tale about Shiva. A hunter finds himself alone and far from home at nightfall so he climbs for safety into a tree. Then he weeps because his wife and children have no food and will be going to bed hungry. His tears fall on a *linga* of Shiva which is hidden beneath the branches of the tree. Shiva accepts the hunter's tears and his fast as authentic worship and rewards him by allowing him to be reborn as a great king.

Ramakrishna Utsav (20 February)
Ramakrishna's birthday, like Gandhi Jayanti, is included as an example of a modern festival independent of the ritual and agricul-

tural calendar. Born in a west Bengali village on 20 February 1833, Ramakrishna was of the most important Indian mystics of modern times. Many of his teachings were formalised within a framework of neo-vedantist philosophy by his disciple Swami Vivekananda whose writings present the view that the main world religions are simply different paths leading to the same goal.

Devotees of Ramakrishna go in procession from the Kali temple at Dakshineshwar, where the mystic had a vision of the goddess, and through the main streets of Calcutta. Ramakrishna's birthday is also celebrated wherever there are branches of the Shri Ramakrishna Math, both inside and outside India.

Holi (February/March)
Holi is a spring festival observed widely in north India, though it is celebrated in many different ways and its origins are obscure. The date of the first day of the festival – the full moon of Phalguna – around the time of the spring harvest, the building of a bonfire and some relaxation of accepted social hierarchical norms are the commonest features. The festival's association with stories about a demoness, often called Holika, is also common.

The length of the festival varies but in rural north India it goes on for at least two or three days giving ample time for festivities. Typically these include the lighting of the bonfire, the offering of coconuts, grain, and so on, which are partially roasted on the fire before being shared and eaten as *prasada* (holy food), and the (usually good-hearted) spraying of coloured dye or powder, often indicating a certain amount of inter-caste or inter-sex rivalry. In villages the direction of the bonfire flames is sometimes thought to indicate the land which will be especially fertile during the following year. The paint throwing can degenerate literally into mud-slinging, and the inter-sex and inter-caste antics sometimes include beatings, usually of the men by the women. Erotic dancing, on occasion, highlights the festival's association with fertility and spring, and the shouting of obscenities is not uncommon. The temporary relaxation of normal rules of behaviour has been variously interpreted as helping to maintain the established social order or as providing the means for the whole community to go through a period of ritual pollution which, for a time, removes most of the barriers that hold people apart.

In some areas, for example Gujarat, babies and young children are carried around the bonfire, a ritual intended to protect children from harm and sometimes associated with the story of Krishna and Putana (see below).

The festival is sometimes associated with Krishna because the squirting of coloured dye is, by some, traced back to Krishna's frolics with the *gopis* or cow-herd girls and because the story of demoness Putana, who was slain by the infant Krishna, is connected with the festival in some places. It should be emphasised that myths, customs and rituals associated with Holi vary considerably from place to place.

Perhaps the myth most commonly told at Holi is the story of Prahlada and Holika – a tale which has many regional variations, although the central plot remains more or less the same. King Hiranyakashipu had a son called Prahlada who, instead of worshipping his demon father, was a devotee of Vishnu. Hiranyakashipu tried various manoeuvres to get Prahlada to change his ways, all to no avail. Finally the king sought the aid of his sister Holika, who could resist fiery flames because of a boon granted in view of her devotion to the fire god Agni. Because of Prahlada's devotion to Vishnu he survived while his demon aunt perished in the flames. Vishnu triumphed over Hiranyakashipu; good triumphed over evil. The bonfire motif clearly links the story with the festival.

On the same date as Holi, Dola Yatra is held in parts of west Bengal and Orissa, for example. At dawn on the full moon day, images of Krishna are placed on swings and set in motion for a short period. The ritual is repeated at noon and at sunset. Other practices, such as the sprinkling of coloured powder or water are similar to those performed at Holi, and in some places the two festivals are indistinguishable.

New Year festivals (dates vary)
There are several New Year festivals associated with the various Indian calendars (see The Hindu Calendar).

According to the solar reckoning, the first day of the year is the spring equinox (Mesha Sankranti), the day on which the sun enters the zodiacal sign of Aries (Mesha) – a date which falls around 12 April. In some north Indian states, for example the Punjab, the day is called Vaisakhi or Baisakhi (see entry below).

In most states which use luni-solar calendars the New Year begins on the day following the new moon immediately after Mesha Sankranti (see The Hindu Calendar). Thus in the southern state of Andhra Pradesh, for example, the New Year festival of Ugadi (see entry below) takes place on the day after the new moon day of Chaitra. In some states this day is not celebrated as a festival even though it marks the beginning of the religious year.

In Gujarat where an early form of the Vikram reckoning is still used (see The Hindu Calendar) the year begins in the month of Karttika (October/November), and so Divali (see entry below) is a

New Year festival there. Indeed Divali is still regarded as a New Year festival in some areas that have for centuries placed the beginning of the year in Chaitra (March/April).

In Kerala, the year begins with the Malayalam month of Chingham (August/September) and the New Year festival is Onam (see entry below).

Vaisakhi (Baisakhi) (approximately 12 April)

In some north Indian states, including the Punjab, Haryana and Himachal Pradesh the solar New Year, which occurs at the spring equinox, is celebrated as a festival known as Vaisakhi. In the Punjab Vaisakhi marks the ripening of the rabi harvest and is an occasion when spectacular Bhangra dancing is performed by troupes of men.

The festival is especially important for Sikhs, since on Vaisakhi day in 1699 Guru Gobind Singh formed the Khalsa, a martial brotherhood of Sikhs pledged to defend themselves and their faith from oppression (see chapter on Sikh Festivals).

Ugadi (March/April)

Ugadi, celebrated on Chaitra, *shudi* 1, is a New Year festival in the southern state of Andhra Pradesh. In rural areas a drink called *bevu* is prepared from fresh tamarind pulp, jaggery (molasses), pieces of green mango and leaves or flowers of the neem tree – ingredients which are the products of spring and symbolise newness of life and energy. Householders offer the drink to relatives, neighbours and friends as a gesture of good will. Traditionally there is a recitation, given by the family head or a brahmin, of the previous year's events as they have affected the family.

In the village of Shamirpet all the responsible village elders and representatives of the main agricultural families meet in the evening and a brahmin priest, consulting his almanac, makes predictions for the year. His forecasts concern such matters as crop levels, the health of residents and their cattle, and the possibility of epidemics or accidents. After the meeting small groups of people reminisce about past years and, in the light of the brahmin's predictions, comment on future possibilities (Dube, 1955).

Basora (March/April)

Basora (sometimes called Sidhi or Satain), celebrated on Chaitra, *shudi* 7, is a festival confined to parts of Uttar Pradesh, but included here since it has a common Indian village theme – the propitiation of a smallpox goddess. Lewis records that some inhabitants of the village he calls 'Rampur' travel thirty miles to Gurgaon to seek protection from Gurgaon-wali Mata, a smallpox goddess. Others, in extended family groups, visit a small shrine to this goddess on the outskirts of 'Rampur'. Offerings of food and water are made and songs in praise of the goddess are sung including such words as 'O Mata, you gave us children; now protect them from disease!' (Lewis, 1958).

Rama Navami (March/April)

The festival of Rama Navami (Rama ninth) falls on Chaitra, *shudi 9*, and is celebrated in most parts of India, particularly by Vaishnavites. On this day Rama Chandra, the seventh *avatar* of Vishnu is said to have been born at Ayodhya in what is now Uttar Pradesh at exactly twelve noon. Ceremonies re-enacting the birth of the god are held in many temples. Typically an image or a picture of the infant Rama is placed inside a small covered cradle. At noon the covering is removed, *bhajans* (religious songs) are sung and the god is worshipped by devotees who sometimes take turns in rocking the cradle. Special *prasada* is offered to Rama and this may then be shared among the worshippers. In parts of Gujarat the *prasada* consists of ginger, molasses and dill grains, all associated with the birth of children. At a celebration of the festival in an English city by a community of expatriate East African and Indian Gujarati Hindus the pattern outlined above was followed, though the *prasada* consisted of ground coriander seeds mixed with soft brown sugar and sweetened milk mixed with yoghurt.

At Ayodhya, Rama's birthplace according to the *Ramayana*, a large bathing fair is held and in some places images of Rama, Sita, Lakshmana and Hanuman are carried in procession around the streets.

Hanuman Jayanti (March/April)

In some areas the birth (on the full moon of Chaitra) of Hanuman, the monkey god of strength and great devotee of Rama, is celebrated. The *Ramayana* and *Hanuman-Chalisa* are recited in the home and in some temples, and occasionally a fair may be held near a Hanuman temple. Hanuman Jayanti is an important temple festival in some Maharashtrian villages, with the whole population taking part.

Akshaya Tritiya (April/May)

This north Indian festival, celebrated on Vaishaka, *shudi 3*, both marks the beginning of the agricultural season and, like various other festivals such as Mahalaya and Pitra, is concerned with the worship of ancestors. The name of the festival, which means 'inexhaustible third', perhaps refers to the bountiful harvest that is hoped for later. In some parts of central India the festival involves the ritualised gift of water to a brahmin, to a temple or to one's daughter, and also marks the beginning of the agricultural year.

In some states, for example parts of Gujarat, the festival is also important as the birthday of Parashu-Rama, the sixth *avatar* of Vishnu.

Chittrai (April/May)

The name of this festival, local to the south Indian city of Madurai, is the same as that of the Tamil month in which it occurs. Chittrai is celebrated on the full moon day and is really an amalgam of two festivals, the first being a celebration of the wedding of Shiva and Devi, known under the local names of Sundareshvara and Minakshi respectively, the second a re-enactment of the journey made by the god Vishnu, under the local name of Alagar, to the Vaigai river which borders on the old city of Madurai and of his return to his Vaishnava temple at Alakarkovil, twelve miles north of the city.

These two festivals have been combined into a two-scene drama enacted by the priests and servants of the two temples, and a local oral myth explains the fusion. In this, Alagar is portrayed as Minakshi's brother. Although he has been invited to Minakshi and Sundareshvara's wedding, he has been given the wrong time. He draws near to Madurai only to discover that the wedding has already taken place. Insulted, he goes instead to spend the night in Madurai with his mistress before returning to his own temple.

At the high point of the festival a crowd, estimated at around 500,000 people, gathers to participate in the auspicious presence of divinity.

Ganga Dasa-hara (May/June)

This festival celebrated on Jyaishtha, *shudi* 10, is especially popular in Uttar Pradesh. The name of the festival – literally 'Ganges ten-lost' – refers to the five major and five minor sins of body, mind and spirit which may be removed by bathing in the Ganges on this occasion. Bathing also takes place in other rivers such as the Yamuna (Jumna) on this day. Lewis reports that in 'Rampur' where the festival is called Jaith-Ka Dasahra, it is believed that bathing in the Yamuna removes sins such as killing ants or beating oxen incurred during agricultural work (Lewis, 1958). There are other bathing festivals in various locations on different dates.

Nirjala Ekadashi (May/June)

See Ashadhi Ekadashi (below).

Snan-yatra (May/June) and Ratha-yatra/Jagannatha (June/July)
The procession of a deity's *murti* (image) on a vehicle through the streets of a town is a feature of a number of festivals. Nowhere, however, is there such a spectacular display as that at the Ratha-yatra (pilgrimage of the chariot) festival in the city of Puri in Orissa. The deity is Krishna, known under the name of Jagannatha, attended by his sister Subhadra and his brother Balarama.

On the full moon day of Jyaishtha the festival of Snan-yatra takes place. The image of Jagannatha, which has been kept in its shrine since the previous year, is brought outside the temple and on a high platform is bathed, anointed with oil and clothed by priests in view of a vast crowd of people. After this the image is held up for all to see, and a great shout goes up from the people, many of whom believe that a sight (*darshana*) of the god will remove all of their sins.

For fifteen days the image of Jagannatha is kept out of public view and is cleaned and repainted. Then on the second day of Ashadha the images of Jagannatha, Subhadra and Balarama are brought out of the shrine and placed in enormous wooden cars about fifteen metres high which are towed by hundreds, or even thousands, of people to another temple in the city. The images are housed in this temple for a period of days before being returned to the cars and pulled back to Jagannatha's shrine.

Large-scale Ratha-yatras are also held in other places such as Calcutta, and in recent years the festival has become important outside India for members of the neo-Hindu Hare Krishna sect who hold Ratha-yatra festivals in such cities as London and New York.

The English word 'juggernaut' is derived from the name of the god, though it clearly refers to the enormous vehicles used to transport the deities rather than to the images themselves.

Ashadhi Ekadashi/Toli Ekadashi (June/July)
Ekadashi means 'eleventh', and this day in both the 'bright' and the 'dark' half of each month is traditionally a holy day. Particularly important eleventh days include Ashadhi Ekadashi (Toli Ekadashi in parts of south India) celebrated on Ashadha, *shudi* 11, Devuthna or Karttika Ekadashi, which takes place four months later (October/November), Nirjala Ekadashi, celebrated in Jyaishtha (May/June) in Gujarat and Madhya Pradesh for example, and the south Indian Vaikuntha Ekadashi observed in Margashirsha (November/December). All of these festivals share the common austerity of fasting (*upavas*).

Toli Ekadashi is celebrated in the southern state of Andhra Pradesh and marks the beginning of agricultural operations. In the village of Shamirpet members of the top three castes (Brahmins,

Komtis and Reddis) fast on this day in honour of Vishnu, although the fast is only kept strictly by all the brahmin adults. Some people fast totally until the evening even though certain foods are allowed to be eaten. In homes and at village shrines, images of Vishnu and his *avatars* are worshipped and offerings of such foods as dates and coconut are made to them (Dube, 1955).

In parts of north and central India this day is known as Ashadhi Ekadashi. In the village of Chhattisgarh it is said that Vishnu goes to sleep on this day and does not wake up until Devuthna Ekadashi (Karttika, *shudi* 11), four months later, after the rainy season (Babb 1975). This four-month period is commonly known by the Sanskrit word *chaturmas*, and is regarded by many Hindus as a period of self-control. On certain days and times during this period, particular foods may be avoided, fasts are held and there may be abstention from sexual intercourse. In some areas marriages are not conducted during *chaturmas* since Vishnu is asleep and unable to give his blessing and protection to the couples.

In the state of Maharashtra on Ashadhi Ekadashi large numbers of pilgrims from many parts of western India gather at Pandharpur to touch the feet of the image of the god Vithoba. The pilgrimage is repeated four months later at Karttika Ekadashi (Kartikka, *shudi* 11) after *chaturmas*.

Teej (Tij) (July/August)

Teej, celebrated on Shravana, *shudi* 3, is a north Indian festival popular in Rajasthan, but also celebrated in such states as Uttar Pradesh and the Punjab. The festival marks the beginning of the monsoon rains and, in its swinging rituals, has an ancient connection with fertility.

'After the hot summer months the monsoon rains have finally come, and now the air is cool and everything is green. Millet has been planted, sugar cane cultivated and the villagers are in good spirits. Tij is meant to express this mood.'

Lewis, 1958

Early in the morning men go out to hang swings from tree branches for their sisters or for other young women. In the afternoon, in an atmosphere of mild flirtation, young women go out to have swings and to sing appropriate folk songs. (Another example of a swinging festival is Dola Yatra, see under Holi.) At Teej young brides receive

Opposite: *Festival cars are common in the streets of Puri during Ratha-yatra. The car on the right is that of Jagannatha (Krishna) and is about 15 metres high.*

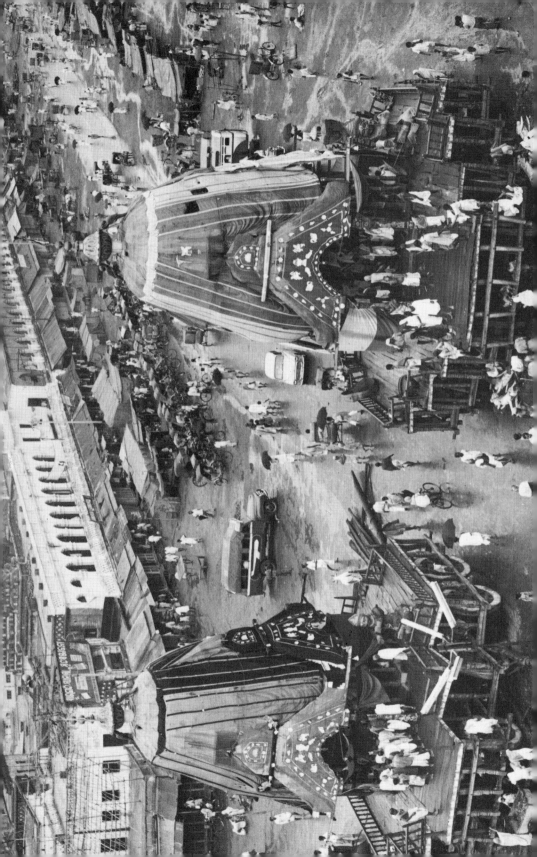

presents of clothing from their fathers-in-law. Presents may also be sent to daughters and daughters-in-law. In some areas married women fast for the long life and prosperity of their husbands, while unmarried women fast in order to get a good husband.

In many places the festival is associated with the goddess Parvati who, according to mythology, undertook severe austerities in order to secure her marriage to Shiva. In Jaipur a richly clad image of Parvati is borne around the city in an impressive procession which includes dancers, elephants and camels.

Naga Panchami (July/August)

This festival, falling on Shravana, *badi* 5, is widely celebrated, though the precise name and date vary. Naga Panchami means 'snakes fifth'; other names for the festival are Vishari Puja (*visha* means 'poison') and Guga Naumi, the latter being used, for example, in the Punjab and Uttar Pradesh, where the celebration takes place on Bhadrapada, *badi* 9 (September/October).

The festival has a number of associations, perhaps the most basic being the fear of snake bite. In west Bengal and parts of Orissa and Assam the snake goddess Manasa is worshipped to protect devotees from snake bite. It should be noted that Shravana coincides with the beginning of the rainy season when snakes come out of their holes and are therefore more of a threat to humans. In some places water is poured over images of snakes and offerings of food and water or milk are left by the holes where snakes are known to live.

Snakes are also associated with certain deities, particularly Shiva who wears a necklace of cobras and Vishnu who, according to the account of the creation of the universe given in the *Vishnu Purana*, sleeps upon the sea on the coiled body of his great snake Shesha, protected by a canopy formed by Shesha's thousand heads. Thus Vishnu observes the world as it passes through successive cycles of creation and destruction. In some areas Naga Panchami commemorates the victorious return of Krishna from the river Yamuna after he overcame the serpent Kaliya.

The snake is also associated with fertility, possibly because the animal is regarded by some as a phallic symbol. In some places infertile women, or women whose children have died soon after birth, worship the cobra in the hope of conceiving and giving birth to healthy children.

Raksha Bandhan/Shravana Purnima/Salono/Rakhi Purnima (July/August)

The festival of Raksha Bandhan takes place on the full moon of Shravana; *raksha* means 'protection' and *bandhan* means 'to tie'. In north India girls and married women tie a *rakhi* (amulet) on the right wrists of brothers, wishing them protection from evil influences of various kinds. In return the girls receive cash and gifts. Amulets are purchased from colourful stalls which offer a wide selection for sale and are sometimes sent through the post to brothers who live some distance away.

Various myths are associated with the festival in different places. In one, during a war between the gods and the demons, the consort of Indra tied a silken amulet around his wrist. As a result of this it is said that Indra won back his celestial abode. One explanation of the festival's origin given in a village in Uttar Pradesh traces it back to a warrior in the *Mahabharata* epic called Abhimanyu who was given an amulet by his grandmother. Although immune from harm while wearing it, he was overpowered when it broke in battle.

Raksha Bandhan is also a time when family priests visit their clientele to receive presents, and in some regions the occasion on which brahmins and members of other 'twice-born' castes change their sacred threads. In the village of Shamirpet in Andhra Pradesh, where the festival is known as Rakhi Purnima, twice-born castes put on new sacred threads and some of the occupational castes tie multi-coloured threads to their tools of trade. Work is suspended for the day and a festive meal is shared.

Onam (August/September)

Onam is a popular New Year festival widely celebrated in the south Indian state of Kerala in the Malayalam month of Chingham. The festival takes place in the middle of the harvest season. Houses are cleaned and decorated, new clothes are worn and there is a customary exchange of gifts between the head of each matriarchal clan and his dependents.

The festival is associated with a Puranic myth about Mahabali (Great Bali), a demon king who ruled in south India. Mahabali, surprisingly, followed the path of *dharma* and was a good ruler, bringing prosperity to his subjects. The gods, having become jealous of Mahabali's status, decided to send Vishnu to earth as Vamana, a dwarf. Vamana asked Mahabali for a piece of land – as much as he could pace out in three strides. Seeing how small Vamana was, Mahabali granted the request. Vamana then grew into an immense giant, measured the whole earth in two strides and with his third pushed Mahabali down to the nether world – but not before granting the demon king permission to come and see his people once a year.

For ten days leading up to the festival clay images of Mahabali are worshipped and beautiful floral decorations are made in honour of the king whose return is celebrated on the second day of the festival.

A spectacular feature of the festival is the snake-boat race, held at various places such as Aranmula and Kuttanad. Huge boats, covered with green and scarlet umbrellas are rowed by about a hundred oarsmen. The Prime Minister's Trophy boat-race at Alleppy has become a feature of Independence Day (15 August).

Ganesha Chaturthi (August/September)

This festival, on Bhadrapada, *shudi* 4, celebrates the birth of Ganesha, the elephant-headed deity. In origin Ganesha may well have been a local deity of the west of India but he has become absorbed into Hindu mythology as a son of the great god Shiva. The *Shiva Purana* tells the story of how Shiva's wife Parvati asked her son to stand guard over her room and to allow no one to enter whatever his rank or station. Parvati's husband, Shiva, came along and insisted on going in to Parvati but the boy refused to allow his father to enter. The *Purana* gives a long account of various attempts by Shiva to get past Parvati's son, employing the help of other Hindu deities. Finally, in a bloody fight, the boy is beheaded by Shiva's trident and lies dead on the battlefield. Parvati insists that Shiva undoes the wrong that he has done by replacing the boy's head with the head of the first living being that Shiva meets. Because Shiva encounters an elephant first, the boy receives an elephant's head.

In popular Hinduism Ganesha's importance is great, for he is the remover of obstacles who is prayed to by Hindus before they undertake any new or important enterprise such as getting married, taking examinations or moving house.

Ganesha Chaturthi is especially popular in western and central India, in Rajasthan and in the southern states of Andhra Pradesh and Tamil Nadu. It is not celebrated in several north Indian states, but is an important festival for Shaivites in the southern state of Tamil Nadu. It is an important festival in the village of Shamirpet in Andhra Pradesh, where it is called Chauti. Images of the deity are brought from the city of Hyderabad, or home-made ones of clay are used. Brahmin and Komti castes perform different and more complex festival rituals from those of other castes, and untouchable castes take no part. Each family worships its image of Ganesha and he is offered sweets. The image is kept in place and worshipped daily for three to twenty-one days. It is then taken to the village tank and immersed in water.

In the western state of Maharashtra, particularly in and around Bombay, the festival is celebrated enthusiastically. Clay images of Ganesha are worshipped and taken out in procession accompanied by the sound of drums and cymbals. The images (sometimes as much as eight metres high) are eventually immersed in a 'tank' or in the sea.

Janamashtami/Krishna Jayanti (August/September)

This festival, on Bhadrapada, *badi* 8, commemorates Krishna's birth, traditionally said to have been on the eighth night of the dark fortnight of Bhadrapada. Janamashtami means 'eighth day of birth'. Like Rama, Krishna is an *avatar* of the god Vishnu and is of immense importance in Vaishnavite Hinduism. Krishna is a many faceted deity. In the Indian classic the *Mahabharata* he is fundamentally an epic hero, while in the *Bhagavad Gita* – a later text which has been incorporated into the *Mahabharata* – Krishna is identified as God. In the *Gita*, Krishna is *the* incarnation of Vishnu, being fully personal and accessible and yet having divine attributes. In certain texts called *puranas*, Krishna is a young child who can get up to pranks and also astound his mother and others with his divine power. As a young man, Krishna plays amorously with the *gopis* (cow-herd girls), who gave their love selflessly to him. In one *purana*, Radha emerges as the most important *gopi* – she is Krishna's self-giving lover and the symbol of the worshipper in relation to God. Devotees of Krishna worship him in an intense and emotional manner, singing devotional songs and at times dancing in their expression of loving devotion to their lord. All kinds of human love are taken as parables or metaphors of Krishna's love for the devotee and the devotee's love for Krishna. This may be the deep affection felt by a lover for his or her loved one or it may be a mother's love for her child or devotion between friends. Different kinds of human love become idealised and serve as a means of concentrating the worshippers' thoughts on the divine person of Krishna.

Krishna is said to have been born at midnight, so many Hindus fast and stay up until that time in order to greet the baby Krishna with singing and dancing, and with offerings of butter and curds. The festival is celebrated with great enthusiasm at such Krishnaite centres as Mathura, Krishna's birthplace, and Vrindaban where Krishna is said to have spent his childhood. Pilgrims from all over India are attracted to these places for the festival where night-long prayers are recited and devotional songs are sung in the temples, which are decorated for the occasion with flowers and fruit. The festival is also celebrated in the home, where an image of the baby Krishna may be placed on a small swing or in a cradle, and pictures showing important incidents from Krishna's life may be displayed.

One of the myths often told about the festival's origin tells how the demon king Kamsa decided to kill all the children born to his sister Devaki, because he had been told by his advisers that he would be in mortal danger from one of them. Kamsa imprisoned his sister and brother-in-law and killed each child immediately after birth. Just before the birth of her eighth child, Krishna, Devaki persuaded her sister to exchange babies. Thus Krishna survived and later killed the demon king.

Mahalaya/Shraddha/Pitri Paksha/Kanagat (September/October)

This ritual occasion lasts sixteen days, from the full moon of Bhadrapada to the new moon of Ashvina. It is known by a variety of names including Mahalaya (the new moon day at the end of the fortnight is called *Mahalaya amavasya*), Pitri Paksha (a name for the whole fortnight), Shraddha and Kanagat. Every new moon day is important for ancestral offerings, but *Mahalaya amavasya* is especially important. Families who can afford to do so engage brahmin priests to recite the correct *mantras* (sacred words or syllables) and perform the *tarpana* rites or *shraddha* which reaffirms lineage ties. Performers generally mention the name of the original (mythical) lineage ancestor (*gotra*) and the names of the ancestors of three generations.

In some villages in Uttar Pradesh, the observances take place on any half day in the fortnight, according to the day on which the ancestor to be honoured died. Food is offered to brahmins on behalf of the dead person (usually deceased sons over eighteen, parents or grandparents). On the day of the ceremony the brahmin arrives at the family home early in the morning and takes a bath. From rice, milk, flour and ghee he makes rice puddings and chapatis. The eldest son bathes in the village pond before taking part in the ritual. The brahmin reads aloud some *mantras* while the son, facing the sun, pours water from a pot on to the floor. The brahmin offers rice pudding to a cow and chapatis to crows, and then he eats. It is believed that the dead person being honoured receives the benefit of the food. Members of some castes (usually lower ones) sometimes dispense with the services of brahmin, with the eldest son performing the rituals but not reciting the *mantras*.

Navaratri/Durga Puja/Dassehra (September/October)

Navaratri (also known by colloquial names such as Norta) and Durga Puja are the first nine nights of the bright fortnight of Ashvina (Puratacci in Tamil Nadu). Dassehra ('the tenth') is the day after Navaratri and in some areas refers to the whole ten day period.

Navaratri (nine nights) is one of the few genuinely all-Indian festivals and not surprisingly its modes of celebration vary widely. The main themes are the worship of the Goddess in various forms – especially in the form of Durga who, according to mythology, slew

Hindus from Bengal, now living in Delhi, transport an image (murti) of the goddess Durga which will be worshipped for nine days during the festival of Durga Puja.

the 'buffalo' demon Mahishasura – and celebration of the victory of Rama over the demon king Ravana on Dassehra, the tenth day.

The myth concerning Durga tells how Mahishasura once defeated all the gods who subsequently decided to kill him by sending Durga, armed with an especially powerful weapon from each of the deities. These included Shiva's trident, Vishnu's disc, Yama's spear, Agni's dart, a magical bow from Vayu and a quiver full of arrows from Surya, a sword and shield from Kala, a club from Kubera and Indra's thunderbolt. Riding on a ferocious lion provided by Himavan, and wearing beautiful jewellery as well as armour provided by Vishnu, she rode into battle and destroyed the demon.

In West Bengal and surrounding states the festival is known as Durga Puja, and the goddess's victory is central to the festival. Images of Durga, showing her dressed for battle and riding her lion, are worshipped for nine days and on the tenth day (Dassehra) they are taken to a river or pond and immersed in the water.

Another place where the Durga/Mahishasura myth is prominent is the Minakshi temple at Madurai in Tamil Nadu, where Minakshi is identified with Durga. On the first night of Navaratri the portable image of Minakshi, used in festivals, is placed in a special shrine to the goddess and an amulet, believed to protect the goddess in battle, is tied around the left wrist of the image. On the eighth night the decoration in the shrine depicts Minakshi beheading Mahishasura, and on the ninth night she is shown worshipping Shiva. On the tenth day, a ritual representing the washing of Minakshi's hair is performed, and then the goddess and Shiva (Sundareshvara) are carried in procession around Shiva's part of the temple. Local tradition says that Mahishasura was a devotee of Shiva, so that in killing him, the goddess caused Shiva offence. By worshipping Shiva and by having her hair washed (symbolising the removal of taint caused by killing the demon) Minakshi makes double reparation to Shiva, and is thus able to join him in a procession which expresses their unity.

In addition to Durga, other major Hindu goddesses are also honoured at Navaratri, particularly Saraswati, goddess of learning, the arts and beauty, and in many places Saraswati Puja is celebrated on the first night of the festival. An image of the goddess is placed on top of a pile of the various sacred books in the house and she is worshipped over a three day period (see also Vasanta Panchami).

In Gujarat state the festival has become especially important as a time when such traditional dances as the *dandia ras* (stick dance) and the *garba* are performed. These dances have been preserved by migrant Gujarati communities and are performed enthusiastically in temples and at cultural gatherings on each night of the festival.

As well as honouring the well known Indian goddesses, Navaratri, when celebrated in the village, is also likely to include veneration or propitiation of *mata*, local goddesses whose names may be known only in the immediate locality, although on occasion a *mata* will be identified with one of the major Hindu goddesses. The *mata* are thought to be less powerful than the great *devas*, but they may be of enormous practical and immediate importance, for example in identifying the source of an illness or finding a piece of lost property. The *mata* are often served by non-brahmin priests, many of whom become possessed by the *mata*, and in a state of trance answer questions put by worshippers. In Sundarana, a village in Gujarat, Navaratri is the special season of the *mata* and three different ceremonies are held in honour of various *mata*, two of them involving mediumship, on the eighth night of the festival. In 'Rampur', a village in Uttar Pradesh, Oscar Lewis reports that the principal object of worship during Navaratri is a local *mata* called Sanjhi who appears to be the ghost of a weaver's wife murdered in the village many years earlier. Worship of the *mata* is performed by women and children only (the men are busy with the harvest) and there is no worship of major Hindu goddesses (Lewis, 1958).

In some parts of north India, for example Uttar Pradesh, the festival is closely associated with the epic story of Rama – of his birth, exile, the abduction of his wife by the demon king Ravana, her subsequent rescue and the couple's return to the city of Ayodhya. Troupes of players tour the villages performing *Ram Lila*, plays based on the *Ramayana* story. In Delhi an impressive *Ram Lila* is held annually and the various episodes of the Rama story are unfolded over the ten-day period, the climax being Dassehra on which an arrow shot by the actor playing Rama sets fire to a huge firework-filled effigy of Ravana.

In many places Dassehra is also a day on which artisans and farmers worship their tools and traditionally warriors worship their weapons. This latter activity is linked both with Durga's slaying of Mahishasura and with Rama's defeat of Ravana.

Gandhi Jayanti (2 October)
Mohandas Karamchand Gandhi (later popularly titled Mahatma – 'great soul') was born on the second of October, 1896 at Porbandar in Gujarat. His non-violent contribution to the struggle for Indian independence was highly influential on the nationalist movement. Gandhi took the view that India's struggle was moral and religious, and in his personal conduct he set an example to others through his simple living, his fasts and his appeals to Indians to return to the spirit of their pre-industrial past.

As well as drawing on some features of Hinduism (and criticising others such as untouchability) Gandhi took inspiration from Christianity and Islam, being particularly influenced by the Sermon on the the Mount. He hoped for a tolerant India with its religions working side by side. It was partly this open-mindedness that led to his assassination at the hands of an ultra-orthodox Hindu on 30 January 1948.

Although Gandhi's ideas are no longer widely influential, he is nevertheless revered as a great man and a saint and his birthday is observed as a national day.

Divali/Deepavali (October/November)

Divali or Deepavali (both names mean a row or garland of lights) is probably the most widely celebrated Hindu festival of all – though like Navaratri/Dassehra it is best described as a complex of festivals. The festival varies in length from two to five days, being celebrated between Ashvina, *badi* 13 and Karttika, *shudi* 2, (and always includes the new moon day of the month Karttika, which marked the beginning of the New Year according to the pre-medieval version of the Vikram system of dating, and still is New Year in the state of Gujarat). The lighting of *divas*, lamps, is all but universal, and although the festival may include a host of varied local or regional rituals and celebrations, it is often related to one or more familiar all-Indian themes – the defeat of the demon king Mahabali by the dwarf avatar of Vishnu (see Onam) or the return of Rama and Sita to Ayodhya after the defeat of Ravana, and more commonly the yearly coming of Lakshmi, goddess of wealth. *Divas* or *deeps* – small earthenware bowls – are filled with oil or *ghi* and supplied with cotton wicks. These are placed in extended rows inside and outside houses and are lit in the evening. Sometimes rows of small electric lights are used. The lightning of the lamps is sometimes associated with the welcome given to the returning king Rama.

Lakshmi *puja* is a common feature of the festival, though it takes place on different days in different places. In some areas members of trading castes close their accounts at this time before taking part in Lakshmi *puja*. At home, or in a temple, coins may be piled on ledgers and an image of the goddess placed on top prior to worship. In many areas, Lakshmi *puja* is the central event of the festival and the lighting of *divas* is said to help the goddess to find her way into the homes of worshippers.

Gambling is a familiar pastime and other customs include the drawing of colourful designs by women on the floor near the threshold of houses, the sending of Divali cards to relations and friends as a gesture of goodwill and the distribution of sweetmeats.

As part of the Divali celebrations of a Hindu family in Britain, puja *is performed before a picture of Lakshmi, goddess of wealth.*

At the Shree Krishna Temple in Coventry, England, Divali is celebrated by Gujarati Hindus over a two-day period. On the first evening shopkeepers and businessmen bring their account books along to the temple to be inscribed by the brahmin priest with sacred *mantras*. Then two members of the community, acting on behalf of the whole congregation, perform a special *puja* to Lakshmi, assisted by the priest. The priest ties red amulets around the right wrists of all of the men, who vow that they will be honest and hard-working in their business dealings over the next year. They also hope that their prayers to Lakshmi at the beginning of the commercial year will bring them good fortune in their business life. On the following evening (New Year's Day: Karttika, *shudi* 1) a large congregation of men, women and children appears at the temple for the celebration. A long table is set up at the front of the temple and on it are placed a selection of Indian sweets and food. The table is surrounded by candles which are lit during the evening's celebrations.

The second day of the bright half of Karttika – in many places the fifth or last day of Divali celebrations – is known in different parts of north India by such names as Bhatri Dwitiya and Bhaia Duj. Like Raksha Bandhan it is a family festival where girls wish good health and welfare to their brothers. In some places the day is called Yama Dwitiya and recalls the story of the god Yama who dined with his sister Yamuna on this day and commanded everyone else to do the same. All males are supposed to dine in the house of a female relative and to give her presents.

Chhath (October/November)

Chhath (sixth) is a festival peculiar to the north Indian state of Bihar and is celebrated on Karttika, *shudi* 6. The festival, which may last as long as six days, is in honour of Surya, the sun god, and is celebrated thoughout the state, although the Sun temple in the village of Surajpur-Baragaon is a special centre having a large fair and attracting many visitors. After a period of fasting devotees go at sunset and at sunrise to make offerings to Surya at a river or a tank (a cross between a pond and a small lake).

Something of the atmosphere of the festival is captured by an observer who visited India in 1981.

'When I was taken to the Chhath celebrations at one Bihari village, where it was difficult to move because of the thousands assembled, all of whom were camping there for the festival, I understood how devotion can grip a multitude.'

Gould, 1982

Elsewhere the same observer describes the sunset oblations on one day of the festival.

'The worshippers immersed themselves in the tank with hands folded upwards (as pilgrims do in the Ganges at Varanasi) and after plunging themselves into the water several times they pushed their way through the throngs to the temple of the sun god, crawling outstretched the not inconsiderable distance along the wet, muddy path. After their oblations the devotees broke their fast by taking *prasada*.'

Gould (personal communication)

In some areas the festival is also concerned with family welfare and offerings are made to the goddess Shasti in order to protect children from harm.

Karttika Ekadashi/Devuthna Ekadashi/Tulsi Ekadashi (October/November)
This important eleventh day marks the end of *chaturmas*, a period of four months during which Vishnu is said to sleep (see Ashadhi Ekadashi, above). In some areas the marriage of Vishnu to the goddess in the form of the tulsi (holy basil) plant is celebrated on this day.

Karttika Purnima/Tripuri Purnima (October/November)
In some places this day, the full moon in the month of Karttika, commemorates the goddess Kali's slaying of the demon Tripura and Shiva's destruction of the demon's three cities of gold (heaven), silver (earth) and iron (hell). The occasion is often marked by the lighting of lamps and fireworks.

Elsewhere the day is associated with Vishnu, especially with the Matsya (fish) *avatar* of the god. In the village of Shamirpet in Andhra Pradesh the day is observed in the home by high-caste women who bathe early in the morning, fast, apply turmeric paste to their bodies and wear yellow clothes. The tulsi plant (sacred to Vishnu) is worshipped and offerings are made of twenty-one threads, twenty-one flowers (preferably different varieties) and twenty-one garlands.

Hoi (October/November)
This local festival, celebrated on Karttika, *badi* 7 in the region around the village of 'Rampur' in Uttar Pradesh, is included as an example of the countless celebrations concerned with protecting family members from harm. In this case the festival is concerned with the protection of children. The women of the village bathe and fast until late afternoon. In each home a small pitcher is filled with water and another with grain, and both are placed near the hearth. The water is kept for use in a later festival but the grain is used in a ritual

performed by the women in the afternoon during the recitation of an edifying story on the theme of protection of children.

Skanda Shasti (October/November)
This seven-day temple festival, occurring during the Tamil month of Aippaci, is popular with many of south India's Tamil people and has special significance to the devotees of Skanda or Subramanya, known more commonly by his Tamil name of Murukan. He is a son of Shiva, but is also linked in various ways with Vaishnavite tradition – for example in the *Bhagavata Purana* he is said to be an incarnation of Vishnu. The festival, which takes place in Murukan temples throughout Tamil land, is a re-enactment of the mythical six-day career of the god, including his birth and maturation, and climaxed by his conquest of evil cosmic forces and his marriage to his two consorts. It is intended to constitute a new beginning both in the sense of bringing the god into being again (there are complex temple rituals which include the dressing and ornamentation of the divine symbol) and in affording the cosmos and the human community an opportunity to start afresh. Skanda Shasti illustrates well the pattern of Tamil festivals. It reconstructs the mythic seven-day life of the god: he is ritually brought into existence, he matures, on the sixth day he overcomes the demonic *asuras*, on the seventh day he is married to his consorts and is taken out on a triumphal procession through the streets.

Since Subramanya-Murukan, to some extent, symbolises the Tamil cultural heritage, independent of the Sanskrit mainstream, the festival is an expression of Tamil self-consciousness.

Vaikuntha Ekadashi (November/December)
See Ashadhi Ekadashi (above).

Lakshmi Puja (date varies)
Lakshmi Puja is frequently celebrated as part of Divali celebrations, but in some areas of India the beautiful goddess of wealth is honoured at different times of the year. In west Bengal and Himachal Pradesh, for example, Lakshmi Puja is held on the full moon day of Ashvina (September/October). In the eastern state of Orissa the festival is held on the full moon day of the month of Agrahayana or Margashirsha (November/December). In a Government of India Anthropological Survey it was noted that of the thirty-three villages in Orissa studied, fifteen celebrated Lakshmi Puja. In Orissa, in some villages, the rice harvest takes place at the time of the festival. Housewives, having cleaned their houses, decorate the floors and walls with intricate rice-paste designs. Small feet are drawn on the

doorsteps and floors in the hope that Lakshmi will follow the footsteps and enter the house. A symbolic image of the goddess is made from newly harvested rice, coins, gold ornaments and a red silk sari. Food, made with new rice, is offered to Lakshmi and then shared by close relatives on the father's side of the family. Some of the women read the *Lakshmi Purana* in the evening.

Table of Hindu festivals

January Makar Sankranti/Til Sankranti/Lohri, Pongal, Kumbha Mela at Prayag (every twelve years)

January/February Vasanta Panchami/Shri Panchami/Saraswati Puja, Bhogali Bihu, Mahashivratri

20 February Ramakrishna Utsav

February/March Holi

March/April Ugadi, Basora, Rama Navami, Hanuman Jayanti

April Vaisakhi

April/May Akshaya Tritiya, Chittrai

May/June Ganga Dasa-hara, Nirjala Ekadashi, Snan-yatra

June/July Ratha-yatra/Jagannatha, Ashadhi Ekadashi/Toli Ekadashi

July/August Teej, Naga Panchami, Raksha Bandhan/Shravana Purnima/Salono/Rakhi Purnima

August/September Onam, Ganesha Chaturthi, Janamashtami/Krishna Jayanti

September/October Mahalaya/Shraddha/Pitri Paksha/Kanagat, Navaratri/Durga Puja/Dassehra, Lakshmi Puja (West Bengal and Himachal Pradesh)

2 October Gandhi Jayanti

October/November Divali/Deepavali, Chhath, Karttika Ekadashi/Devuthan Ekadashi/Tulsi Ekadashi Karttika Purnima/Tripuri Purnima, Hoi, Skanda Shasti

November/December Vaikuntha Ekadashi, Lakshmi Puja (Orissa)

7 Jaina Festivals

PADMANABH S JAINI

Jainism

Jainism today is a religion whose followers are few in number, only about four million throughout India. Along with Buddhism it was one of the two most prominent Shramana or non-Brahmanical religions that originated in the Ganges valley during the sixth or seventh century BCE, but its history differs from that of Buddhism in two striking respects: Buddhism was destined to spread throughout south-east and east Asia, while Jainism never left the subcontinent; secondly, Buddhism declined and almost disappeared from India, while Jainism survives in almost all parts of India, especially in the western states (Punjab, Rajasthan, Gujarat) and the Deccan (Maharashtra and Karnataka).

Jainism is recognisable as an Indian religion, espousing the doctrine of *samsara* (the cycle of birth and death). This doctrine holds that all living beings are bound by their *karma* (effect of past deeds), which leads to their successive re-births in different bodies, but that there is a possibility of salvation in the form of freedom from the cycle of birth and death. Nevertheless, it rejects the authority of the Vedas and related texts, the efficacy of sacrifice, the existence of a creator-god, and the underlying rationale of the caste system. The human model emulated by the Jainas is that of the perfected ascetic, whom they call *Jina* (Victorious), whence the name Jaina is derived, or *Tirthankara* (Maker of a bridge across the river of *samsara*).

The Jainas, who hold to a variation of the typically Indian scheme of beginningless, cyclical time, believe that in each of an infinite number of cosmic cycles there is an ascending and descending phase, and in each phase twenty-four Tirthankaras teach the Jaina path. We are currently near the end of the descending phase, the first teacher of which was named Rishabha, and the last Vardhamana Mahavira. Only legendary accounts of the first twenty-two Jinas exist, while the twenty-third Jina, Parshva, is considered an historical figure, since his followers, known as *Niganthas*, are mentioned in the Buddhist Tripitaka. Mahavira, the last Tirthankara and the supreme teacher of the present day Jainas (599–527) BCE), flourished in the tradition of Parshva and was a contemporary of Gautama the Buddha.

According to the canonical texts of the Jainas, their community at the time of Mahavira was comprised of lay votaries and mendicants, with as many as 14,000 monks (*sadhus*) and 36,000 nuns (*sadhvis*). Around 300 BCE the once unified Jaina monastic community was split into two major sects known as *Digambara* and *Shvetambara*. The Digambara (Sky-clad) monks claimed that total renunciation of clothing – as practised by Mahavira himself – was a prerequisite for being a Jaina monk and therefore adhered to the practice of nudity. The Shvetambaras (White-clad) maintained that nudity was forbidden to the members of the ecclesiastical community and adopted the practice of wearing white (cotton) garments. The two mendicant sects eventually rejected each other as being apostates from the true path, compiled their own scriptures, and ceased to perform their common rituals, such as confession, together. The lay followers, called *shravakas* (hearers of the law), of these two sects also formed their own social groups. They are distinguished mainly by the images of the Tirthankaras that they worship; the Digambara images are naked, while the Shvetambara images are decorated with ornaments of gold and silver. In the sixteenth century, moreover, there arose within the Shvetambara community a reformist movement (*Sthanakavasi*) that condemned the worship of images. Thus, in spite of a basic agreement about the fundamental teachings of the Jina, there have been sectarian differences regarding the manner in which the Jaina festivals are celebrated.

Notwithstanding these sectarian differences the Jainas have been able to preserve their separateness from the Hindus, primarily because of their sizable monastic community. According to the most recent count it includes about two thousand monks and five thousand nuns, who form the most important element in supervising the major Jaina festivals. During the course of more than two thousand years of close contact with the Hindus, especially the merchant castes, the Jaina lay people have adopted many of the Hindu social customs, such as the caste system; and participate in Hindu festivals such as Vijaya-dashami (Dassehra) and Divali, which have become Indian national holidays. But the major Jaina festivals are observed exclusively by the Jainas, since they are celebrations of the holy careers of the Tirthankaras and of ascetic practices that emphasise non-possession (*aparigraha*) and non-violence (*ahimsa*), the two most important features of the Jaina teachings.

The Jaina era and calendar

The Jainas have traditionally reckoned the era of Mahavira (*Vira-samvat*) to have begun in 528 BCE, the year after Mahavira's death. This era, also known as the *Vira-nirvana* era is, however, employed by Jaina authors only to indicate the dates of major events in the history of the Jainas (major schisms, councils, compilation of texts, and so on). For all other purposes the Jainas have used the *Vikrama-samvat* (beginning in 58 BCE), prevalent among the Hindus of western India. Thus the holidays described below follow the traditional Hindu calendar (*pancanga*).

New Year's Day has no special religious significance for the Jainas, since it is not associated with the holy career of the Jina. The birthday of Mahavira (Mahavira-jayanti), the only Jaina holiday recognised by the Government of India, therefore functions as the first of the annual cycle of Jaina festivals.

The festivals

Mahavira-jayanti (April)
Mahavira-jayanti, or the celebration of Mahavira's birth, takes place on the thirteenth day of the waxing moon of Caitra. Although the annual festival of confession, the last day of the Paryushana-parva is the holiest, Mahavira-jayanti is the most important festival in social terms. All Jainas, regardless, of sectarian affiliations, come together to celebrate this occasion publicly, taking leave from work and school to participate in the activities.

According to tradition Mahavira was born in 599 BCE in Kunda-grama, a large city in the kingdom of Vaishali (near modern Patna in the state of Bihar). His father, named Siddhartha, is said to have been a warrior chieftain of the Jnatri clan. His mother, Trishala, was the sister of the ruler of Vaishali. The Jaina myths say that five events in the life of a Jina are the most aupicious occasions (*kaly-anas*), on which the gods come down to earth and attend upon him. His descent from heaven into his mother's womb (*garbha*) is the first occasion. At this time his mother has sixteen dreams, in which she sees sixteen auspicious objects, such as a white elephant, a lion, the full moon, the rising sun, an ocean of milk, and so on. The second auspicious event is his birth (*janma*). Indra, the king of gods, and his consort, Indrani, come down to the royal palace and transport the baby to Mount Meru, the centre of the Jaina universe, and sprinkle him with water from all the oceans. Thus they declare the advent of a new Tirthankara.

During the Mahavira-jayanti, these two auspicious events are celebrated with great pomp by the Jaina laity in the form of a ritual which may strike an outsider as a dramatic re-enactment. The festival begins in the early part of the morning with the arrival of the Jainas at their local temple. On this day gold and silver images, which represent the objects in Trishala's dreams, are prominently displayed in order to suggest the conception of Mahavira. A newly married or a wealthy couple will volunteer to assume the roles of Indra and Indrani, and will worship a small image of the Jina by placing it on a pedestal (serving as Mount Meru) and pouring perfumed water on it, and anointing it with sandalwood paste. Those who play these roles distribute large amounts of money for charitable purposes as well as for the upkeep of the shrine. The other members of the community join in this ritual by chanting the holy litany while showering flowers on the image and waving lamps (*arati*) in front of it.

If a monk or a nun happens to be in residence at that time, he or she will add to the occasion by reading the *Kalpasutra*, the biography of Mahavira, and describe the three remaining *kalyanas* of his spiritual career: Mahavira's renunciation of household life (*diksha-kalyana*) at the age of 30 his severe austerities for a period of twelve and a half years culminating in his enlightenment (*kevalajnana-kalyana*), and finally his death (*nirvana-kalyana*) at the age of 72. The ceremony concludes with the chanting of the holy Jaina hymns in the praise of Mahavira and the lay people returning to their homes to enjoy a feast in honour of Mahavira's birth.

Akshaya-tritiya (April/May)

The holiday of Akshaya-tritiya (Immortal Third) falls on the third day of the waxing moon of Vaishakha. Akshaya-tritiya celebrates the first instance of alms being given to a mendicant, in this case the first Tirthankara of this cycle, Rishabha. After his renunciation, Rishabha went without food for six months, since none of his contemporaries knew the proper foods acceptable to a mendicant. A Jaina mendicant, who by law must be a vegetarian, observes a great many other dietary restrictions. He may not eat raw vegetables nor fruits like figs, which contain many seeds. Tradition has it that a prince named Shreyamsa dreamed that in a past life he had offered alms to a Jaina monk. This dream led him to recognise the kind of food acceptable to a Jaina mendicant. He then offered a pitcherful of sugar-cane juice to Rishabha, who, by drinking it, broke his six-month fast. The gods celebrated this event by showering jewels on Shreyamsa's household, and that day thus became known as the Immortal Third.

A devotee makes offerings at a Jaina temple in Bombay on the occasion of Mahavira-jayanti, the birthday of the founder of Jainism.

The present-day Jainas celebrate the first gift of alms to a Jaina mendicant by publicly honouring lay men and lay women, who undertake fasts similar to that of Rishabha. In almost all major centres of Jaina population several elderly Jainas of both sexes vow to fast on alternate days for periods of six months or a year. The last day of these fasts (*varshi-tapa*) falls on the Akshaya-tritiya, when the elders of the Jaina community, under the supervision of a monk or a nun, honour these devout Jaina lay people by feeding them spoonfuls of sugar-cane juice, thus helping them to break their fasts. This action recalls Shreyamsa's giving alms to Rishabha and emulates the examples of the first Jaina ascetic in undergoing austerities on the path of salvation.

Shruta-pancami (May/June)

Shruta-pancami (Scripture-Fifth) is celebrated on the fifth day of the waxing moon of Jyeshtha. It commemorates the day on which the Jaina scriptures (*shruta*) were first committed to writing. At first the teachings of Mahavira were handed down orally; since they were sacred, Jaina teachers were not willing to commit them to writing. It was, however, not easy to maintain this oral tradition, since those monks who had committed the teachings to memory gradually died off, and, because of adverse conditions few new monks were trained.

The Digambara tradition maintains that around 150 CE two Jaina monks, Bhutabali and Pushpadanta, compiled those teachings that were available and wrote them down on palm leaves. The 'Scripture-Fifth' is said to be the day on which this scripture, entitled *Shatkhanda-agama* (Scripture in Six Parts), was completed. The Shvetambaras, however, have a different set of scriptures called *Dvadasha-anga-shruta* (Scripture in Twelve Parts). These were compiled under the supervision of their pontiff (*acarya*) Devarddhigani Kshamashramana, *c*.450 CE. This event occurred at a different time of the year, and hence it is celebrated on the fifth day of the waxing moon of Karttika (October/November). The actual celebrations, nevertheless, are almost identical.

On this day elaborately decorated copies of the scripture are displayed in Jaina temples, and devotees sit in front of the pedestal on which they are placed. They then sing hymns in praise of the Jinas who preached the teachings and the mendicants who faithfully preserve them. On such occasions it is customary for rich lay people to commission new, illustrated copies of certain texts, especially the biographies of the Jinas such as the *Kalpasutra*, and distribute them to the general public. Jaina children participate in this festival by copying the Jaina litanies and by giving gifts of paper and pens. The

145

ceremony concludes with a sermon by a monk or a nun about the importance of reading scriptures in the search for knowledge. The public then recites a formula in veneration of the teachers. For this reason this day is also known as *Jnana-pancami* (Knowledge-Fifth) or *Guru-pancami* (Teacher-Fifth).

Paryushana-parva/Daksha-lakshana-parva (August)
The festivals described above last only a day and are associated with some historical event. On the other hand Paryushana, which means 'passing the rainy season', is dedicated to the cultivation of certain religious practices of a longer duration. The Jaina monks and nuns, unlike their counterparts in other religions, do not have permanent abodes in the form of monasteries and nunneries; they are obliged by law to stay only a few days or weeks at a time in any one place. During the four months of the rainy season (*caturmasa*), however, they are required to choose a fixed place of residence and spend their time within the boundary of that village or town. The presence of nuns and monks (who must always live separately and in groups of a minimum of three persons) during the rainy season thus affords great opportunities for the lay devotees to undertake a variety of religious practices. The elders in the Jaina community plan for this occasion a year in advance by inviting a particular group of monks or nuns to come to their town for the rainy season. Since the Jaina mendicants must travel by foot, they set out on their journey early enough that they may arrive before the onset of the rainy season, which officially begins on the fourteenth day of the waxing moon of Ashadha (June/July). On that day lay people visit the mendicant teachers and resolve to lead temporarily a life of restraint which may include dietary restrictions (such as not eating certain kinds of foods or not eating at night time), sitting in meditation in a regular manner every day, or the study of a particular scripture.

Participation in these religious observances becomes more intense during the week-long celebration of the Paryushana-parva. For the Shvetambaras this begins on the twelfth day of the waning moon of Shravana (August) and ends on the fourth day of the waxing moon of Bhadrapada. The Digambaras celebrate the same festival a week later, for ten days.

During these eight or ten days many members, young or old, of the Jaina community observe some form of restraint regarding food. Some may eat only once a day, or fast completely on the first and the last days; others refrain from eating and drinking (except for boiled water) for the entire week. These latter spend most of their time in temples or monasteries, in the company of monks. All participants attempt in these various ways to emulate the life of a mendicant for however short a time, detaching themselves from worldly affairs and leading a meditative life. Each day monks and nuns give sermons, placing special emphasis on the life and teachings of Mahavira. For a second time the Shvetambaras celebrate the birth of Mahavira by reading the *Kalpasutra* in public, thus rededicating themselves to his ideals.

The Digambaras refer to the festival of Paryushana-parva also by the name *Dasha-lakshana-parva*, or the Festival of Ten Virtues: forgiveness, humility, honesty, purity, truthfulness, self-restraint, asceticism, study, detachment, and celibacy. They dedicate each day of the festival to one of the virtues.

The celebration of Paryushana-parva comes to a climax on the last day, when Jainas of all sects perform the annual ceremony of confession, *Samvatsari-pratikramana*. This is the holiest day of the year for the Jainas, who take leave from work or school on this occasion to participate in the activities. On the evening of this day (on which almost all participants have fasted) Jainas assemble in their local temples, and, in the presence of their mendicant teachers, they confess their transgressions by uttering the words *miccha me dukkadam* (may all my transgressions be forgiven). They then exchange pleas for forgiveness with their relatives and friends. Finally they extend their friendship and goodwill to all beings in the following words:

> 'I ask pardon of all living creatures;
> May all of them pardon me.
> May I have a friendly relationship with all beings,
> And unfriendly with none.'

Vira-nirvana (November)

The festival of Vira-nirvana, or the anniversary of the death of Mahavira, occurs on the fifteenth day of the waning moon of Ashvina. On this night in the year 527 BCE Mahavira, at the age of 72, entered *nirvana* (the state of immortality that is freedom forever from the cycle of birth and death), in a place called Pavapuri, near modern Patna. Towards the dawn, his chief apostle (*ganadhara*) Indrabhuti Gautama, a monk of long-standing, is said to have attained to enlightenment (*kevalajnana*), the supreme goal of a Jaina mendicant. Tradition has it that Mahavira's eighteen contemporary kings celebrated both these auspicious events by lighting rows of lamps. This act of 'illumination' is claimed by the Jainas as the true origin of Divali, the Hindu Festival of Lights, which falls on the same day. The Hindus, of course, have a different legend associated with Divali, and their festival probably antedates Mahavira's *nirvana*.

Devout Jaina lay people observe Vira-nirvana by undertaking a twenty-four-hour fast, and spend this time in meditation. It is considered highly meritorious to keep vigil throughout this holy night, especially at the actual site of Mahavira's *nirvana*. Those who cannot make the pilgrimage perform a memorial worship in their local temple by lighting lamps in front of an image of Mahavira. This solemn service takes place early in the morning of the next day, the first day of the waxing moon of Karttika, prior to the breaking of the day-long fast. The ceremony concludes with a public recitation of an ancient hymn addressed to all 'liberated beings' (*siddhas*), including Mahavira:

'Praise to the holy, the blessed ones, who provide the path across, . . . those who are endowed with unobstructed knowledge and insight . . . the Jinas, who have crossed over, who help others cross, the liberated and the liberators, the omniscient, the all-seeing, those who have reached the destiny of the *siddha* from which there is no return and which is bliss immutable, inviolable, imperishable, and undisturbed; praise to the Jinas who have overcome fear. I worship all the *siddhas*, those who have been, and those who in future will be.'

Karttika-purnima/Ratha-yatra (December)

The festival of the Karttika-purnima, or the Jaina Car Festival (Ratha-yatra), occurs within a fortnight of Divali, on the full moon day of Karttika. This marks the end of the rainy season. On the following day the monks and nuns, who have stayed in retreat for four months, must resume their wanderings. At the same time the lay people are released from the various vows which they had undertaken for the duration of the season. The festival of Karttika-purnima provides them with an opportunity to thank the monks and nuns for their sermons and counsel.

The lay people celebrate this day by putting an image of the Jina into an immense, beautifully decorated wooden vehicle (*ratha*) and pulling it by hand through the streets of the city. The procession, headed by monks and nuns, begins at the local temple and winds its way through the city to a park within the city limits. Here a prominent monk gives a sermon, and the leading lay people call for generous donations in support of the various social and religious projects (such as building temples, libraries, or hospitals) that have been inspired by the presence of the mendicants. The procession then returns of the temple, and the people go home in a festive mood.

Bahubali-mastaka-abhisheka (every twelve years, February)

Finally, we may mention a special ceremony, which, although not part of the annual cycle, is the most famous and by far the most spectacular of all Jaina festivals. This is called Mastaka-abhisheka (Head-anointing), and is held every twelfth year at Shravanabelgola, in Karnataka, in honour of the Jaina saint and hero, Bahubali. The most recent performance of this very popular ceremony took place in February 1981 CE, and was especially dramatic, since it fell on the thousandth anniversary of the consecration of Bahubali's statue, which was installed by the Jaina general, Camundaraya. Hundreds of thousands of Jainas from all over India came to the small town of Shravanabelgola, in order to anoint and to meditate before this monumental statue of Bahubali, which stands fifty-seven feet tall and was carved out of granite on a hill-top just outside of the town. The statue depicts Bahubali, the first man to attain to *nirvana* in our present time cycle, as standing erect, completely naked, immersed in deep meditation. Bahubali is believed to have held this posture, oblivious to the vines and snakes gathering around him, for twelve months, in a heroic effort to root out the last vestiges of impurity. In order to honour his achievement and to gain great merit for themselves, the faithful come to Shravanabelgola every twelve years, and erect a temporary scaffolding behind the statue, with a platform at the top. From this platform they anoint Bahubali with pitcherfuls of various ointments consisting of yellow and red powder, sandalwood paste, milk, and clear water; the colours of these materials symbolically represent the stages of purification of Bahubali's soul as it progresses towards enlightenment.

Table of Jaina festivals

February Bahubali-mastaka-abhisheka (every twelve years)
April Mahavira-jayanti
April/May Akshaya-tritiya
May/June Shruta-pancami
August Paryushana-parva/Daksha-lakshana-parva
November Vira-nirvana
December Karttika-purnima/Ratha-yatra

8 Japanese Festivals
MICHAEL PYE

Introduction

Japanese religion consists of a complex tapestry of traditions. The three main elements are Shinto, whose origins are lost in the mists of prehistory; Buddhism, imported from China via Korea; and a wide range of new religions which have become more and more important in recent decades. The number of religious organisations is very large. It is common for the ordinary person to have something to do with more than one temple or shrine, for example to be married in a Shinto ceremony, to have Buddhist scriptures recited for the deceased, and in case of special need or sickness to seek help at a branch of some independent new religious movement. The various religions borrow from each other and share symbols and practices of many kinds. In this context it is possible to speak of Japanese festivals as a single theme.

The common word for 'festival' in Japan is *matsuri*, which implies a combination of ritual celebration and bright public good cheer. The festivals of Japan are most closely linked to the indigenous religion, Shinto. However the various schools of Buddhism also contribute in their own way to the annual round of festivals in which the public participate. So too do the new religious movements, and even Christmas, thanks mainly to commercial attention, is becoming established as a *matsuri* festival falling just before the all-important New Year.

Strangely enough, New Year itself is not usually referred to as a *matsuri*, but it certainly does belong to the annual round of festivals and indeed sets the tone for the rest of the year. It is the most universally observed of all Japanese calendrical events.

The festivals of Japan are one of the common threads which link together the otherwise varied and separately organised religious traditions of the country. Some festivals, such as the Bean Scattering Festival (*Setsubun*), are not particularly related to any one religion at all. Others are celebrations pertaining to particular Shinto shrines, or representing particular points in the Buddhist year. These differences will be indicated below. It is generally felt, however, that a *matsuri* is open in principle to all. There is therefore a feeling that the annual round of festive occasions is something which links all the people of Japan, and indeed visitors too, who are always welcome to share in them.

It may be debated whether all the festivals listed below are really 'religious'. This is a particularly difficult problem in the Japanese context for two reasons. First, there are many different possible degrees of participation: people may attend because their families expect them to, even though they would say that they have little in the way of a religious belief system. Returning to one's home town, or going away on an excursion, because of a *matsuri*, is simply an opportunity for travel and relaxation, and for meeting relatives and friends. In some cases it may be purely tourism. Participation is often light-hearted, nevertheless the total number of people involved in festivals in Japan for one reason or another is very large, and certainly includes the majority of the population. Secondly, the annual observances are so closely intertwined with everyday life that it is impossible to say clearly and definitely where religion begins and ends. Even the apparently secular holidays of the modern Japanese state are still enmeshed in the overall apprehension of the calendrical year which carries all before it. In spite of the constitutional separation of religion and state which concerns specific religious bodies, several of the national holidays are of definite religious origin and in a broad sense are still to be understood as part of the Japanese religious tradition.

The essentially religious meaning of *matsuri* is given in the Shinto religion. As representatives of the Association of Shinto Shrines stated a few years ago:

'It is usual for *matsuri* in Shinto to mean the ceremonies of group worship. But, in the spiritual sense, *matsuri* is to approach the Divine, to attain accord with the Divine, and to live in dependence on the Divine.

'In *matsuri* is included thanksgiving for the fact that one's entire life is a life in accordance with divine blessings, joy at being able to live in accordance with the divine will, and confident trust in thus being able to obtain blessings.
Shinto Committee for the Ninth International Congress for the History of Religion, *An outline of Shinto Teaching*, Tokyo 1958, p 10

The social meaning of festivals was even more strongly emphasised by Mr M Sonoda, a priest of the Shinto shrine in the city of Chichibu in eastern Japan.

'The essential motif of the *matsuri* is the renewal of lifepower among the *kami* and human beings in a given life-space. This renewal occurs through a set of symbolic actions in which people collectively welcome and extend hospitality to the *kami* in an effort to enrich his benevolent power and appropriate this power in their own lives.' [The word *kami* here refers to divinities in the Shinto sense.]
'The Traditional Festivals in Urban Society' in *Japanese Journal of Religious Studies* 2.2–3 (1975) p 103

Such thoughtful definitions are not necessarily present in the minds of all those who participate in the often colourful and noisy occasions in question. Nevertheless they do indicate the power which *matsuri* carry for those who take part in them, whether they have strong or clear religious beliefs or not.

Many of the best known festivals in Japan are regional festivals which have become nationally well known and which attract visitors from other parts of the country, national television coverage and so on. The Chichibu night festival with its procession of heavy, lantern-laden wooden vehicles is a clear example. This means that personal involvement in many cases is optional. More obligatory are the small-scale village festivals, often just called, for example, Summer Festival (*Natsu-matsuri*). These really do require the participation of and financial contribution from the relevant villagers. They provide an almost compulsory celebration of the unity of the village and, incidentally, of the prevailing kinship and property-owning hierarchy. Because of the immense variety of all these festivals, which make up a large part of the religious life of Japan, it is quite impossible to provide a comprehensive list on a calendrical basis. For this reason only festive seasons and festivals with a national Japanese meaning are given, interspersed with a few examples of regional festivals which have achieved a national reputation for their display and drama.

It is not really possible to separate the festivals or *matsuri* mentioned above from various other annual observances of a related character. These are generally referred to in Japanese as *nenjū gyōji*, which may be translated as annual observances, ceremonies or functions, many religious institutions give their own list of *nenjū gyōji*. Such lists have some common elements. For example they very often include the Bean Scattering Festival (*Setsubun*). However they also vary a great deal because of their specific religious interests. Thus a Buddhist temple might list the Flower Festival (*Hana-matsuri*) celebrating the birth of the Buddha, while a Shinto shrine would list the Rice-planting and Harvest Festival with considerable prominence. These variations are another reason why the list below can only be a representative compromise.

Some annual events are still influenced by the older lunar calendar. Because of this some festivals now falling in early spring must be understood as having once been connected with the New Year. The Buddhist O-bon Festival is celebrated at different times in different places because some hold to the older date. Also influential on Japanese ways of thinking is the designation of years by the Chinese-derived cycle of sixty combinations of written characters. At public level this is retained only in the form of the twelve zodiacal animal signs which appear in turn on postage stamps for New Year. Many commercial calendars further indicate the sequence of auspicious and inauspicious days which varies slightly from year to year. In general, however, the Japanese year is conceived nowadays in terms of the western-derived solar calendar with its seven-day week.

The list below includes nationally celebrated festivals of various kinds, national public holidays, and some regionally celebrated festivals of national prominence. The summer and autumn festivals typical of Shinto shrines up and down the country cannot be incorporated because of their great variety.

The festivals

New Year (1–3 January)
New Year's Day itself, the first of January, is known in Japanese as *Ganjitsu* and is a public holiday. New Year celebrations are, however, spread over the first three days of the month. Many institutions and businesses are closed on January 1st and or 2nd as well as on the official public holiday. The season as a whole is called *Shōgatsu*.

New Year is celebrated in many Shinto shrines, but also as a national and domestic festival. The national focus is provided by the appearance of the Emperor before great crowds of well-wishers in the grounds of the Imperial Palace in Tokyo. The Post Office issues a stamp depicting the zodiacal animal of the year and with exactly the right postage. Millions of these are printed with lottery numbers which may benefit their recipients.

The main outward signs of the season are the arrangements of pine and bamboo (known as *kadomatsu*) placed in front of houses and or shops. These two trees, together with the early-flowering plum (*ume*) are key New Year symbols. The evergreen pine has the meaning of continuity, the sharply cut bamboo has the meaning of straightness and cleanness, or sincerity, and the early plum blossom (which does not actually flower until early February, the old New Year) indicates new life.

Smaller, more colourful, arrangements (*kazari*) hung on doors are considered to invite well-being and to ward off misfortune. Paper elements may incorporate the Japanese flag as a motif, or a crane symbolising longevity. Rice-straw is a common component in these decorations, indicating the traditional link with rice-based agriculture. In some areas a rice-cake such as offered to the *kami* (Shinto divinities) is built into the arrangement.

In the home New Year is a time of rest when the family is gathered together. Special food includes rice-cakes (*o-mochi*) and a special soup (*o-zōni*). Traditional games are played including card-matching games (*karuta*) and a simple form of badminton using wooden bats painted with designs reflecting New Year. In this way traditional themes are reinforced at family level.

Central to New Year is the first visit of the year (*hatsumōde*) to a Shinto shrine. Some enthusiasts journey through the night to be at a particular shrine in the early hours or to view the sunrise from a mountain-top shrine. At such visits amulets and a variety of other religious accessories of the past year are returned for burning. New ones are purchased to ensure protection and well-being throughout the coming year. The atmosphere is cheerful and festive with one or two moments of serious reflection or self-dedication before the shrine. For smaller numbers services within the shrine building are held, during which prayers (*norito*) and branches of the *sakaki* tree are offered, and after which small cups of rice-wine are distributed to the participants. Such 'first visits' can also be made during the whole of the day or on the following two days. Traditional kimonos are often seen during this period as small family groups put on their traditional best for the leisurely visit. Now a few Buddhist temples also attract their followers for a 'first visit': particularly notable are the crowds who flock to the Shingon temple Sensōji at Asakusa in Tokyo.

Seven Herbs (7 January)
A minor date in the Japanese calendar is Seven Herbs, as it is here called for convenience after the seven herbs (*nanakusa*) of spring which may be used in a soup. The day is notable as the first of a series of five of which the rest are 3 March, 5 May, 7 July and 9 September. These are known together as the five seasonal days (*gosekku*).

Opposite: Shōgatsu . . . celebration of the Japanese New Year. Traditionally homes are decorated with pine (symbolising stability) and bamboo (symbolising righteousness). The spirit of New Year is one of renewal and energy.

Adults' Day (15 January)

Adults' Day (*Seijin no hi*) is a modern public holiday which celebrates the coming of age of young men and women who in the past year have attained the age of twenty. It provides another occasion for the girls to wear their traditional but brightly coloured kimonos as they go to public ceremonies of congratulation.

Bean Scattering (3 or 4 February)

Bean Scattering is a convenient English name for *Setsubun* which was originally a new year's custom in the traditional Chinese calendar dividing the year into twenty-four sections. The connection can also be seen from the fact that the festival precedes *risshun*, the establishment of spring and beginning of the new year in the older calendar. The person or persons selected to scatter the beans of good fortune are known as the *toshi-otoko* (year man). The word *setsubun* itself simply refers to the division of the seasons.

In its simplest form today the eldest son of the house, or another male, scatters some roasted beans from a wooden box made in the size and form of one of the traditional measures, and says loudly 'Demons out, happiness in' (*oni wa soto, fuku wa uchi*). Members of the household eat one bean for each year of their lives plus one more for the new year about to begin.

Buddhist temples and Shinto shrines often hold a public bean-scattering ceremony at which guests scatter the beans from a raised platform and members of the public scramble to catch them. Those who catch them feel that they will be protected from ill and enjoy good fortune.

Snow Festival (5–7 February)

The Snow Festival (*Yukimatsuri*) at the city of Sapporo on the northern island of Hokkaidō is famed for the scale and elaborate workmanship of its snow sculptures depicting a wide range of themes. It is one of the more secular of Japan's festivals but contributes to the identity of what, by Japanese standards, is a recently developed area.

Other 'snow festivals' of various kinds are celebrated in Japan's often neglected 'snow country', see for example the Igloo Festival.

National Foundation Day (11 February)

The Day for Commemorating the Foundation of the Nation, as the Japanese name *Kenkoku kinen no hi* means in full, is a modern public holiday. It falls on the same day as the pre-war public holiday celebrating the accession of the Emperor Jimmu, the legendary grandson of the sun goddess Amaterasu. In the modern holiday the

The Gion Festival in Kyōto. Thirty-one floats escort the divinity Susanoo around various parts of the city.

accent has shifted away from mythological origins but it remains a reminder of Japanese national unity.

Igloo Festival (15 February)
The Igloo Festival (*Kamakura-matsuri*) is celebrated in various places where heavy snow lies well into the early spring months, that is, above all in Akita Prefecture in northern Japan. The celebrations in the city of Yokote are particularly well known. The city is dotted with igloos in which children stay up all night and receive visitors. They give their visitors a cup of sweet rice-wine (*amazake*) and toasted rice-cake (*o-mochi*), while the grown-ups for their part give the children some money. Inside the igloo is a small altar (*kamidana*) on which the water god (*mizugami*) is celebrated with candles, oranges and so on. The igloo is in effect a temporary shrine and the custom is related to that of other villages where shrines are carved out of snow at the same season.

The festival is interpreted as a supplication to the water god to maintain a supply of water even in the season of deep snow and hard frost. However it also has features reminiscent of New Year, particularly the idea of seeing through the night.

Dolls' Festival/Girls' Day (3 March)
Girls' Day is the second of the five seasonal days (*gosekku*) of old tradition, the others being 7 January, 5 May, 7 July and 9 September. As Japanese months are named by number, 'first month' for January, 'third month' for March, and so on, this represents a steadily ascending sequence of numbers. This seasonal day is associated with peach blossom. Although a day of widespread observation it is not a public holiday.

The most usual name for the festival is *Hinamatsuri*, which means Dolls' Festival. Emperor and empress dolls with retinue, modelling the ancient Japanese Heian court, are presented and displayed in the home. Offerings of peach blossom, rice-wine and rice-cakes are placed before the stand.

An older form of the custom, still practised in some places, is to release straw floats on a river with paper or clay dolls set on them. It is believed that these will carry away with them any illness which is afflicting or threatening the daughters of the house. Even where this is not the practice, the day is used to pray for daughters to grow up healthily and dutifully.

It is thought that the picnics associated with the outdoor practice and the playing with dolls enjoyed by the children led to the usual modern indoor version of the custom. Today the picnic food is replaced by the miniature multi-coloured sweetmeats available especially for this festival.

Spring Equinox (21 March)
Spring Equinox Day (*Shunbun no hi*) is a public holiday, but the Buddhist observance on which it is based is spread over three days. The Buddhist name for this time is *Higan* (further shore), and it is a time when people have *sutras* recited on their behalf for deceased family members and go to visit family graves. Here they offer incense and flowers and anoint the memorial stones with water.

Higan in spring (and again in autumn, see Autumn Equinox) is together with *O-bon* in midsummer the busiest time for Buddhist priests in charge of temples with a parish system.

Flower Viewing (1–8 April)
The above dates are approximate for this custom, as they vary slightly throughout the country in accordance with the appearance of the cherry blossom.

Originally the spring flower viewing was a celebration of the activities of the gods (*kami*) in blessing the hillsides and fields with new growth. Today it is more of a celebration of the cherry blossom itself as a symbol of Japanese national pride and hope. People get together in parks where cherry blossoms are out, drink plenty of rice-wine as they sit about in little groups on the ground and generally give themselves a jolly party.

Flower Festival (8 April)
The Flower Festival (*Hanamatsuri*) celebrates the birth of the historical Buddha Shakyamuni (the name generally used for him in Japan). The legend from India relates that immediately after his birth the infant Buddha took seven steps in each of the four directions, north, south, east and west, raised his right hand to heaven while pointing with his left to the earth, and declared, 'In heaven and on earth only I am to be revered.' This dramatic declaration of the superior claim of Buddhism over other faiths is held fast in the images of the infant Buddha venerated on this day. Placed on a small stand decorated with flowers, and positioned out in front of a Buddhist temple for all to see, the image is anointed with fragrant tea (*amacha*) reminiscent of the perfumed water provided by the heavenly spirits (*devas*) for the Buddha's first bath in India.

Children take a particular delight in anointing the infant Buddha with the sweet liquid. The flowers recall the flower-decked garden in which the Buddha was born. At the same time the ceremony falls at a season when Japanese people are in any case thinking of the spring cherry blossoms.

Emperor's Birthday (29 April)
Tennō Tanjōbi, the birthday of the reigning emperor, Hirohito, is a
public holiday.

Constitution Day (3 May)
This is a public holiday named literally Constitution Commemoration Day (*Kenpō kinenbi*) but implying recollection of the day on
which the present post-war constitution was promulgated.

As three public holidays fall close together on 29 April, 3 May and
5 May respectively, and as people tend to be out and about enjoying
the sunshine of advanced springtime, the seven days spanned by
these holidays are popularly called Golden Week.

Children's Day/Boys' Day (5 May)
Now generally known as Children's Day (*Kodomo no hi*) this day has
traditionally been the boys' counterpart to *Hinamatsuri* (Dolls' Day),
and is indeed the next seasonal day of the five mentioned in that
context above.

Boys' interests are presumed, traditionally, to be martial, and on
this day models of samurai helmets and armour are commonly
presented and displayed. In modern times the custom is not
restricted to houses of samurai heritage.

It is also the time at which huge cloth streamers are flown from
poles. The streamers are made in the shape of carp, a fish known
for its active bravery and long life. Wherever these streamers are
seen flying high above the house there is a boy down below whose
parents and relatives wish these qualities for him. Unlike Dolls' Day,
this is a public holiday.

The flower traditionally associated with 5 May is the iris. At about
this time it is still customary to make a special point of viewing large
collections of irises, for example in the park of Meiji Shrine in
Tokyo. Traditionally iris and mugwort leaves were hung from the
eaves on this day to ward off the onset of the summer heat. The
strong smell was thought to ward off evil and ill-health. A health-
giving food eaten at the same period is rice-cakes wrapped in oak
leaves. This, too, reinforces the overall idea of health and strength
which is celebrated at the festival.

Hollyhock Festival (15 May)
The Hollyhock Festival (*Aoi matsuri*) is one of the three great festivals
of the former capital city of Kyōto. It is essentially a procession from
the court to the Kamo Shrine (Shinto) so that a court messenger can
give thanks for the protection vouchsafed to the city by the divinity
of that shrine. Since the processants ornamented their clothes and

head-dresses with hollyhocks (*aoi*) the festival is now popularly named after this flower. With its one-thousand-year history the festival is one of the leading attractions in the city's calendar, even though the court has now moved to Tokyo.

Ise Rice Planting (15 June)
The Ise Divine Rice Planting (*Ise Jingū O-taue Shinji*) may be taken as representative of many other similar ceremonies indicating the link between the traditional rice economy and the Shinto religion. Ise Shrine has its own special rice field for this purpose and the rite is said to be over one thousand five hundred years old.

Star Festival (7 July)
Tanabata is the common name of this colourful festival which, though not a public holiday, nevertheless attracts widespread interest as a kind of giant outdoor party in the streets of certain towns. The most famous celebration is in the city of Sendai, to the north of Tokyo, where the streets are hung with colourful streamers cut with great variety and skill from paper. The display at Sendai is reckoned as one of the three great festivals of the north-east.

The Star Festival is linked to the story of the love between two stars, a legend deriving originally from China. The story is about a cowherd and a weaving girl in the heavenly regions who were so fascinated by each other that they neglected to do their work properly. This angered the god of the skies who ordered them to be set apart at opposite ends of the milky way. They were to work hard at their trades and see each other only once a year, on 7 July.

People celebrating the festival pray for skills in weaving and in farming if they have any connection with these occupations. However this does not exclude other petitions being written on the little slips of star-spangled paper which find their way into the decorations, and which are often home-made by children and young people.

As the seventh day of the seventh month *Tanabata* also counts as the fourth of the five seasonal days (*gosekku*), the others being 7 January, 3 March, 5 May and 9 September. In some places it is also treated as more or less belonging to the *O-bon* season (see below) and used as a day for cleaning tombstones and Buddhist house altars.

Nachi Fire Festival (14 July)
Nachi Shrine is celebrated for its high waterfall under which austerities have been practised for centuries for the attainment of heightened powers. The shrine is the dwelling of twelve 'manifestations'

(*gongen*) deriving ultimately from the Buddha-nature of the universe. These are borne, on 14 July, in twelve palanquins (*mikoshi*) to the waterfall. Here they are received and purified by twelve huge and heavy flaming torches from the associated Flying Waterfall shrine. The dramatic spectacle is a reminder of the close association between Shinto and Buddhism in Japan, a link which at Nachi was particularly strong in medieval times.

O-bon (13–15 July)

O-bon is a Buddhist community festival at which the spirits of the departed are welcomed back to their home area amid feasting and dancing. It extends over three days, like the Buddhist *Higan* periods in spring and autumn. The first day, 13 July, is a day of welcoming (*mukae-bon*). The second day, 14 July, is the central day of association between family members, present and past, and may be thought of as *O-bon* proper. The third day, 15 July, is for seeing the spirits safely away again (*okuri-bon*). In many places *O-bon* is celebrated one month later. The prefix *O-* in the name *O-bon* is a common prefix indicating respect, and the name may be met with elsewhere without it.

The spirits of the departed are attracted into the home by placing freshly gathered herbs and flowers before the family altar (*butsudan*) or on a special *bon*-shelf set up for the occasion. Small fires may also be lit for this purpose, and again for seeing the spirits away on the third day. In the meantime food is also set out for their enjoyment.

In some places, such as Hiroshima in south-western Japan, the fires take the form of small lights in tiny receptacles which are allowed to float away down-river. In other places a large communal fire is lit on a mountain-side. A well-known example of this is the large fire on a hillside overlooking Kyōto, which takes the form of a Chinese character meaning 'large' (referred to as the *daimonji*).

The most general form of celebration at *O-bon* is the dance. On the second day, *O-bon* proper, whole villages gather in the open to enjoy a slow dance in which all participate. The dancers form a large circle around a high central stand festooned with lanterns and on which the musicians are mounted. The atmosphere is one of relaxed good humour and various snacks and amusements ensure a pleasant time for all.

Less obvious but equally important are the rounds of the Buddhist priests who at this time have a heavy schedule of parochial visits. Each house linked to the priest's temple is visited briefly, and the priest recites a short scriptural passage (i.e. from a Buddhist *sūtra*, referred to in Japanese as *o-kyō*) before the family altar. The passage selected varies from denomination to denomination, but as it is read in a form derived from Chinese the lay people do not directly understand it as recited. The importance for them lies rather in the performance of the rite as an acknowledgement of the care due to the memory of the ancestors.

Although *O-bon* is a major Japanese festival, almost comparable in importance to New Year, it is not a public holiday. Many people take a few days' holiday at this time to return to village homes with which they still have links.

Gion Festival (17 July)

The Gion Festival is one of the three major festivals of the former capital city, Kyōto. Consisting of various rites, it extends over a whole month from 1 July to 30 July. However the high point is the parade of floats on 17 July. Thirty-one of these huge vehicles on wooden wheels, heavily decorated, and carrying a considerable number of fan-waving, music-making Shinto parishioners, are dragged through the streets. These represent the community centred on the Yawata Shrine of Kyōto. Technically the floats are out to meet and escort three other conveyances (*mikoshi*) which carry the divinity Susanoo and his family from the shrine, around the various parts of the town where parishioners reside, and back home to the shrine again.

Modelled on this Gion Festival in Kyōto are some three thousand other Gion festivals which take place across the country. Thus in its own way the Gion Festival has become a national institution.

Nebuta Festival (2–7 August)

This is one of the three major festivals of north-eastern Japan and takes place in the city of Aomori, related festivals taking place elsewhere in the region. Huge pictures of men, women and animals are painted on great wooden frames and carried illuminated through the streets, commemorating a military decoy used to crush a rebellion. Nowadays the festival is a great opportunity for artistic tradition and inventiveness to vie for attention on the famous throwaway displays.

Lantern Festival (5–7 August)

The Lantern Festival (*Kantō-matsuri*) at the city of Akita is another of the three great north-eastern festivals. During the festival the streets are filled with huge bamboo frames with some forty glowing lanterns suspended from them. Each is carried by just one man. The festival was originally meant to celebrate, and pray for, the ripening of the rice harvest. Each frame with its crosspieces represents a well-filled ear of rice and each hanging lantern represents a grain.

Chrysanthemum Day (9 September)

Known informally as *Kiku no sekku*, this is the fifth of the five seasonal days (*gosekku*), the others being 7 January, 3 March, 5 May and 7 July. The appropriate observance is a chrysanthemum-viewing party, and this sometimes takes the form of a major chrysanthemum show in the grounds of a Shinto shrine. The sixteen-petalled chrysanthemum is a symbol of the Emperor Meiji who ruled the country during its rapid modernisation in the nineteenth century.

Respect for the Aged Day (15 September)

This day is a modern public holiday reflecting a traditional Japanese value and balancing the days assigned to children and young people. The Japanese name is *Keirō no hi*.

Moon Viewing (15–20 September)

The most beautiful moon is that of the night of 15 August according to the old lunar calendar. This now falls between 15 September and 20 September of the new calendar.

The central practice, shared with China, was always to drink rice-wine while looking at the moon and composing songs. However it was also an opportunity for praying to the moon for a good rice harvest and the aversion of typhoons which tend to arrive in Japan at about this time. The shadows on the moon were presumed to be a rabbit engaged in making rice-cakes or making medicine from the leaves of a wonderful tree which induces long life. This festival, known in Japanese as *Tsukimi*, is nowadays less observed than some others.

Autumn Equinox (23 September)

Autumn Equinox Day (*Shūbun no hi*) is, like the Spring Equinox, a public holiday, but in autumn too the Buddhist observance is spread over three days. In detail Buddhist practice is similar to that at the spring *Higan*, and visits to the graves and *sutra* recitations are the main activities.

Physical Fitness Day (10 October)

Physical Fitness Day (*Taiiku no hi*) is a public holiday intended to increase awareness of the importance of physical fitness. Various events are staged but many people just treat it as a day off.

Opposite: *Sightseers view a huge, finely detailed snow sculpture featuring the ancient castle of Osaka-jo on the opening day of the 32nd Sapporo Snow Festival. The five-day festival attracts two million people.*

Period Festival (22 October)
The Period Festival (*Jidai-matsuri*) of the Heian Shrine is one of the three great festivals of Kyōto. The festival, and indeed the shrine itself, is a modern foundation dating from 1895. Enshrined at the building are the first and last emperors to have reigned in Japan from the former capital, Kyōto. The festival consists of a huge procession of participants dressed in costumes of the various periods of Japanese history. It is thus a celebration of Japan's past as a shared theme overruling the divisions and conflicts of particular periods. At the same time it represents the whole of Japan's past up until the restoration of imperial power under the Emperor Meiji as a closed chapter, thus endorsing the modern power structure based on an imperial presence in the new capital, Tokyo. Other Period Festivals take place in other cities.

Culture Day (3 November)
Culture Day (*Bunka no hi*) is a public holiday designed to promote and celebrate the arts, but most people just treat it as a day off work.

Seven-Five-Three (15 November)
The name Seven-Five-Three (*Shichi-go-san*) refers to girls aged seven, boys aged five and girls aged three. On this day they are supposed to be dressed in new clothes and taken to a Shinto shrine for prayers that they will grow up healthy and strong. This custom is not universal and the day is not a public holiday.

Labour Thanksgiving Day (23 November)
Labour Thanksgiving Day (*Kinrō kansha no hi*) is a public holiday designed to encourage appreciation of all forms of work done by others. It more or less concludes the extended harvest season.

Chichibu Night Festival (3 December)
The Night Festival (*Yo-matsuri*) at the city of Chichibu is one of the more famous festivals in eastern Japan. It celebrates the meeting of the divinity (*kami*) of the city shrine with the divinity of a nearby mountain which dominates the city's skyline. Huge floats are dragged through the streets from the shrine to the meeting point. The last heave, up a steep slope, is particularly dramatic and strenuous. The floats are followed by the palanquin (*mikoshi*) bearing the *kami* of the shrine, and the celebrant Shinto priests arrive in the same procession. As fireworks burst overhead the union of the *mikoshi* with a framework symbolising the temporary residence of the *kami* of the mountain is effected.

Heroes Festival (*14 December*)

Heroes Festival seems the best English name for the *Gishi-matsuri* in memory of the forty-seven samurai who came to a tragic end avenging the honour of their master. *Gishi* means 'righteous samurai', but the fame of the forty-seven samurai lies in their need to reconcile two loyalties, even at the cost of their own lives.

The well-known story, subject of a *kabuki* drama and much else, runs in outline as follows. The feudal lord Asano, in whose service the samurai were retained, was due to present himself at the court of the Shōgun in Edo (modern Tokyo). The man responsible for the ceremonies was himself a powerful man at the Shōgun's court and was used to receiving large-scale presents for his services in preparing incoming lords from the provinces. Asano was not well advised on this point and so the master of ceremonies, the lord Kira, gave him inappropriate instructions on purpose. As a result Asano appeared wrongly dressed. In his anger he attacked Kira on the spot but was restrained so that the latter escaped with a cut. For violating the Shōgun's rule of order in the court Asano was ordered to commit suicide, which he did. His spirit was laid to rest at the Buddhist temple called Sengakuji in Edo (Tokyo).

This left his followers bereft of leadership and they determined to avenge their master. This was naturally not unexpected, so to lull Kira into a false sense of security the forty-seven *rōnin* (leaderless samurai) as they were now called, led a life of dissolution, brawling, petty commerce, and indeed anything which would lead people to believe they had abandoned the duty of loyalty to their deceased lord, Asano. This programme was masterminded by a leading samurai named Ōishi.

At last, on 14 December (hence the date of the festival), the opportunity presented itself when Kira and his retainers were themselves engaged in enjoying their revels. The forty-seven *rōnin*, under the leadership of Ōishi, burst in and killed Kira on the spot. Taking his head they then proceeded to the temple Sengakuji and reported their achievement at the tomb of their master.

Alas, they too, though acting in accordance with the code of the time, had offended against the rule of the Shōgun himself by killing one of his direct followers. Hence they also had to commit suicide, which they all did in samurai fashion.

The resultant forty-eight memorial stones (including that of Asano himself) are now the focus of much devotion as Japanese people consider their actions to be the epitome of 'sincerity', which in Japanese terms means being true to one's appointed duty and role. On 14 December each year a group of men make their way to the temple dressed as samurai (though they travel part of the way by underground railway) and re-enact the deed. The general public flock in behind and burn incense at the forty-eight memorial stones, one stick of incense for each so that the air is heavy with the thick scent of it.

Year End (31 December)
The last day of December, known as *Ōmisoka* in Japanese, is important as a day of preparation for the New Year. Home shrines (Shinto-related) and altars (Buddhist-related) are cleansed ready for the *kami* of New Year and for the ancestors. Of the many beliefs and practices associated with these preparations the most prominent is undoubtedly the sounding of the Buddhist temple bells. These are struck 108 times shortly before midnight to symbolise the driving out of evil and impurities. This striking of the bells is known as *Joya no kane*.

Table of Japanese festivals

1–3 January   New Year
7 January   Seven Herbs
15 January   Adults' Day
3/4 February   Bean Scattering
5–7 February   Snow Festival
11 February   National Foundation Day
15 February   Igloo Festival
3 March   Dolls' Festival/Girls' Day
21 March   Spring Equinox
1–8 April   Flower Viewing
8 April   Flower Festival
29 April   Emperor's Birthday
3 May   Constitution Day
5 May   Children's Day/Boys' Day
15 May   Hollyhock Festival
15 June   Ise Rice Planting
7 July   Star Festival
14 July   Nachi Fire Festival, O-bon
17 July   Gion Festival
2–7 August   Nebuta Festival
5–7 August   Lantern Festival
9 September   Chrysanthemum Day
15 September   Respect for the Aged Day
15–20 September   Moon viewing
23 September   Autumn Equinox

10 October Physical Fitness Day
22 October Period Festival
3 November Culture Day
15 November Seven-Five-Three
23 November Labour Thanksgiving Day
3 December Chichibu Night Festival
14 December Heroes Festival
31 December Year End

9 Jewish Festivals

ANGELA WOOD and HUGO GRYN

The Jewish calendar

The Jewish calendar is lunar, that is, it is based on twelve months and each month is marked from new moon to new moon – the time it takes the moon to travel around the earth, which is twenty-nine or thirty days. Twelve such months total 354 days, some eleven days shorter than a solar year (the time it takes for the earth to travel round the sun). Many Jewish festivals rely for their mood and their expression on observance at a particular time of year: for example the Passover (*Pesah*) is a spring festival; Tabernacles (*Sukkot*) celebrates the autumn harvest; and Lights (*Hanukah*) is only meaningful in winter. So, if these eleven days were allowed to 'accumulate' over the years, festivals would be celebrated at quite inappropriate seasons. To avoid this, adjustments are made in the calendar: it has been calculated that the addition of an extra month in each of seven years in a cycle of nineteen years solves the problem. Thus, the third, sixth, eighth, eleventh, fourteenth, seventeenth and nineteenth years are all 'leap years'. In these, the twelfth month, Adar (February/March), is repeated: it is called Adar 2, or Adar Sheni. When there is a second Adar, Lots (*Purim*) is held over from the first Adar and celebrated in Adar Sheni.

The flexibility in the nineteen-year cycle means that other adaptations can be made: specifically, the coincidence of a particular annual festival or fast with the Sabbath (*Shabat*), or the day before or after it, might involve a conflict, a violation of the day or some infringement of it. For example, if the Day of Atonement (*Yom Kippur*) were to come on a Friday or a Sunday, it would be impossible to keep the Sabbath: there would be no time to make the preparations for one on the other. Candles cannot be lit on the Day of Atonement to usher in the Sabbath or on the Sabbath to usher in the Day of Atonement. The same applies to domestic cleaning, personal bathing and a host of other important preparatory tasks.

The only solution is to avoid altogether the coincidence of the two.

Another necessity for a unified calendar that would have general agreement and common usage among Jews is the determination of the new moon. The central question is: When is a moon 'new'? In biblical times, when two reliable witnesses had actually observed, in Jerusalem, the new moon in the sky it was proclaimed as *Rosh Hodesh* (New Moon). Beacons were lit on the Mount of Olives and, by a chain of bonfires, the communities even outside Israel would learn the news. Further afield, Jews were told of the new moon by messengers. However, there were often delays and the method became confused and inaccurate. Because a month can be either twenty-nine or thirty days, Rosh Hodesh could be on either of two particular days; there arose the custom, therefore, of 'double days', that is of celebrating Rosh Hodesh on both possible days to cover both possibilities. By extension, major festivals were also doubled – with the exception, on grounds of health, of the Day of Atonement, a day of total fasting. These practices were established by the second century CE, but even when it later became possible to calculate the movements of the moon, the system remained: those in the Diaspora continued to observe festivals for double days, partly because of the force of tradition and the fact that liturgical arrangements had already been made for both days (spreading the readings over the two days), and partly because communities were reluctant to relinquish a day of rest and joy! Today, the calendar is based on calculation rather than observation, and progressive Jewish communities do not observe double days; nor do Jews in Israel, except all the celebration of the New Year (*Rosh Hashanah*).

The Jewish year has many beginnings: trees are 'celebrated' on 15 Shevat, cattle on 1 Ellul! The first month is, strictly speaking, Nisan, (March/April) but *the* New Year – a moment of theological, ethical and legal significance, falls on the first day of the seventh month, Tishri (September/October). The Jewish era counts the years from this date, beginning in the year equivalent to 3,760 BCE; thus the Gregorian year 2,000 will have 5,760 as its equivalent in the Jewish Calendar. The exact reference point for the starting of this count is not known: it is suggested that it was the creation of the world. Clearly, the universe is considerably older than that but it is also possible to see that period of time as the minimum amount of human history as recorded by Jews. The essential point is that history is not seen by Jews as beginning with the birth, death or other experience of a specific human being or even of a whole people. Rather the idea is that human history became possible when God created the universe.

Jews nevertheless live in a non-Jewish world and their calendar is not the dominant one. Invariably they use the Gregorian model in everyday life, as more than one calendar and era would be confusing. A *luah* is a conversion calendar which shows the equivalents of Hebrew and Gregorian dates: a Jew may use this to plan work and religious observances in advance – years ahead if need be. Jewish days begin at sunset – when almost everyone is awake and able to experience them: this must be taken into account and an adjustment made when using a *luah*.

The Hebrew months

Nisan	March/April
Iyar	April/May
Sivan	May/June
Tammuz	June/July
Av	July/August
Ellul	August/September
Tishri	September/October
Cheshvan	October/November
Kislev	November/December
Tevet	December/January
Shevat	January/February
Adar	February/March

In leap years there are two months of Adar (1 and 2)

The festivals

Through the weekly festival of the Sabbath – the model of all festivals – the monthly *Rosh Hodesh* and the *Yomim Tovim* (Good Days), the cycle of annual celebrations of sadness and gladness, Jews bring ideas of eternity into time. Through them can be seen the most important Jewish beliefs, rituals and customs, satisfying individual and communal needs.

All festivals – to some extent or other – originate with specific events in the past which have significance for the Jewish people. But Jews do not simply recall these incidents at the intellectual level: rather they enact them dramatically so as to recreate, as far as possible, the original situation and to engage the full range of emotional responses through social interaction. For Jewish history is not only past, it is also present; the situations are not completed, they are ongoing; and certain key experiences are relived at all times and in all places. Through the past and the present, Jewish festivals point to the future, to a point of eternity beyond time, when the universe will finally be completed and human society perfected. The Jewish idea of history is not a straight line but a spiral: it is a movement in human affairs that goes not only onwards but also upwards.

Each Jewish festival contributes to the overall pattern of the continuing years. Thus, the festivals are traditionally linked: the feasts of the Passover, Weeks (*Shavuot*) and Tabernacles form a group, together celebrating liberation from slavery, revelation from God and settlement in the homeland. They are known as the three pilgrim festivals (*Shalosh regalim*), occasions to visit the Temple in biblical times. Passover and Weeks are literally connected by the counting of the *omer* (measures of barley) for forty-nine days; the New Year and the Day of Atonement form a pair held by the ten days of repentance, thus making a ten-day season beginning and ending with a festival.

The Jewish tradition has developed other connections between festivals through customs: some communities have the habit of saving the palm-branch (*lulav*) from Tabernacles to use as a broom for the ritual removal of leaven before the Passover. They will also need light and they may well have kept a candle from *Hanukah* for this. In ways such as these, the many phases of the Jewish calendar acquire continuity, shape and wholeness.

Shabat (Sabbath) (weekly)

'The children of Israel shall keep the Sabbath, observing the Sabbath as a timeless covenant for all generations. It is a sign between me and the children of Israel for ever . . .'

Exodus 31: 16–17

Shabat, the Sabbath, is a day of rest for the Jews. Work is not permitted and there are statutory religious services. According to Abraham Heschel, the Sabbath is more than an interlude in the week or even an armistice in life's battle: it is a conscious harmony of world and people and a profound sense of what unites heaven and earth. For centuries, Shabat has been seen as a glimmer of heaven and a taste of perfection. It is said that on Shabat Jews gain an additional soul. This is not a 'bit' added on to them but rather a new dimension, a real self, a deeper state of consciousness. This image is carried to the end of Shabat: a metaphorical explanation as to why Jews feel sad on Saturday evening when Shabat ends is that the additional soul is leaving and they hate to see her go! Every seventh day, a miracle takes place: the soul of humanity and of the world, according to a mystical view, is resurrected.

The image of Shabat as a bride is a strong one: one tradition suggests that the universe without Shabat would be like a bridal-chamber without a bride; another speaks of the Jewish people as perpetually in love with Shabat. But Shabat is also a queen and this is appropriately echoed in the meaning of Kabbalat Shabat – the Friday evening service. It refers to welcoming, greeting, and receiving a *person*, but also to accepting a *law* as binding and taking an obligation upon oneself. Clearly Kabbalat Shabat is both these; Shabat is both queen and bride. The experience is both one of outward observance in actions and inward reflections in feelings. Jews are commanded both to 'observe the Sabbath day and keep it holy' (Deuteronomy 5: 8) *and* to 'remember to keep the Sabbath day holy' (Exodus 20: 8), thus achieving balance of their outer and inner selves, of law and love, of body and spirit.

In terms of law, the Bible gives very little clue as to what constitutes work and therefore what is avoided on Shabat. There are only two specific prohibitions: travelling outside the town where you live or are staying (Exodus 16: 29), and lighting fires (Exodus 35: 3). It is clear that both these activities are hard work not only in terms of the effort they require but, more importantly, as activities directed at the material world and the attempt to conquer it.

On the same principle and by a process of deduction, the rabbis were able to formulate a comprehensive classification of the categories of work. They noticed that the Sabbath commandment was repeated to Moses immediately *after* the instructions for building the worship tent (tabernacle) and again by Moses to the Israelites immediately *before* he communicated the building instructions. Not believing that this was merely a coincidence and definitely not a writer's error, the rabbis queried the juxtaposition of the two messages and wondered if there was a connection between them. They concluded that the tabernacle was a sanctuary in space and Shabat a sanctuary in time! On this basis, they analysed the building of the tabernacle, discovered thirty-nine different activities or actions and decided that Jews should therefore refrain from these on Shabat in order to experience its holiness. These thirty-nine kinds of work can be grouped, for simplicity, under five headings:

1 Producing food (ploughing, baking, etc.)
2 Making cloth (shearing wool, sewing, etc.)
3 Writing (making parchment, writing, etc.)
4 Building (lighting and extinguishing fire, demolishing, etc.)
5 Carrying in a public area

All of these reinforce the idea of work as essentially constructive and potentially destructive: Jews who refrain from such production efforts on Shabat are avoiding the week-long temptation to remake or reshape the things of space and to conquer nature.

The rabbis developed comprehensive guidelines for behaviour on Shabat partly with the purpose of establishing a universal pattern that would last forever, preserve Jewish values and ensure the survival of Jewish identity. One famous dictum says: 'More than Israel has kept the Sabbath, the Sabbath has kept Israel.' The rabbis were keen to preserve the unique holiness of Shabat by suggesting, in general terms, ways in which to prevent weekly matters from encroaching upon it and specifically by erecting a fence, that is, by developing disciplines which prevent forgetful or absent-minded breaking or desecration of the Sabbath. Lastly, conscious that 'the Sabbath is given to you, not you to the Sabbath' and that to become mental slaves to the idea of rest would be a contradiction in terms, the rabbis wanted to remove the burden of trying to work out how to observe Shabat. The idea behind their pattern for Shabat was that it alleviated anxiety and apprehension, and liberated people for joy.

For all their love of Shabat, there was and is one area in which it is not only allowed to desecrate the Sabbath, it is *commanded*: that is, for purposes of saving life. Thus doctors, nurses, and the like, may work on Shabat and emergency services operate: it is not only a privilege, it is a duty (*mitzvah*).

The Sabbath is, of course, itself a form of life: indeed, a life-giving force, and Jewish time revolves around it. It is the only day of the week to have a Hebrew name: all others are simply numbered. Elaborate preparations are made for Shabat in most Jewish homes, and a great deal of work is involved in arranging for the day of rest! In hard times families would save their tastiest food for Shabat, eating very simply all week, and anyone given a new item of clothing would save it to wear for Shabat. The mood on the eve of Shabat is one of domestic bustle, of cooking, washing, bathing and putting out the best, and ideally everyone in the family should make some contribution to the day in honour of the Sabbath, by polishing candlesticks, preparing a special dish, laying the table, arranging flowers and so on. Intimate spiritual readiness must take place, too: some time should be left to cast away thoughts and worries from the week so as to honour the Sabbath not only in the home but also in the heart. Of the three-way relationship between God, Torah and Israel, which characterises so much of Jewish life and thought, each element is reflected in the mood of a particular phase of Shabat. Friday evening's meal is flavoured with 'Israel': it is a light, social, unifying time. The two candles are lit just before sunset in observant homes, usually by women. Synagogue services are short and generally attended mostly by men and boys. The central prayers of the Shabat service avoid petitions which are linked to everyday worries. The celebratory glass of wine (*kiddush*) traditionally entered the synagogue at this point for the benefit of travellers but it came to stay, although in token form.

At home, the returning father may bless his children – hoping that the boys be like Menasseh and Ephraim and the girls like Sarah, Rebecca, Rachel and Leah. The wife and mother may well be serenaded by her husband and children with a passage from Proverbs 31 which sings the praises of 'A woman of worth . . . more precious than rubies'. The recital of *kiddush*, usually by the father of the house, over wine or any drink except plain water, sanctifies the day.

After ritual washing of hands, the breaking of bread (the *hamotzi*) is made. The special loaves (*hallot*) are reminiscent of the Temple offering. In preparing *hallot*, a tiny piece of dough is torn off, not eaten and burnt. Traditionally, it is a dough enriched with egg or possibly a little sugar. The loaves for Shabat are usually plaited – to suggest God-Torah-Israel – and may be sprinkled with seeds and glazed. Loaves are served in pairs, partly to recall the double portion of manna which Moses told the Israelites to collect on Friday so they would not work on the Sabbath. The loaves should be covered by a cloth (*dekel*): it is said that this is to shield the feelings of the loaves which may feel unimportant because they are preceded by candles and *kiddush*; the point is to transfer this protective principle to human beings. Many regional customs attend the breaking of bread; it should either be broken by hand or, if cut, a 'non-weapon' should be used, that is, either a knife with a blade of silver or some other precious metal, or a knife which has a sheath or cover. The idea is that on the day of peace, there should be no weapons on the table. Salt is sprinkled on the bread before eating for a number of possible reasons: to recall that human beings earn their bread by the sweat of the brow (sweat is salty!); as a token of human dignity, for only human beings spice their food and are not content merely to satisfy hunger; there is also possibly a play on Hebrew words, the word for salt being *melah*, and one of the names for God being *Meleh* – Ruler or King.

The meal will be a special one and there may well be table songs (*zemirot*) between courses – or sometimes even during! These reflect Jewish ideas about the value and beauty of Shabat. A longer version of the thanksgiving for food is used for Shabat, which begins with

Opposite: *When Shabat is over, the evening service is followed by Havdalah which separates the holiness of Shabat from the week ahead.*

Psalm 126, recalling the return of exiles to Zion. One of the additional phrases refers to Shabat as an image or model for the time being of the eternal day of peace which is for all people and is a perpetual Jewish hope. It is 'a day that shall be entirely a Sabbath'.

The week's major synagogue service is on Saturday morning: the structure is identical to the service on any morning, but there are extra psalms and such prayers as 'The breath of all living shall praise God'. The heart of the service is the reading from the scroll of the weekly Torah portion and the *haftarah* (completion). Before the scroll is returned ceremonially to the Ark it is dressed and held while an additional portion of the prophets' prayers are said (in the vernacular) for the country or the head of state; for the welfare of community, workers, for the sick or the troubled. It is often the practice to draw attention to individual celebrations or commiserations such as weddings and bereavements. On the Shabat before Rosh Hodesh, the new moon, there is a simple, moving prayer asking God's blessing for the month ahead.

The mood of Torah continues into lunch, which is introduced by *kiddush*. The meal has not, in Orthodox homes, been cooked on Shabat. It may be a cold meal, one which can be warmed on a fire that was lit before Shabat or a dish that has been cooking continuously since before Shabat. *Cholent* is a bean casserole, sometimes made with meat, potatoes or barley, which has been slow-baked at a very low temperature since Friday afternoon. Among Jews of the Orient *hamim*, a similarly prepared dish utilising rice, is often eaten. Discussions at the table centre on the weekly Torah portion and possibly the sermon which was based on it.

The third phase – Saturday afternoon – is devoted to the individual's relationship with God: it is a quiet time of sleeping, strolling, private reading and intimate relations. The third meal is simple and reflects this mood: bread, cheese, herrings and maybe cake are served. There is no *kiddush* before but a complete thanksgiving afterwards.

The final ritual of Shabat actually takes place after it is over. *Havdalah* (distinction) is a ceremony which focuses on pairs, which are actually not separate but, paradoxically, merge: Shabat and weekdays, holy and profane, day and night, Israel and the nations. The cup of salvation is raised and wine is drunk; a spice-box is sniffed deeply so as to take from the Shabat the fragrance and delight of the day. All who are gathered round also stretch out their hands towards the light (so as to use it), which is in the form of a long candle, made of plaited tapers, bringing together the 'threads' of Shabat. Shabat has come and gone and the Messiah has not actually come (although the taste of things to come has been very strong indeed): the song *Eliahu haNavi* (Elijah the Prophet) yearns for Elijah to bring the Messianic Age very soon. *Havdalah* is recited standing up because it bids goodbye to the Sabbath and it is polite to stand up when a guest leaves.

'The children of Israel shall keep the Sabbath, observing the Sabbath as a timeless covenant for all generations . . .'

Exodus 31: 16 *et seq*

This passage generally forms part of the noon *kiddush* on Saturday and encapsulates the meaning of Shabat.

The three pilgrim festivals

'The Lord said to Moses, "I come to you in a thick cloud, so that the people may hear when I speak with you and may also believe you for ever." And Moses told the words of the people to the Lord.'

Exodus 19: 9

Pesah (Passover) (March/April)

Pesah is celebrated from the fifteenth or sixteenth to the twenty-first or twenty-second day of the Hebrew month of Nisan. The first and last days are days of rest; no work may be done and there are statutory religious services.

The first words of the Ten Sayings ('I Am the Lord your God who brought you out from the land of Egypt, from the camp of slavery') proclaim God's connection with the Exodus and the importance of freedom in Judaism. The experience of slavery in Egypt and the act of redemption have never been regarded as isolated incidents in Jewish history or merely as the 'birthday' of Israel; rather, the theme of God's work of liberation in human society is constantly recurring in Jewish life and thought, in the content of many prayers and songs, in the Zionist movement. There is a particular political interpretation of Pesah which views oppressors, tyrants and racists of any age as 'pharaoh' and totalitarian, and godless regimes as 'Egypt'. At Pesah, when Jews recall how the angel of death passed over (*pesah*) their first-born, they are aware not only of God's saving work but also of the violation of human rights in the world today. This gives a special meaning to the passage in the *Haggadah* (the Telling, the Story), the book read at the Passover supper, which prompts all Jews to identify and become involved with the experience: "In every generation, everyone should regard himself as if he personally had come out of Egypt": the message of Pesah has to be applied to the life of every Jew.

179

In their hurry to escape from Egypt, when the chance came, the Israelites did not wait for dough to rise but simply baked flat loaves – *matzot*. As a reminder and a re-enactment, Jews eat *matzah* (unleavened bread) at least once at the *seder* (order) during Pesah, and throughout the week-long festival they do not eat or drink any form of *hametz*, that is, food which involves fermentation such as 'ordinary' bread, biscuits or cakes, pasta, yeast extract or malt vinegar, beer or whisky. There is thus at Pesah an intense physical experience of change or renewal as well as some intellectual awareness of liberation.

Domestically, the time before Pesah is the busiest in the year: it is appropriately a period of refreshing the home – Pesah is also the Spring Festival – and of the self-evaluation that comes with turning out cupboards and pockets! All the *hametz* must be eaten up, given to non-Jews (large quantities can be sold) or taken outside on the evening before Pesah. On the morning before, the last bits are burnt or thrown to the wind or water. From that moment on, for the next week, only food or drink which is acceptable to the Passover is consumed. Families may even have special sets of cutlery, crockery and cooking utensils kept just for this festival; otherwise, they have to ritually cleanse them, usually by baking or boiling. The point behind the enormous work that is inevitably involved is that release from slavery is *total* and permeates every level of existence: it is as much to do with crumbs under the table as it is with the most abstract thoughts or the most intense emotions.

The focus of Pesah is the Passover supper. It has been called a 'feast of history' because the *seder* has a structure and a process in the reading, singing, talking, demonstration and eating which epitomise and encapsulate the transitions from slavery to freedom. There are fifteen formal rituals in the *seder*, some of them tied to specific items of symbolic significance found on the table – most of which will be eaten at some point in the evening.

Passover suppers (*Sedarim*) are usually large gatherings, mostly held at home (some synagogues hold them communally, also) but no matter how many there are already, there should always be room for unexpected guests: hospitality is not only a joy, it is a religious duty. Near the beginning, the leader of the *seder* – usually the father, grandfather or perhaps the community's rabbi – will issue an open invitation: '. . . let all who are hungry come and eat. Let all who are in need come and celebrate Passover.'

Opposite: *The Passover meal: a time for remembering the deliverance of the children of Israel from Egypt. This meal is being held in Jerusalem, a city special to all Jews.*

There are three vital components of the *seder*: the *pesah* (bone), *maror* (bitter herbs) and *matzah* (unleavened bread) and these should be referred to and explained or discussed. The central focus of the table is the *seder* plate which will have these items:

zeroa a piece of lamb shankbone (which is not eaten) in memory of the ancient Temple sacrifice, also connected with the use of lamb's blood in saving the Israelites in Egypt;

beytza a roasted egg, also not eaten, and symbolising other sacrifices;

karpas a spring vegetable or greenery, usually but not necessarily parsley, which is itself indicative of the time of year and is early on in the ceremony dipped in salt water, for a taste of the Israelites' tears and sweat;

maror bitter herbs or plants, such as radish, horseradish, chives, chicory or indeed any bitter vegetable, but lettuce is specified in some traditions as the most suitable vegetable for it tastes sweet at first and afterwards bitter: such was the life of Israel in Egypt.

Maror thus symbolises the bitterness of Egyptian slavery and must be eaten at the *seder*, however unpleasant. Some tables will have two kinds of *maror* as it is taken twice: once with *matzah* (known as the 'Hillel Sandwich' after the rabbi who used to combine them in order to fulfil physically the biblical idea of eating bitter herbs *with* unleavened bread) and again with *haroset*, a delicious paste of grated apple, ground nuts, cinnamon, honey and wine, symbolic of the mortar used by the Israelite slave builders. Near the *seder* plate and occupying the place of honour will be three *matzot*: two replace the two loaves used on the Sabbath and festivals, while the third emphasises the special blessing for eating *matzah*. It is the bread of affliction, and a token of the broken condition of the Jewish people. Of the middle *matzah*, one half is used for the blessing and the other is hidden for the *afikomen* (dessert): it will be the last bite to be eaten that night so that the lingering taste will be of *matzah*. A popular diversion of children towards the end of the meal is 'hunting the *afikomen*': finding it is said to enable the second part of the *seder* to take place and is usually rewarded!

There will also probably be a bowl of shelled, hard-boiled eggs – one each – to be eaten with salt water (at the beginning of the meal) as a symbol of new life born of sorrow. Historically, it is likely that this reflects, during the Roman Empire, the serving of eggs as *hors d'oeuvres* at a banquet, at which slaves would never sit. Thus, in terms of the dominant contemporary culture, Jews were eating the food of the free.

It is the duty of every man and woman on the first night of Pesah to drink at least four glasses of wine: each glass is poured or refilled at a specific point during the *seder* and it is understood that each one represents a phrase describing redemption: 'I shall liberate you from bondage', 'I shall bring you to the land', '. . . deliver you from Egypt', '. . . take you to me as a people'. Because there is a fifth term, '. . . redeem you from servitude', there arose the custom of the fifth glass of wine – the 'cup of Elijah', filled between the third and fourth glasses and never drunk. Elijah, according to legend, never died and is thought to be the forerunner of the Messiah who will remove suffering and usher in the world to come. The doors are opened at this point: Pesah was a very treacherous time for Jews throughout the Middle Ages, because of anti-semitic attacks at Easter time and so the doors would have been shut. But at this moment they are opened metaphorically to let Elijah enter. The traditional verses spoken (Psalms 79: 6 *et seq*; 69: 25; Lamentations 3: 66) were a cry from the heart, a plea to God to show anger to the godless and the Jew-haters. This does not fit the overall tone of Pesah and some Jews think they should not show or feel revenge; so nowadays there are sometimes prayers instead for universal peace and brotherhood, such as a reflection on the Holocaust:

'. . . We remember with reverence and love the six millions of our people who perished at the hands of a tyrant more wicked than the Pharaoh who enslaved our fathers in Egypt . . . they slew the blameless and pure, men and women and little ones, with vapours of poison and burned them with fire. But we abstain from dwelling on the deeds of the evil ones lest we defame the image of God in which man was created . . .'

The youngest there starts off by asking the traditional four questions in the form of exclamations: 'How different this night is from other nights! For on this night . . . we only eat *matzah* (not *hametz*) . . . we must eat *maror* . . . we dip twice (*karpas* into salt water and *maror* into *haroset*) . . . we all recline (lean over as if on couches at a Roman banquet).' The answers are 'We were slaves' and 'Our ancestors were idol worshippers': the rest of the story is an elaboration and an exploration of these answers. Women as well as men are obliged to narrate the story because they also took part in the miracle. In fact, according to tradition it was through the righteousness of the women in Israel that God freed his people.

'"I will pass through the land of Egypt . . ." – I and no angel; "I will kill every first-born . . ." – I and no seraph; "I will execute judgements . . ." – I and no intermediary; "I am the Lord" – I and no other.'

Moses' name does not appear in the Haggadah, thus stressing that God himself has intervened in the history of the Jews and that the miracle was not performed by a human being. Although Moses is the greatest prophet, in Jewish tradition, the rabbis wanted to play down his role to make sure he was never deified for working wonders.

At the recitation of the ten plagues, everyone spills a drop of wine (from the second cup) either by tipping their glass slightly or by dipping their finger and shaking off the wine or dabbing it on a plate. This is because, although these plagues killed the oppressors, sadness should still be felt at human suffering: the cup of joy therefore cannot be full. The emphasis must rather be on thanking God for positive benefits. *Dayyenu* (It would be enough for us) is a fourteen-verse 'growing' song where the last line of one verse becomes the first line of the next. It recognises that thanks are due for the smallest action God might have performed: so much more for what God actually did in total!

If the first half of the *seder* is concerned with the Passover of the past, the second looks to the future, to the Passover to come, the banquet at which everyone will sit and eat: the liberation from Egypt is a model and an image of the Messianic age in which all will be free. The *seder* ends, therefore, 'Next year in Jerusalem!' and, in Israel, 'Next year in Jerusalem rebuilt!'

Shavuot (Festival of Weeks) (May/June)
Shavuot is celebrated on the sixth day of the Hebrew month of Sivan. It is a day of rest, no work and statutory religious services.

Of all the festivals, this has the most names and these give a useful insight into the meaning of the festival and its main features. It marks the season of the wheat harvest and was originally an agricultural feast known as the Festival of the Harvest. On that day, Israelites offered first fruits of the field as an expression of gratitude to God; hence the name Day of the First Ripe Fruits. In the prayer book, the festival is called 'The Season of the Giving of Our Torah': the reference here being to the historial events concerning the assembly of the Israelites at Sinai, the revelation of God to the people and the giving of the Ten Sayings (Commandments).

As well as names referring to agriculture and the revelation of Torah, two other names link this festival with Passover. The name Conclusion (*Atzeret*) is frequently used in the Talmud and Abraham ibn Ezra, a twelfth-century Spanish scholar, pointed out that it is related to the Hebrew for 'stop'; this may be because there are very few customs and very little ritual connected with this festival, the main observance of it being the stopping of work. However, the Conclusion of Passover (*Atzeret shel Pesah*) puts it at the end of a season of harvests which began at Pesah with barley. There is another kind of 'conclusion' involved: the freedom from slavery which Pesah marks is incomplete without the revelation of the Torah and the ethical ideas it gave; true freedom is a life under God's law.

The most common name for this festival is Shavuot, the Festival of Weeks, so called because a period of seven weeks, known as *Sefirat Omer* (Counting the Omer) is measured from Passover. An *Omer* is a measure of barley. Traditionally, an *omer* was brought to the temple each night for fifty nights, beginning on the second night of Passover. The counting continues for forty-nine days and a 'running commentary' is shown on a board in some synagogues: '. . . you shall count fifty days' (Leviticus 23: 15). This is the origin of the term *Pentecost*; it comes from the Greek for fifty.

The problem of dating Shavuot – which alone of all the festivals has no specific date given in the Bible – comes from an ambiguity about the day on which the *omer* was brought: 'the day after the Sabbath'. 'Sabbath' could literally refer to the weekly day of rest, in which case Shavuot would always begin on a Saturday night and would have a moveable date (anything from the sixth to the thirteenth of Sivan). This would have been an anomaly and the rabbis found it unacceptable that the central Jewish historical experience, the giving of the Torah, should not be celebrated on a fixed date. They took the point of view that 'Sabbath' can also refer to a festival which is a day of rest. So Shavuot was to be celebrated on the fiftieth day after the first day of Pesah.

There is a further strange aspect to Shavuot: whereas the Bible gives it an agricultural significance, it does not state that it is the anniversary of the giving of Torah. Some say this is because the idea of celebrating the Torah came later when an increasingly urban population found agricultural festivals less meaningful. For Jews today living in cities outside Israel, the bringing of the first fruits aspect of Shavuot is not of direct relevance. However, the link with the land is seen in the floral decorations of homes and synagogues and, in some countries, the custom of strewing fresh grass on the floor. This is first a reminder that Mount Sinai was covered with vegetation in honour of the great event of the giving of Torah and secondly, an indication that the world is judged through the fruit of the trees. In the State of Israel today, the agricultural significance and impact of Shavuot has been revived. It is one of the ways in which the Zionist hope of the restoration and reintegration of land and people can be fulfilled. Ceremonies, involving song and dance as well the collection of harvest goods for distribution, take place. Other celebrations and customs of Shavuot reflect its Torah-giving aspect. Devout Jews take the three days before Shavuot as a time of spiritual preparation: this is historically derived from the 'three days of setting bounds' when Moses kept the people from climbing Sinai until after the revelation. These three days culminate symbolically in the spending of the entire night in study on Shavuot itself – quite appropriate for the Festival of the Torah. This aspect of Shavuot seems to be about five or six hundred years old and is connected with a mystical idea that during the night heaven opens to receive prayerful and studious intent. It might also be bound up with the wish to make Shavuot happen over and again in individual lives: the Israelites slept through the night before the giving of the Torah and had to be shaken dramatically with thunder and lightning; the night of study is therefore an attempt to be alert and awake to any and all revelations from God – even the revelation that can come through study and discussion. A special book, an anthology of religious literature called *Tikkun leyl Shavuot*, was devised for the night of study.

Dairy foods are served throughout the night and indeed are characteristic of Shavuot for a number of reasons. First they are suitable for summer weather – cheese cake, for example, is a special Shavuot food. Secondly, until the revelation on Sinai, the Israelites had no commandments about *kashrut* (proper diet), so meat and fish are avoided. Thirdly, the event took place on the journey to the promised land, described as 'flowing with milk and honey'; both of these are symbols of the Torah: 'Honey and milk are under your tongue' (Song of Songs 4: 11).

As might be expected, the synagogue Torah readings include Exodus 19 and 20, which recount the giving of the Ten Sayings, and the congregation stands to hear them. The selections from the prophets are Ezekiel 1, which is concerned with visions of God, and Habakkuk 3, a description of God's power in revelation. The most well-known of Shavuot readings is Ruth – one of the five special scrolls. It is the story of Ruth, a Moabite woman, who marries an Israelite and whose attachment to his family, his people, their beliefs and values does not end with his death. It is therefore read to embellish the idea of Shavuot as a commitment to the Torah. There are other reasons for the choice of Ruth: the story has a harvest theme; it features gleaners (the poor who followed the reapers in the harvest) and the description of the Shavuot offering is followed by the commandment to leave some grain for the gleaners' dignity in filling their needs (Leviticus 23: 22 *et seq*). Yet another association is with David, the great grandson of Ruth and

Israel's favourite king, and also, for many, the model of the Messiah who is to come: the link is that David, according to legend, was born and died on Shavuot. For this reason Psalms are read on the second night.

Above all, Shavuot affirms and enhances Jewish education: it was once the time when young children would be first taken to Hebrew classes – often literally 'with honey on the tongue' or with sweets on their writing-slate. A variation on this theme today is the 'graduation service' in some Reform and Liberal congregations: Jewish teenagers who have reached a certain level of education and who have finished formal lessons as children are honoured collectively, perhaps by leading the services in synagogue, by processing with the Torah, by reading the passages for the day, by initiating a discussion session or by hosting a special celebratory meal for their families and friends.

Sukkot (Festival of Tabernacles/Booths) (September/October)

Sukkot is celebrated from the fifteenth to the twenty-second day of the Hebrew month of Tishri. The first and last days are days of rest; no work may be done and there are statutory religious services.

'Rejoice!' is a strange and seemingly impossible commandment to obey – yet Jews are *obliged* to be happy during the celebration of Tabernacles. It is called *Zman Simhatenu* – the Season of Our Rejoicing. And joy on Sukkot is referred to three times in the Torah: 'You shall rejoice before the Lord your God seven days'; 'You shall rejoice in your festival . . .'; 'You shall have nothing but joy'.

This command is probably the most difficult of all to fulfil, for· human beings might be able to carry out orders which involve *doing* something, but not necessarily observe commands which involve *feeling* something. There is also a problem of knowing whether rejoicing was actually taking place! Yet this is a vitally important reminder of the need for happiness in worship, of loving God with a glad heart (Psalms 100: 2; 68: 3).

The basic idea underlying the command 'Rejoice!' is that feelings not only move from inside out, they also move from outside in; that not only does feeling affect doing, but doing affects feeling; that one can become joyous by behaving joyfully. Certainly, there are stories of Jews in concentration camps who forced themselves, and each other, to be happy; who incredibly managed to dance and sing in the grimmest possible circumstances.

One simple reason for joy is that celebration is total. Some Jews noted that the command to dwell in a *sukkah* (booth, hut, tabernacle) requires the *whole* body. On the Day of Atonement (*Yom Kippur*), the *whole* person is involved in praying and fasting and Sukkot, which follows barely five days later, stresses the union of body and soul intended by Torah and the Jewish tradition for the worship of God and community life. In some families and congregations, it is customary at the end of the Day of Atonement – even *before* breaking the fast with food or drink – to make a token start on the building of the *sukkah*: thus both the connection and the contrast between the two festivals are expressed.

The *sukkah* is a temporary home which recalls the *sukkot* (plural) in which the Israelites lived during their wilderness wanderings between Egypt and their homeland. The commandment concerning this is not to look at a picture of a *sukkah*, build a model and put it on the table or merely sing songs about a *sukkah* but, very significantly, to 'live' in them for seven days. The experience should permeate every aspect of existence and invite the individual to identify with the historical experience. So much happened during that phase of Jewish history that was to have such a formative influence on Jewish culture, and so much was learned about Israel's relationship with God, that to strengthen that influence and to recall what was learned means recreating the original condition – that is, living in *sukkot*. The major message is that the outside of each person's life is weak and fleeting – like the *sukkah* – but inside one is strong and everlasting.

Sukkot falls during the autumn, a time of the year when people are not normally sitting under shade in their gardens or on their roofs or balconies. This draws attention to the festival of Sukkot and points to a different purpose, a spiritual one. There is seldom strong sunshine in the month of Tishri but the 'shade' of the *sukkah* lets in rain and wind and, in stormy weather, eating, drinking and maybe sleeping in the *sukkah* can be scary. The *sukkah* shaking and the leafy coverings rustling evoke a feeling of the vulnerability of human nature and the precariousness of human life.

As a harvest festival, the feast of in-gathering, it is a time of material abundance as well as spiritual significance. The fullness and fruition of the year is all around and Jews might be tempted to see themselves as self-sufficient, but the thin coverings over the *sukkah* encourage them to look up, literally and metaphorically, to gaze at the sky and contemplate their dependence on God. So, at a time of year when they might be expected to leave temporary dwellings for the security of their houses, they leave their houses for the permanent security of God.

The *sukkah* is also a symbol of the cosiness of humanity; the *sukat shalom*, the covering of peace, protects and unites all the peoples of the world. The universalism of Sukkot could be seen in the number of the sacrifices prescribed in the Torah and performed in the days of the ancient Temple: they totalled seventy during Sukkot and these, it was said, corresponded to the seventy nations of which the world was thought to consist. Symbolically, then, these seventy sacrifices were atonement offerings by Israel on behalf of the whole world. Normally, the Hebrew prophets did not call upon non-Jews to carry out Jewish practices but Zechariah (the reading from the prophets for the first day of Sukkot) had a vision of the Messianic Age in which the nations of the world would go on a pilgrimage to Jerusalem during Sukkot: 'On that day, shall the Lord be one and his name one.' The tradition of hospitality during Sukkot, of inviting non-Jews into the *sukkah*, is a foretaste of the world to come.

A *sukkah* can be very simple: there are several rules about its construction in order to ensure that the 'spirit' of the festival is expressed. For example, the *sukkah* should be temporary: it should ideally be erected just for the festival, but if the frame or the walls are left up all year, then the covering or ceiling should be put on freshly each year. The ceiling should be the last thing to go on the *sukkah* – after the walls are finished – so that it *completes* the *sukkah*. It should be made of plant material ('grown from the earth') that is cut down (not still growing) such as fruit or food (although these are frequently used as decoration inside the *sukkah*). Any materials can be used for the walls.

There are stipulations, too, about size. The *sukkah* itself must be large enough to be a 'home', the area defined as such allows a person and a table to be fitted in. The *sukkah* can be as long or wide as necessary: some *sukkot* hold the entire congregation of a synagogue, perhaps several hundred people. There is a minimum height – for the sake of dignity – *and* a maximum, so that the shade comes from the ceiling not from the walls, and also because dwelling in the *sukkah* should be a conscious experience. It could be difficult to be aware of the *sukkah* if it were very tall. No blessing is said for building the *sukkah* because the religious duty is not the constructing of it but the living in it.

Another positive command for Sukkot is taking the four plants (the *arba minim*). These are: the citron, palm, myrtle and willow. Clearly these four species were intended to symbolise the final harvest, the fertility of the land in a ritual of thanksgiving. These four were probably chosen because they would remain fresh throughout the week, and so instill joy in the heart and lift up the spirit. More importantly, they connect the people and the land and this is vital for those who live in cities.

Beyond this, however, there are several traditions which explore the meaning of the four species. One likens them to parts of the body: the citron to the heart, the palm to the spine, the myrtle leaves to the eye and the willow to a lip. All of these should be united in worship of God: a sincere heart, dignified posture, inspiration of the eye and honest words. The most popular way of explaining the meaning is to do with 'use' and 'beauty' – the 'goodness' and 'learning': The palm bears fruit but not flowers, so it is useful but not beautiful; myrtle flowers but bears no fruit so it is beautiful but not useful; the willow neither flowers nor bears fruit and is neither useful nor beautiful; but the citron is both beautiful and useful. These plants are taken to correspond with four types of people with respect to their learning of Torah and their acts of goodness or religious duty – the theory and practice of religion. The ideal, clearly, is the *etrog* (citron), which is a name used to describe an admirable, praiseworthy person who is well-balanced and 'whole'.

Whichever imaginative or evocative explanation is developed, the point behind it is that the four species are held together, the *etrog* in the left hand, and the other three bound together and held in the right hand. The four parts of the body or four kinds of people are one.

The ritual of waving has also grown up as a way of 'taking the *lulav*': the four species are waved three times to and fro in every direction: to the east, south, west, north, up and down. These wavings symbolise the spreading of blessings over all and they are performed every day during the festival (except on Shabbat by Orthodox Jews) immediately after taking the *lulav* and again at several points during the singing of the *Hallel* (Psalms 113–118).

One more ritual remains: on the seventh day of the festival (*Hoshana Raba* – the great Hosanna – 'save us') it is a custom to strike a willow branch upon a hard surface until the leaves fall off. Some suggest this is because willows grow near water and the prayers at this season are for rain. Folklore in the Middle Ages linked Hoshana Raba with Yom Kippur, suggesting that the final 'sealing' was postponed until then.

The real key to understanding Sukkot is expressed by this prayer, which is recited on the first day of the festival.

'May it be Your will, O my God and God of my fathers, that You cause Your divine presence to live among us, and may You spread a covering of peace over us.'

Prayer Book (authors' translation)

Shemini Atzeret (Eighth Day of Conclusion) and Simhat Torah (The Rejoicing in the Torah) (September/October)

'On the eighth day you shall hold an Assembly; you shall not do any laborious work . . .'

Numbers 29:35

Shemini Atzeret falls on the twenty-second day of Tishri (and also on the twenty-third for Orthodox Jews in the Diaspora). It is a day of rest, no work and statutory religions services. It is partly the concluding day of Sukkot and partly a separate day, a festival in its own right. Therefore the blessing *Sheheheyanu* ('. . . who has kept us alive and sustained us and enabled us to reach this season') is said with the candles and the *kiddush* at the beginning of the festival, this shows Shemini Atzeret as an independent occasion. However, Jews do live in the *sukkah* in the sense of eating, drinking and praying there but not sleeping: the blessing for dwelling in the *sukkah* is not said on Shemini Atzeret.

No reasons are given in the Bible for the additional day but an explaining story (*midrash*) connects it with the word *atzeret* which can have the meaning of 'holding back': Sukkot is like a seven-day party given by a king. When the time comes for the guests to leave, the king says, 'I hate to see you go. Won't you stay another day?'

To some extent the Rejoicing in the Torah, *Simhat Torah* could be seen as a way of avoiding an anticlimax. For Orthodox Jews in the Diaspora, the second day of Shemini Atzeret might be very flat indeed, coming as a repetition of the completion of Sukkot, which itself follows only four days after Yom Kippur, the last of the Ten Days of Awe, which began with Rosh Hashanah. There was clearly a human need for a grand finale to the festivals of the month of Tishri!

There originated in Babylon a custom of 'completing the Torah', that is of reading Deuteronomy 33 and 34, on the second day of Shemini Atzeret. It seems to have once been called the Day of the Book but the prayerbook of Rashi, an eleventh-century biblical commentator, refers to it as a *Simhat Torah* (Rejoicing in the Torah). By that time, it was already a habit to hold a special meal because it was like the completion of a piece of study.

It was probably not until the twelfth century that the reading of the first chapter of Genesis was introduced on this day. Two reasons are given for it: first to show that it is a privilege to witness the end *and* the beginning of Torah; and, secondly, to avoid the impression of being happy to *finish* the Torah! Thus the reading of both the end and the beginning of the Torah as a circle, a cycle of revelation that actually has *no* beginning and *no* end.

Because of the image of the Torah as a bride, those who read are referred to as 'husbands' or 'bridegrooms'. The one honoured to read the end is called bridegroom of the Torah (*Hatan Torah*), and the one who reads from the beginning is called bridegroom of Genesis (*Hatan Bereshit*). It is a custom in some communities for one person to play both parts so that the idea of the never-ending circle of the Torah can be most effectively expressed. He will even try not to take a breath between the end of one scroll and the beginning of the next so as to show continuity and wholeness.

The custom most obviously associated with Simhat Torah is that of circuits (*hakafot*). The Torah scrolls are taken out of the Ark and paraded round the synagogue – as a bride might encircle her husband under the wedding canopy – usually seven times. Circuits have been known since ancient times and were recorded in the Bible (for example, by Joshua at Jericho) but they only seemed to begin on Simhat Torah in the late sixteenth century. The popularity of circuits is partly due to the participation of so many, especially of the children. Customs vary – and so does the degree of emotional intensity and religious fervour – but usually the *hazzan* (reader or singer) takes the scrolls from the Ark, hands them out and then leads the procession, singing psalms and folk songs, often with the refrain (in Hebrew) meaning 'Please, Lord, save us. Please, Lord, make us succeed!'

Children join in, carrying miniature scrolls and flags decorated with festival motifs, or perhaps with an apple or a candle on top. In traditional congregations, many people who are not carrying scrolls still leave their seats and form dancing circles, holding hands and linking arms over each other's shoulders; or they might make a chain and weave in and out of the circuits! When each circuit finishes, people pass on a scroll so that everyone who wants the ecstatic joy of carrying one can do so. Sometimes, the circuits extend outside, either by accident or by design. Sometimes the movement inside the synagogue is so expansive that it is *forced* outside!

The wedding canopy (*huppah*) also features largely in Simhat Torah and it may well take the form of a prayer shawl (*tallit*) held up horizontally by four long-armed (and strong-armed!) people who each grasp a corner. In some synagogues, the wedding canopy is appropriately held over the 'bridegrooms' as they read the Torah passages. Frequently the children in the congregation join the 'bridegrooms' as a living symbol of the marriage of the children of Israel to the Torah.

Since 1967, Jews have had access again to the Western Wall in Jerusalem, the last remains of the Temple. At Simhat Torah, it is the scene of a special rejoicing when crowds carrying Torah scrolls under canopies are almost countless.

Of all the festivals in the Jewish calendar, Simhat Torah is the one which today holds greatest meaning for the Jews of the Soviet Union. For more than sixty years the Communist regime has effectively suppressed Jewish culture, forbidding the teaching of Jewish ideas and values, the instruction in Hebrew and the observance of rituals and customs, most synagogues and other institutions having been destroyed or adapted for state purposes. At the same time internal passports are stamped 'Jewish', thus making Jewish identity unavoidable and antisemitism a possibility. In such a climate, the assimilation of young Jews would be understandable but since the 1960s there has been a gradual reawakening of Jewish consciousness in them. Despite the dangers involved, many in their teens or twenties have begun to meet *outside* the remaining synagogues in Moscow and Leningrad on Simhat Torah, as an act of defiance of the Soviet government and as an act of solidarity with the people of Israel who on this day proclaim the joy of being Jewish.

Rosh Hashanah (New Year) (September)

'Sound the horn on the new moon, at the appointed time, on the day of our solemn feast, for this is a statute of Israel, and a law of the God of Jacob.'

Psalm 81:3,4

Rosh Hashanah falls on the first day of Tishri. It is a day of rest and there are statutory religious services. In this festival three themes are woven: the anniversary of the world's creation; the day of judgement; and the renewal of the bond between God and Israel.

Rosh Hashanah exists as a celebration of nature and of divine creativity even without our precise knowledge of the origins of the universe. God is not only creator but also judge and on Rosh Hashanah individual and collective actions are weighed: people are responsible not only for themselves but also for each other. Both these themes are universal but the third embodies the reciprocal relationship between God and Israel: Israel is indebted to God for its existence and God is committed to Israel's preservation. This tempers the idea of judgement and is a reminder of God's mercy.

As it is a *new* year, there are many customs which involve renewal and starting again: many have a haircut just before or buy a special outfit. At the very least, all wear their 'best' clothes. Some wear white to symbolise purity (red is symbolical of sin in the Jewish tradition) or as a token of the funeral shroud (*kittel*), which evokes humble supplication. The traditional greeting on this occasion is

'May you be inscribed in the Book of Life for a good year!' or, now, simply 'Good Year!' (*Shana Tova!*).

Home rituals include dipping an apple in honey (and eating it!) for a sweet year. Some families bake bread of the special shabat dough (*hallot*) in the shape of a crown to recall divine sovereignty, or in the shape of a ladder to link heaven and earth. Some communities eat pomegranates – fruits with many seeds – not only in the hope of fertility but also with the prayer that God may multiply the credit of goodness.

The morning service of Rosh Hashanah includes special Torah readings – Genesis 21 and 22 – which form a single narrative but are divided between the two days. Chapter 21, the reading for the first day, tells of the birth of Isaac and Chapter 22, the reading for the second day, of the binding of Isaac. Congregations which celebrate only one day usually read Chapter 22. There is a clear link between the ram in the story and the *shofar* (an instrument, usually a ram's horn, blown on Rosh Hashanah and at other moments at that time of year) but more importantly, the story is about faith and the acceptance of God's power in relation to human strivings.

The additional (*musaf*) service is divided into three parts, corresponding to the three themes and the three other names for Rosh Hashanah: the Exaltation of God as King (*Malkhuyot*); Remembrance (*Zikhronot*) and Blowing the Horn (*Shofarot*). The *musaf*, like the *shahrit* (morning) service, may include medieval hymns and prayers which explore the uncertainty of life and the inability of human beings to control the forces of change: 'Who will live and who will die? . . . who by fire and who by water? . . . who shall fall and who shall rise? But returning, repentance, prayer and good deeds turn away the evil decree' (Rosh Hashanah Prayer Book).

A fairly widespread custom for the afternoon is the *tashlikh* ceremony: pleading prayers are said at a source of water such as a river, seashore, spring, pond or well; the water should ideally, but not necessarily, be running water. Everyone then empties all the 'bits' out of their pockets into the water, symbolically ridding themselves of the burden of guilt. 'He will again have compassion on us . . . and you will cast all their sins into the depth of the sea' (Micah 7: 10–20).

Moses Maimonides (d. 1204 CE), a philosopher and codifier of Jewish law, explored the role of the *shofar*: he felt that the sounds of this instrument, which are mellow as well as piercing, can stimulate the spirit and move the moral sense. The *shofar* should be curved, not straight, as a token of the Jews' willingness to submit to God or as a sign of the shaping and moulding that God does to people. It should be held to the right, pointing upwards, for its sound is sent to God from the heart; it should be blown at the narrow end so that the sound emerges at the wide end, as a reminder that thoughts should emerge from a broad mind and feelings from a full heart.

Teruah is the technical name for one of the sounds made on the *shofar*: it is a short, wailing note and comes in nines, giving a staccato effect of sobbing. *Shevarim* (from a root meaning 'break') is a group of three longer notes, echoing a broken heart and broken people. The basic, single blast is called *tekiah* and may be thought of as a summons to be alert or as a confident, hopeful note that weeping will become singing. The three notes are blown in succession, in a variety of combinations which are highly stylised and which usually total either thirty or one hundred.

The *shofar* is a ritual object which has been interpreted symbolically more than any other. It is inextricably bound up with Rosh Hashanah and the season of *t'shuvah* (returning), and reveals a great deal about the meaning of the festival. Saadia Gaon (d. 942) is said to have found ten different reasons for blowing the *shofar*:

1 Rosh Hashanah, as the day of Creation, acclaims God's rule. The Israelites became God's loyal subjects and the *shofar* the coronation trumpet.
2 The *shofar* heralds the beginning of the *Aseret y'mei t'shuvah*, the ten days of repentance and returning which end with the Day of Atonement
3 The *shofar* recalls revelation at Sinai, when the Torah was given accompanied by blowing on the horn.
4 Many Jewish prophets compared their ideas with a blast from the *shofar*, thus today the *shofar* can remind Jews of the prophets' words about justice, peace, goodness and mercy.
5 The *shofar* is sounded during battle and it was in battle that the Temple was destroyed and Jewish identity shaken. Now the *shofar* calls for strength and healing.
6 Instead of Isaac, Abraham offered a ram. The *shofar* prompts the giving of self in response to God.
7 The *shofar* is frightening: it represents the evil in the world around us and within ourselves. These evils must be confronted in the New Year if they are to be overcome.
8 The *shofar* calls to mind the Day of Judgement (*Yom Hadin*), another name for this festival. The prophet Zephaniah (1:16) spoke of the 'day of the Lord' as a day 'of the *shofar* and alarm'.
9 'On that day, a great horn shall be blown; and they shall come . . . and they shall worship the Lord in the holy mountain at Jerusalem' (Isaiah 27:13). The exiles – those dispersed throughout

the world – will be gathered in. The Messiah will usher in an era of peace and will banish war. Such is the Jewish idea of God's kingdom on earth.

10 The *shofar* is to be sounded at the resurrection: it is right that on the New Year festival which encourages Jews in self-awareness they should be reminded that their actions have eternal significance.

The *shofar* is first blown not on Rosh Hashanah but during the month of Elul (August/September). Tradition has often seen Rosh Hashanah as a 'palace in time' and often likened God to a 'king' – indeed the 'king of kings'. Elul is thus the court of the palace and the *shofar* is the herald. A fairly widespread *custom* is the daily (except on Shabat) blowing of the *shofar* at or before dawn until Rosh Hashanah. On New Year's Day, the blowing is a matter of *din* (decision or law). Psalm 27 is read at this time.

A custom which reflects the influence of the wider society on Jewish culture is that of sending *Shanot tovot* (Good years) greetings cards. This is especially popular in Europe, North America and Israel today.

Rosh Hashanah is not merely a one- or two-day festival: it is also the beginning of the ten days of returning and of awe which have their climax in Yom Kippur. The heightened spiritual awareness and self-examination which began on New Year's Day should continue throughout the period as individuals and communities prepare for forgiveness and atonement. During this time, *Shabat Shuvah* (Sabbath of the Returning/Repentance) falls: it takes its name from the reading of the prophets in the morning: 'Return, O Israel, to the Lord your God . . .' (Hosea 14: 2–10).

'Awake, you sleepers, from your sleep and you slumberers awake from your slumber. Reflect on your deeds and repent, and remember your Creator. Look to your souls and mend your ways and actions, those who forget the truth because of the empty vanities of life, who all their years go astray following vanity and folly which neither profit nor save. And let each one of you abandon evil ways and thoughts which are not good.'

Yom Kippur (*Day of Atonement*) (*September/October*)

'For on this day he shall make atonement for you, to purify you; you shall be clean from all your sins before the Lord.'

Leviticus 16:30

Yom Kippur is celebrated on the tenth day of Tishri. It is a day of rest and there are statutory religious services.

Teshuvah, the Hebrew for 'repentance', means returning: people have moved away from God because of their sins, but there is no impenetrable barrier between them. Hayyim Luzzatto (d. 1747) compared God's love to the rays of the sun which can only come into the room if the windows are clean. By *teshuvah*, the windows are washed.

Neither *teshuvah* nor Yom Kippur can wipe away the hurt between one person and another until that hurt has been healed. It is therefore a vital custom within the community for Jews to ask forgiveness of each other, on the eve of Yom Kippur, for any wrongs they may have committed or any pain they may have caused. They must mend and heal all that they can, but some suffering cannot be relieved so easily. It is then gracious of the one who has suffered to forgive the one who caused it. After that, all are at liberty to begin Yom Kippur – a day of atonement between people and *God*, a day given in the Torah for human benefit.

An important part of the real repentance (*teshuvah*) is confession: Jews have no human being to confess to, no mediator and no intercessor, for they do not believe that anyone should come between a person and God or that anyone can play the part of God. That means that sins committed against God are confessed directly to God for only God can forgive and take away guilt. However, it is helpful to the individual for the whole congregation to be making the same formal confession: in that way, there is, first, no personal embarrassment and, secondly, every Jew is accepting responsibility for every other Jew's actions by saying 'We have sinned . . .'. There are six major conditions of sinning – three pairs: under compulsion and of free will; secretly and publicly; unwittingly and knowingly.

There are a number of biblical names for sin: *het* is the one most frequently used in the prayers and confessions. There is also *pesha* which is a rebellion: here a person does not recognise God or his teachings and laws and therefore sets himself up as the judge of his own actions. *Avon* (to be twisted or crooked) refers to someone's life being turned away from good. *Het* is the vaguest term: meaning 'to miss', as an archer misses a target, it refers to lack of determination, to carelessness, neglect or over-indulgence.

For the Jewish people Yom Kippur is, above all else, a day of fasting for all adults who are healthy and fit. (There are no strict categories of exemptions from fasting: common sense and medical advice guide the individual's decision about whether or not to fast. Certainly the principle of the preservation of life means that no one should endanger their health by fasting.) The practice of fasting on Yom Kippur is derived from a command in the Torah: 'In the seventh month, on the tenth day of the month, you shall afflict your souls' (Leviticus 16:29) and also from the passage read on Yom

Kippur morning (Isaiah 58:3) which connects fasting and affliction.

'Affliction of the soul' on Yom Kippur means refraining from eating and drinking, washing, anointing, putting on sandals and sexual intercourse. These were the groups of activities defined by the rabbis. The reason for not putting on sandals or, in fact, any leather shoes was that these can only be made from a dead animal and to wear them would not be right on a day of praying for God's mercy, which is for all creatures. 'Anointing' nowadays would include applying make-up, hair or skin cream, or wearing perfume or jewellery.

Four main reasons are given for fasting on Yom Kippur: it is, first, a way of showing sincerity, that the desire for forgiveness is genuine; that the Jew is willing to give something up and feels that punishment would be fair – even though God is *not* punishing him or her. Second, fasting requires self-discipline and this can lead to betterment in other aspects of the personality. Third, if the body is ignored for a day, then the person can concentrate on the spirit. Fourth, fasting can make a person more compassionate, more sensitive to the needs of others (cf Isaiah 58:6 *et seq*). A particular custom which embodies this last ideal is that of sending food – traditionally chicken – to the poor before Yom Kippur. In modern times, there has also developed the High Holy Day Appeal, a concerted campaign to collect money for charity, on the part of many synagogues and other Jewish institutions.

The meal before the fast begins should be festive. Festival candles are lit and so are *yahrzeit* (anniversary) candles because Yom Kippur is a day on which Jews recite *Yizkhor* (Remember) – a memorial prayer for close ones who have died. Jews dress up for it and serve good food. It is a command to eat well, to build up strength for the fast but spicy, sweet or rich dishes create thirst and may be difficult to digest. They might spoil the fast so should not be eaten.

The atmosphere at the synagogue is unmistakeable. The Ark coverings will probably be white and some will wear a *kittel*, which resembles a long white smock. It is also probable that the synagogue will be packed and spilling over into other buildings. The evening service is so closely associated with the sung prayer *Kol Nidrei* (All our vows) as to be known by the same name. Throughout the Ashkenazi world (Jews from central and eastern Europe – the vast majority of Jews) *Kol Nidrei* is sung to the same tune – a haunting, wistful melody – usually by a tenor. It has a tragic connection with Jewish persecution and was composed for the benefit of those Jews who had been forced or pressurised into converting to Christianity, who had made false and unwilling vows. The song is therefore a plea to God for release from them. It also represents the community's recognition and acknowledgement that these secret Jews are actually in synagogue with their people on this, the Sabbath of Sabbaths (*Shabat Shabaton*). There is no provision in Jewish law for annulling vows made to other people: a word is binding: promises must be kept. *Kol Nidrei* is about private promises, vows made to oneself, commitments to God.

The Torah readings on Kippur morning tell of the ancient atonement ritual involving a scapegoat to bear away sins (Leviticus 16) and a description of the sacrifices performed in Temple times on Yom Kippur (Numbers 29: 7–11). The prophetic reading (Isaiah 57:14–58:14) contrasts the meaningless outward fasting with the inner value of fasting – to work for social justice. Many hymns sung on Rosh Hashanah are sung again on Yom Kippur for the two festivals are linked; indeed, the ten days might be thought of as a long semi-festival which begins and ends with a High Holy Day.

The additional service on Yom Kippur is quite distinctive and is concerned with sacrifices and martyrs, which some find outdated. Some Progressive prayer books have therefore adapted the service to include poems about human goodness and offerings to God rather than ones about temple sacrifices, and reflections on the Holocaust in place of tales of martyrs who died for Judaism. Afternoon readings from the Torah are traditionally from Leviticus 18 or Deuteronomy 30, both readings upholding the Torah as *lived*. The well known reading from the prophets is Jonah, a parable about the role of the Jew in human suffering and about God's infinite capacity to forgive all mankind – even those who do not deserve to be forgiven.

Since the second Temple, Yom Kippur is the only day in the year which has five services – perhaps this corresponds to the five afflictions. *Neilah* is the closing or concluding service and it summarises the day. It was once the time when the temple gates were literally shut for the night. It is a closing of the gates of mercy – but not a closing out, a closing in. The mercy of God cannot now be lost. The service ends with the first line of the *Shema*: 'Hear, O Israel, the Lord is our God. The Lord is One'. This is followed by the triumphant shout of Elijah: 'The Lord – he is God!' The *shofar* is sounded after sunset, proclaiming an end to the fast.

Purim (*Festival of Lots*) (*February/March*)

'We thank you for the wonders, for the heroic acts, for the victories, for the marvellous and consoling deeds which you performed for our fathers in those days at this season. In the days of Mordechai and Ester, in Shushan the capital, when the wicked Haman rose up against them, he sought to destroy, kill and exterminate all the Jews, both young and old, little children and women, on one day, and plunder their possessions . . . then you, in your great mercy, upset his plan and overthrew his design, and made his acts recoil upon his own head. And you performed a wonder and a marvel for them, therefore we thank your great name.'

Prayer Book

This prayer not only summarises the events which Purim marks (as recorded in the biblical book of Ester) but also indicates a Jewish response to such occurrences: that God is to be thanked for making them happen. This festival falls on the fourteenth day of Adar.

Eating and drinking are characteristic of Purim because the word *mishteh* (a feast or drinking party) occurs twenty times in the Book of Ester – as many times as it occurs in all the rest of the Bible put together! One of the *mitzvot* (commandments) of Purim is the festive meal (*seudah*) which begins at midday and which may include some entertainment lasting for hours. The occasion is enhanced by candles, 'for the Jews had light and joy'. Some families serve dishes of legumes in memory of Ester who avoided eating non-permitted meat in the palace. By contrast, it is also customary to fast the day *before* Purim as a token of her three-day abstention. Another command is that of the sending of gifts (*mishloah manot*), usually via the children, between families. These are often goodies such as three-cornered pastries filled with a rich paste of poppy seeds and honey. Purim became known as (*Eid al-Sukar*) (Festival of Sugar) by some Arab communities because of the cakes and sweets which Jews sent to them. Equally important is the giving of charity to the poor in the hope that all may enjoy the festival. Purim falls in the month of Adar – hence the expression 'When Adar approaches, joy increases' and the popular greeting 'Be happy – it's Adar!' The month is ushered in by a special Sabbath when the readings are concerned with offerings.

The central celebration is the reading of the Book of Ester in the synagogue, evening and morning. Everyone should be there and women have a special reason as the reading tells how the Jews were saved through Ester, a brave woman of independent spirit. The reading should be from an actual scroll – which is written in the same way as a *Sefer Torah* (a scroll of Peutateuch read publicly in the synagogue) – and the reader may open it out and fold it like a letter. The name of Haman is mentioned many times and those present try to drown its sound, by using *graggers* (rattles) or modern variants such as cap-pistols or alarm clocks, by writing the name on the soles of their shoes and literally stamping it out or simply by booing or hissing. The reason for this raucous behaviour is that Haman is thought to be a descendant of Amalek, who had brutally attacked the Israelites. However, the reader should try to say the names of

Haman's ten sons in one breath, not because they were all hanged together, but because Jews should not gloat over the misfortunes of others, even enemies.

The Jewish tradition is opposed to alcohol abuse, but Purim is one time where there is encouragement to drink until you do not know the difference between 'Blessed be Mordechai' and 'Cursed be Haman'. In Israel today, there is a fancy-dress parade or street carnival.

Another feature of Purim is the *Shpeel*, a satirical or farcical play. Students traditionally 'send up' their teachers and elect a 'Purim rabbi' for the day. Purim is not an obligatory day of rest but ideally only vital work should be done. Certainly, it is a day off for pupils and students.

'These days of Purim should never fall into disuse among the Jews, nor should the commemoration of these days cease among their descendents'.
Ester 9:28

Hanukah (Festival of Lights) (December)

'When the Greeks were gathered round in
 the Maccabean days,
Broke my towers to the ground,
Spoilt the oil used for your praise
Your sign then guided our fate,
One day's oil lasted for eight.
Our wise men
Established then
This festival we celebrate.'

This is the last verse of *Maoz Tzur*, (Fortress Rock, a name for God here) a special hymn for Hanukah, celebrated from the twenty-fifth day of Kislev to the second of Tevet, The verse summarises the historical events which gave rise to the festival. The events are recorded in the books of the Maccabees (not found in the Bible).

These events involve a battle ostensibly between Jews and Antiochus Epiphanes when he became king of Syria in 175 BCE. (In reality it involved a struggle on a wider and deeper scale – a clash between Hellenistic and Jewish values.)

Since the time of Alexander the Great, Jews had been influenced by certain Greek ideas and the contact between the two cultures had been of mutual benefit. But political independence and religious autonomy were brought to an end by Antiochus; he prohibited Jews, under penalty of death, from living Judaism. It was not primarily an antisemitic motive which prompted Antiochus but rather a desire for conformity and unquestioning obedience from all his subjects – even to the point of bowing down and worshipping Greek idols, and the enforced eating of pork.

When such idols – notably that of Zeus – were placed in the Temple at Jerusalem, some Jews were so incensed at the sacrilege that they resolved to make a bold bid for freedom. The struggle of these Jews, known as the *Maccabees* (Hammers), was concerned with the symbol of faith and survival – the jar of oil, undefiled by the enemy and with the seal unbroken – and involved a physical miracle: that even though there was only enough oil to kindle the perpetual lamp and to keep it burning for one day it continued to burn brightly for eight days until fresh supplies of oil arrived. For some, the miracle has a deeper significance: the light of Jewish faith and hope seemed doomed – there were enormous pressures on Jews to assimilate and it would have hardly been surprising if Jewish identity and ideals had *not* withstood the strain – but it was not extinguished.

The leader of the Jewish uprising was Mattathias, a priest. He was joined by his sons and a small number of like-minded Jews who used the deserts and mountains as bases for guerrilla attacks on Greek army units. At the same time, these Maccabees were engaged in a battle of wits with fellow-Jews who had been lured by the attractions of the Greek life-style to abandon Jewish beliefs and rituals. Mattathias himself died after a year but he had already ensured that the leadership would continue: Judah Maccabee is the best known of his sons and was respected not only for his courage and clear-sightedness, but also for his strength of purpose.

The day Judah Maccabee chose for the rededication (*Hanukah*) of the Temple in 164 BCE coincided with the third anniversary of the decree by Antiochus that idolatrous sacrifices were to be offered on the temple altar. The twenty-fifth of Kislev is thus a doubly significant date: the *Hallel* (Psalms 113–118) was chanted and celebrations lasted for eight days, but no special dedication customs or rituals are mentioned. However, Judah did decree that the days of rejoicing and the festival of dedication should be commemorated by future generations.

The central ritual of Hanukah is the kindling of lights. Some have suggested that it was already a folklore practice in many societies to light fires at that time of the year, mid-winter, to summon the light of the sun and draw the summer nearer. In this view, Hanukah

Opposite: *The festival of Purim is a joyous, noisy festival. The synagogue resounds to the sounds of shouts and rattles – a great time for children to legitimately make as much noise as possible.*

represents a Jewish adaptation and reinterpretation of this custom: to proclaim the miracle! For this reason, the Hanukah lamp should be lit soon after sunset, ideally outside but otherwise at an open door or in the window. If there is a risk of attack from non-Jews, the lamp can be put on a table and the curtains closed to avoid identifying the household as a Jewish one and thereby endangering life. The lighting of the lamp should happen before anyone – even the youngest child – goes to bed, so that all may witness the event and know the miracle. The lamps should burn for at least thirty minutes; traditionally, it consists of a wick burning in olive, oil, but wax candles, gas burners or electric lamps can also be used.

The lighting is followed by the reading of *Hanerot halalu* ('We kindle these lights') which offers an interesting insight into the role of light:

'. . . these lights are holy and we are not permitted to make use of them, but only to see them in order to thank your name for the wonders, the victories and the marvellous deeds.'

Prayer Book

The Hanukah lamp (*hanukiyah*) consists of eight individual lamps or candles and a servant candle (*shammas*) from which the others are lit. On the first night one lamp is lit, on the second two, and so on until the last night, when all eight lamps burn. The standard procedure is to light the lamp on the extreme right on the first night, moving one lamp towards the left on each successive evening. It is also customary on any given night to light first the lamp occupying the 'new' position. After the lamps have been lit, the *shammas* is returned to its own position, which is a little higher than the other eight. All in all, including the *shammas* on each night, forty-four lights are kindled during Hanukah.

Hanukah is celebrated today even by secularised Jews, who now minimise or ignore other festivals, because it represents a serious attempt by a minority group to uphold its religious and cultural individuality in a wider society. In Israel today, lamps are lit on top of the *Knesset* (parliament building) and at the Western Wall of the Temple. Some journey to Mod'in, the home of Mattathias, where a torch, as a *shammas*, lights lamps at sites thought to be the burial places of the Maccabees. The torch is carried on the first night, in relays, to Jerusalem where, as a *shammas*, it kindles a large lamp at the President's home.

Hanukah has become a time of personal rededication: Israeli soldiers renew their allegiance at the time; Jews in the West strengthen their solidarity with those in the Soviet Union; and it is always auspicious if a community celebrates a *Bar* or *Bat Mitzvah* during Hanukah. But for all this, Hanukah remains a season of simple family gatherings on long winter nights in a mellow mood. Traditional foods are those fried in oil, such as *latkes* (potato pancakes) or, in Israel, doughnuts. It is party time, especially for children, and an occasion for exchanging gifts: some children receive a small present on each of the eight days. In her diary, Ann Frank evoked the special nature of the festival by describing how, even when hiding from the Nazis, she improvised gifts for those around her.

The *dreidel* is a clever invention which adds to the fun of Hanukah celebrations, alongside card games and other forms of gambling, but also has a serious purpose. Essentially, it is a four-sided spinning top with a Hebrew letter on each side – the Hebrew equivalents of 'n', 'g', 'h' and 'sh'. These spell the Hebrew phrase *Nes gadol haya sham*: 'A great miracle happened there'. The letters are also the initials of the Yiddish words used in a game in which everyone puts up stakes and there is a central 'pot': *nichts* (nothing), *ganz* (all), *halb* (half) and *shtell ein* (put one in). But the essential meaning of Hanukah is that individuals and groups have the right to uphold their uniqueness, to define and determine themselves and that God works with those who take a positive stand on those very values which oppression threatens to destroy. The reading from the prophets for Shabat during Hanukah is a passage from Zechariah:

'Not by might, nor by power, but by My Spirit, says the Lord of Creation'
Zechariah 4:6

Minor festivals and fasts

The minor festivals described in this section are not prescribed in the Torah, with the exception of the celebration of the New Moon, *Rosh Hodesh*, some commemorate a biblical events. Unlike most of the major festivals, these are not days of rest, though part of the day is set aside for family and/or communal celebrations, usually centring on one of the day's prayer times, and followed by a festive meal. There is no ultimately authoritative liturgy for these days, but certain readings and songs have become associated with them and some have been decreed by rabbis in the past. Candles are not lit for minor festivals.

The minor fasts are usually for mourning or pleading. With the exception of *Tisha B'Av*, these fasts are not from sunset to sunset, but from dawn to sunset; they involve only abstaining from food and drink. In this way the 'minor' status of these fasts is expressed.

Rosh Hodesh (Festival of the New Moon) (monthly)
The celebration of the New Moon, Rosh Hodesh, is the one
exception to the principles and practices of minor festivals: it is, by
definition, monthly! It is given in the Torah, and there is a fixed
liturgy for its celebration. It is not a major festival, however,
for it is not an obligatory day of rest and it is not ushered in with
the lighting of candles. Nowadays the new moon is heralded by
special prayers on the previous Shabat:

'May the new month bring up a life of fulfilment and peace, a life of goodness and blessing; a life filled with awe of God and fear of sin; a life without
self-reproach and shame; a life marked by love of your teaching; when the
desires of our hearts may be fulfilled for good . . .'

Prayer Book

It has been customary on Rosh Hodesh itself to recite a shortened
form of Psalms 113–118, which is part of the festival liturgy which,
with Psalm 104, centres on the glorification of God's beauty, majesty
and wisdom.

Taanit Behorim (Fast of the First-born) (March/April)
Taanit Behorim, the Fast of the First-born, takes place on the fourteenth day of Nisan, the eve of Passover. It commemorates the fact
that the 'first-born' Israelites were not killed in Egypt. Strictly
speaking, those involved nowadays do not observe the fast but they
do remember the day.

Yom Ha-Shoah (Holocaust Day) (April)
Yom Ha-Shoah (Holocaust Day), observed on the twenty-seventh
day of Nisan, is a memorial to the victims of Nazi atrocities and an
opportunity for Jews to reaffirm their opposition to racism, tyranny
and fascist rule, in all places and at all times. In 1951, 27 Nisan
became an official 'Remembrance Day for the Holocaust' in Israel;
a later law passed by the *knesset* (parliament) forbids public entertainment on the evening of 27 Nisan, so that the dignity and
solemnity of the moment can be respected.

Yom Ha'Atzmaut (Independence Day) and Yom Ha'Zikharon
(Remembrance Day) (April)
Yom Ha'Atzmaut (Independence Day) falls on the fifth day of Iyar,
the anniversary of the creation of the modern State of Israel in 1948.
Public celebrations in Israel today include the kindling of twelve
torches (symbolising the tribes of Israel and, therefore, Jewish
unity). Many people hold parties or picnics and public firework
displays and parades are common. By 1949, rabbis in Israel had

worked out a pattern of prayers for Independence Day on the theme of redemption and national restoration.

The joy of Independence Day is offset by Remembrance Day (*Yom Ha'Zikharon*) which precedes it: a parent in Israel who has lost a child in Israel's defence either before, during or after its independence, hands a lighted torch to the president who lights a memorial flame. Similarly, memorial candles are lit in homes throughout the country. On this day there is no public entertainment in Israel.

Outside Israel, Jewish communities also mark these two days of sorrow and joy in synagogues, communal institutions and private homes. It is customary to eat Israeli food and to hold special services and celebrations expressing their identity and solidarity.

Lag B'Omer (April/May)

Lag B'Omer, the thirty-third day of counting the *omer* (see Festival of Weeks) falls on the eighteenth day of Iyar. It was a much loved festival in the Middle Ages, but the original reason for the festival is long forgotten. There are no special rituals, although customs associated with it still persist. It is a break and a relief from the semi-mourning period between Pesah and Shavuot – perhaps this is the reason for its existence – and is a popular day for getting married. It is a scholar's holiday and Jewish barbers experience brisk trade. Orthodox boys aged 3 have their first haircut on this day.

Yom Yerushalayim (Jerusalem Day) (May)

Yom Yer Shalayim falls on the twenty-eighth day of Iyar and is the most recent addition to the Jewish calendar. It marks the third day of the Six Day War (1967) when Israeli forces moved through the Lion's Gate of the Old City of Jerusalem to which Jews had been denied entry for nineteen years. Jerusalem Day is thus a day of thanksgiving.

Fast of 20 Sivan (June)

This is one of the fasts that has no name – only a date recalling two separate occasions. In Blois, France, in 1171, a small Jewish community were accused of drowning a Christian child: they were given the chance of reprieve if they would collectively convert to Christianity. They refused and were burned at the stake. In 1648, on the same day in the Ukraine, 10,000 Jews were massacred by Chmielnicki's Cossacks. Altogether in that uprising 100,000 Jews died.

Fast of 17 Tammuz (June/July)

This fast begins a three-week period of mourning called 'Between the

September/October   (1/2 Tishri) New Year (*Rosh Hashanah*), (3 Tishri) Fast of Gedaliah (*Tsom Gedaliah*), (10 Tishri) Day of Atonement (*Yom Kippur*), 15/16–22/23 Tishri) Festival of Tabernacles (*Sukkot*), (22/23 Tishri) Eighth Day of Conclusion (*Shemini Atzeret*), (23 Tishri) Rejoicing in the Torah (*Simhat Torah*)

November/December   (25 Kislev – 2 Tevet) Festival of the Dedication of the Temple/Festival of Lights (*Hanukah*)

December/January   (10 Tevet) Feast of 10 Tevet

A note on the Muslim Festivals chapter

Changes have been made to the text of *Muslim Festivals* without the approval of the author. These changes have resulted in errors which, we regret, are impossible to correct at this stage. We leave them to the discretion of the reader. The following should be noted:

page		
	211 line 1	*for* uttered by *read* given to
	211 line 7	*for* of *read* to
	211 line 26	*for* revealed *read* delivered
	213 line 6	*for* three *read* two
	216 line 8	*delete* usually
	216 line 35 to 217 line 4	*delete from* The ritual prayer *to* du'a *and insert* The Prayer consists of two rakas after the sermon. A rakah is a series of movements and recitations from the Qur'an. The sermon is delivered in two parts with a short interval in between for personal supplications (Du'a).
	218 line 1	*for* he *read* He
	220 line 13	*for* sunrise *read* dawn
	222 line 6	*for* sunset *read* sunrise
	224 line 19	*delete* shaving of the head for men *read* as a sign of the completion of the Hajj men should shave or cut their hair
	224 line 24	*for* Mecca *read* Mina
	226 line 1	*delete* only
	228 line 7	*delete* negotiation *insert* struggle
	228 line 26–27	*delete* The sudden . . . *to* . . . of *read* After the death of Muhammad there developed dissident
	233 lines 2–3	*delete from* his . . . *to* . . . established *read* Muslims consider Muhammad as the greatest of the prophets rather than the equal of others
	233 line 24	*delete* New Year Festival (Muharram) *insert* 'Ashura' the Martyrdom of Hussein celebration

10 Muslim Festivals

RIADH EL-DROUBIE

Islam

The religion of Islam is based on the revelations uttered by the Prophet
Muhammad in Arabia during the seventh century CE, but the religion is considered by its adherents, who are called Muslims
('submitters'), to have originated with the creation of man. It is the
religion revealed by God to all the prophets from Abraham to
Muhammad, the last and final one. The Qur'an, in which the
revelations of the Prophet are collected, refers to this in the third
chapter:

> 'In the name of God, the Most Beneficent, the Most Merciful
> Say: "We believe in God and the revelation given to us;
> We believe in the revelations given to Abraham,
> Ismael, Isaac, Jacob and the tribes,
> And to Moses and Jesus and the other prophets.
> We make no distinction between them
> And we bow to God."'

Qur'an 3: 83

Islam calls for complete surrender and submission to God through
acceptance of the Qur'an and the Tradition (*Sunnah*) of the Prophet
Muhammad. Through the Qur'anic revelations God awakens man to
His sovereignty and guides him in all aspects of life – social,
economic, political, moral and spiritual.

Islam emphasises two elements – faith and action. The fundamental doctrine is that there is one God only, who is creator of the
universe. He is omnipotent and omniscient, and every human being
will be accountable to Him alone on the Day of Judgement. Faith
also involves belief in all of God's messages (revealed books), in the
prophets who revealed them, and in God's angels, the chief of
whom is Gabriel.

The religious duties of the believer are called 'the Pillars of the

211

Faith'. These five pillars of action are intended to purify man, to regulate his relations with God and society, and to enable him to do good for the sake of God alone.

1 Repetition of the statement of faith. 'There is no God but the One God; Muhammad is the Prophet of God.' Through repetition of these phrases the Muslim bears witness that there is none worthy of worship except God and that Muhammad is the last messenger of God.
2 Prayer (*salat*). This is performed five times daily at prescribed times with physical movements in the direction (*qiblah*) of the Ka'aba, the sacred mosque at Mecca. The prayers are preceded by ritual washing (*wudhu*). Additional or 'superogatory' prayers are recommended; a Muslim can turn to God at any time to ask for the granting of his wishes, for forgiveness or for guidance, by raising his hands.
3 The purification of wealth (*zakat*). *Zakat* is an obligation on each and every Muslim who possesses more than he needs to give a specified portion for the relief of the poor and needy. It is levied on all kinds of material goods – money, gold, silver, land, houses and cattle, but is neither a tax nor a charity; rather it is a 'loan' to God. Receivers of *zakat* fall into eight categories listed in the Qur'an, and it can be distributed to no others.
4 The fast of Ramadan (*siyam*). During the month of Ramadan it is obligatory to fast each day from dawn to sunset. This involves total abstinence from food, drink, tobacco and sexual relations. Those who are sick or on a journey may be exempted, but are required to make up for it by fasting an equal number of days at a later stage. The fast ends with the Festival of Breaking the Fast (*Eid-ul-Fitr*), which takes place on the first day of the following month.
5 Pilgrimage (*hajj*). At least once in a lifetime every Muslim is required to undertake a pilgrimage to Mecca during the month of Dhul-Hijjah, provided that he or she has the means to do so. The observances of the pilgrimage take place on the eight, ninth and tenth days of the month, culminating in the Festival of Sacrifice (*Eid-ul-Adha*).

In addition to these five duties, Islam lays down certain other obligations on believers. Together with the normal prohibitions concerning unlawful or immoral acts, such as perjury or slander, the Qur'an forbids the consumption of pig's flesh, the drinking of alcohol, the practice of usury, gambling and sex outside marriage. An important rule for day-to-day living is that everything is lawful (*halal*) unless it is either explicitly forbidden (*haram*) or would lead

212

to the occurrence of something explicity forbidden. Good intentions do not justify unlawful or unethical conduct.

The development of Islam

The death of Muhammad, with no appointed successor nor rules for the governing of the community he had established, led to the development of three main political groups. The Sunnis, or followers of the Tradition (*Sunnah*), formed the majority. They placed the unity of the community above all else and would only accept the authority of those who could maintain it. Opposed to them were the Shi'ites, who held that the only legitimate heads of the community were Muhammad's descendants through his daughter Fatima and son-in-law Ali. The Kharijites rejected both these positions, maintaining the right of the community not only to elect its own head, but also to depose him.

Later, when the political controversies had subsided, these dissident groups developed and formulated their own doctrines and interpretations of the Qur'an and the Tradition, and within each group different schools of thought emerged. The majority of Muslims today are Sunnis, who are divided into four schools of thought all based directly on the Qur'an. Most other Muslims are Shi'ites, of whom the Imamites form the largest sect, counting almost the entire population of Iran amongst their number. The Kharijites were always a small minority group, and are now found only in Oman, Zanzibar and southern Algeria.

In the early years of the religion, during the seventh and eighth centuries CE, Islam spread swiftly owing to the conquests of the Arabs in western and central Asia, North Africa, Sind and Spain. From the eleventh century it spread into southern Russia, India and Asia Minor, and in the fourteenth century, largely as a result of missionary work, into Indonesia and China. Thus today there are Muslims living all over the world and their number is increasing, particularly in East and West Africa. The practices and customs of Muslims naturally vary from one country to another, but all are based on the teaching of the Qur'an and the Tradition of the Prophet.

The Muslim calendar

The Muslim era is based on the 'emigration' (*hijrah*) of the Prophet Muhammad from Mecca to Medina in the year 622 CE. This year was later adopted as the first in the Muslim era. The Muslim calendar is a lunar one, having twelve months which are counted from one new moon to the next. The names of the months are:

1 Muharram	7 Rajab
2 Safar	8 Sha'ban
3 Rabi' ul-Awwal	9 Ramadan
4 Rabi' ul-Thani	10 Shawwal
5 Jamada al-Awwal (Jamada al-Ula)	11 Dhul-Qi'da
6 Jamada al-Thani (Jamada al-Akhira)	12 Dhul-Hijjah

As the average interval between consecutive similar phases of the moon is twenty-nine days, twelve hours and forty-four minutes, the months have either twenty-nine or thirty days. The extra forty-four minutes each month amount to eleven days over a period of thirty-years, and so the calendar is arranged such that there are eleven leap years during each thirty-year period. There being twelve months in the calendar, the number of days in a Muslim year is 354, or 355 in a leap year.

To determine whether a given year AH (*al-hijrah*) is a leap year, the number of the year is divided by 30. If the remainder is 2, 5, 7, 10, 15, 21, 24, 26 or 29, then it is a leap year. There are various methods for finding out the *hijrah* year corresponding to a given year in the Gregorian calendar, and vice versa. The following formula is the simplest:

Hijra year $= 1.0307$ (Gregorian year $- 622) + 0.46$

The fact that the Muslim year is ten or eleven days shorter than the solar year means that the months rotate around the seasons. Thus in 1982 the month of Ramadan began on 22 June, in 1983 on 11 June and in 1984 on 30 May. The beginning of the new month depends on the sighting of the moon by the naked eye a few minutes after sunset. If the new moon is sighted on the evening of the twenty-ninth day of the month, that night will be the first of the new month. If the new moon is not sighted, the night following the thirtieth day will automatically become the first night of the next month, no further observation of the moon being required. Thus the night of any given date in the Muslim calendar is the night preceding the day of the same date.

Reliance on the sighting of the new moon to determine the day on which a new month begins clearly leads to difficulties concerning the advance determination of the exact dates of Muslim festivals according to the Gregorian calendar. The table at the end of the chapter shows the approximate dates of festivals and important events in the Muslim calendar from the year 1984 CE to the year 2000 CE, together with the movements of these festivals with respect to the Gregorian calendar throughout these years.

The festivals

The festivals of Islam are called *eid* (or *id*), an Arabic word from a root explained as 'periodically returning'. Hence *eid* indicates a periodical festivity or something which gives unusual pleasure through a ceremony or entertainment. An incident describing a visit to the Prophet's house one *eid* day by Abu Bakr, who became the first caliph after the Prophet's death, demonstrates the importance of festivity on these occasions. On entering the house and finding two women singing and playing musical instruments, Abu Bakr exclaimed: 'An instrument of Satan in the house of the Messenger of God!' the Prophet replied: 'O Abu Bakr! All peoples have their festivals and this is ours . . . There is in our religion an ampleness . . . I was sent with the true religion of tolerance.'

The festivals are times for reducing tension in the community and for establishing new relations in an atmosphere of joy and festivity: the poor must share in the festivity; the lonely and the stranger must feel at home among others; the orphan must feel the love of others; the quarrelsome must make peace and broken relations must be mended. The festivals begin with an act of devotion and prayer. Individual Muslims remember God at home, at school, in the office or at the local mosque. On the two major festival days, the Festival of Breaking the Fast after Ramadan and the Festival of Sacrifice after the pilgrimage, a larger gathering is held, embracing the entire community. It takes place in the biggest mosque of the locality or outside, so that everyone can be accommodated. At least once in their lifetime, if they have the means to do so, Muslims should make the pilgrimage to the heart of Islam at Mecca. There they join with other Muslims from all over the world in a series of ceremonies and festivities.

Besides the Festival of Breaking the Fast and the Festival of Sacrifice, Muslims celebrate many of the events which occurred during the life of Muhammad and throughout the history of Islam. The religion of Islam embraces many countries and races, and through the centuries, rituals and customs have developed which vary from country to country and nation to nation. Thus, whilst all agree on the importance and the spiritual significance of the events they commemorate, the festivals are celebrated by Muslims according to their countries' customs. For this reason the descriptions give a general picture without going into too many details which may vary from one place to another.

Day of Assembly (Friday)

The Day of Assembly (*Yawm al-Jumu'a*) is the sixth day of the week, Friday. The name *al-Jumu'a* comes from the root *jama'a* meaning 'bring together, collect', and the Friday prayer is the principal congregational service of the week when all the faithful assemble in the mosque, usually at noon. The importance of the Friday worship is referred to in the Qur'an:

> 'In the name of God, the Most Beneficent, the Most Merciful
> O believers, when you are called to prayer on Friday
> Hasten earnestly to the remembrance of God
> And cease your trading.
> That is best for you if you but knew it.
> Then, when the prayer is finished,
> Disperse and go in search of God's bounty.
> Praise God always, so that you may prosper.'

Qur'an 62:9

This Qur'anic verse, revealed to the Prophet soon after his migration to Medina, points to the balance necessary between worldly and spiritual activities in order to maintain both society and the individual. The Muslim is not required to take the entire day off work for religious purposes, but should have enough time to join in the prayers at the nearest mosque.

Before prayer the Muslim is required to perform ablution of the face, head, forearms, ankles and feet, a pool or fountain being provided in every mosque for this purpose. Ideally the Muslim should pare his nails, shave, have a bath, wear perfume and put on his best clothes before leaving for the mosque. The Prophet was reported to have said:

'If a person takes a bath on Friday, washes himself thoroughly, oils his hair, uses such perfume as is available, sets forth for the mosque, does not intrude between two persons, offers the prescribed prayer and listens in silence to the *imam* (prayer leader), his sins, committed since the previous Friday, are forgiven.'

Hadith

Friday prayer is like any other congregational prayer except for the sermon given by the *imam* after the call to prayer. The ritual prayer consists of a fixed number of *rakas* (prostrations), the number depending on the time of day or occasion. A *raka* is a series of movements and recitations: whilst raising the hands to the ears, the phrase *Allahu akbar* (God is Most Great) is uttered in a loud voice

A festival is a time for being together. In London's 'Mosque in the Park' crowds celebrate with dignity and passion.

after the *imam*, seven times during the first *raka* and five times during the second and subsequent *rakas*. The sermon is read in two parts with a short interval in between for personal supplication (*du'a*). The *imam* reminds Muslims of their duties toward God and their fellows, and will then speak on current affairs and the problems of the community, offering guidance and advice. Qur'anic verses suitable to the subject of the sermon are read and explained. The sermon is always read in the language of the assembly, except for the introductory and closing remarks, which are spoken in Arabic.

It was reported that the Prophet said:

'The promised day is the Day of Judgement, the witnessed day is the Day of Arafat and the bearer of witness is Friday. The sun has neither risen nor set on a better day than Friday. Therein is an hour in which a believing servant praying to God for good things finds God responding to him; he seeks not refuge from anything, but He gives him refuge therefrom.'

Hadith

Ramadan

Observance of the annual fast of the ninth month of the lunar year, Ramadan, is the fourth 'pillar' or duty of Islam. Fasting involves total abstinence from food and drink from dawn to sunset for the whole of the month. Those who are sick or travelling during this period may be exempted, but are required to compensate by fasting for an equal number of days at a later time. Since the lunar year is shorter than the solar year, the month of Ramadan rotates through the seasons. It is considered by Muslims to be a mercy of God that fasting does not always occur at the same time of year.

Ramadan is associated with the greatest of events in the history of Islam: the start of the revelation of the Qur'an to the Prophet Muhammad, who was then forty years old. The night on which the Prophet received the first revelation, which was communicated by the Angel Gabriel, is known as the Night of Power (*Lailat-ul-Qadr*). The first verses recited were:

> 'In the name of God, the Most Beneficent, the Most Merciful,
> Proclaim in the name of thy Lord and Cherisher who created,
> Created man out of a clot of blood.
> Proclaim, for thy Lord is Most Bountiful,
> He who taught by the Pen,
> Taught man that which he knew not.'

Qur'an 96: 1–5

These verses stress that it is the duty of every Muslim to seek knowledge and to discover God's creation. The Qur'anic revelations continued at brief intervals during the course of the next twenty-three years.

Other major events in the history of Islam also occurred during the month of Ramadan. Three important battles took place after the emigration of the Muslims to Medina, where they went from strength to strength. The third battle was the conquest of Mecca and the destruction of idols and idolatry. The following passage from the Qur'an refers to this day:

> 'In the name of God, the Most Beneficent, the Most Merciful,
> When comes the Help
> Of God, and Victory,
> And thou dost see
> The people enter God's Religion
> In crowds.
> Celebrate the praises

Of thy Lord, and pray
For His Forgiveness:
For He is Oft-Returning
(In Grace and Mercy).'

Qur'an 110: 1-3

The month of Ramadan is also the month of forgiveness and charity. Muslims must pay *zakat-ul-fitr*, which is a charity given as an act of purification. This is equivalent to the price of one good meal for each member of the family, and is used for the relief of the poor and needy, enabling them to share in the festivities.

The observance of Ramadan varies from one place to another, but the objective is the same throughout: the fulfilment of God's commands of discipline, piety and collective worship. Mosques and minarets are lit up, and restaurants and coffee bars are closed during the daytime. Muslims follow the Prophet's tradition by breaking the fast each day at sunset with dates and water at the mosque. After sharing food together, Muslims join in the *maghrib* (sunset) prayer, then they all return home for their main meal. In Mecca it is the custom for people to bring food to the Grand Mosque of the Ka'aba before sunset. When the call to prayer has ended and the cannon signalling the end of the fast for the day has been fired, the food is shared among all. Prayer is said after eating.

In Malaya, Muslims prepare themselves for several weeks before the beginning of Ramadan, stocking up shops and homes with food and other necessities. The main dish during this period is rice and yoghurt with meat or chicken. Religious competitions are held, especially in the recitation of the Qur'an. Older people spend the evenings at the mosque while the younger ones and children tour the streets singing. The same pattern is followed in most of south-east Asia. In Indonesia, the largest Muslim country of the area, houses and mosques are decorated and lit up during the month of Ramadan. During the latter part of the night people are woken for their last meal before dawn by *al-musaharati*, who tour the streets beating and chanting; the job is a voluntary one, but people make donations to these men on Eid day, the day of breaking the fast of Ramadan. Qur'anic teaching circles are held in every mosque and the government collects *zakat-ul-fitr*.

In Sierra Leone Ramadan is a time to forgive and forget. *Imams* from other Muslim countries come during this month to teach and preach at different mosques in the country. At prayer times the mosques are full of people and all roads leading to them are covered with prayer mats. The *sheikh* (leader) of the district invites people to break fast with him, and religious poetry and other readings are chanted everywhere.

219

In Tanzania, Kenya and Zanzibar, the head of the family presents a copy of the Qur'an to each member of his family on the day before Ramadan begins. He offers them advice and teaches the principles of fasting. Afterwards they all join in prayer either at home or in the mosque if it is not too distant. All go to the nearest mosque in the evening. In Turkey, life during Ramadan centres around the mosque. Men, women and children attend prayers daily, and the women compete with each other in preparing different dishes, especially pastries.

Whatever the local customs may be during the month of Ramadan, all Muslims will share the joy of the fulfilment of fasting and the purification of body and soul through the abstinence from food and drink between the hours of sunrise and sunset.

Festival of Breaking the Fast

The fast of Ramadan ends with the Festival of Breaking the Fast (*Eid-ul-Fitr*) on the first day of the following month, Shawwal. The festival is also known as the Small Festival (*Eid-ul-Sagheer*), lasting only three days compared with the four days of the Festival of Sacrifice (*Eid-ul-Adha*), the other major festival of Islam. It is also known as *Bairam* or *Eid Ramadan*.

The festival is an occasion for celebration and rejoicing in God's favour for his revelation of the Qur'an, and a thanksgiving by individuals for having the strength to complete the fast and thus to fulfil their duty. About this day the Prophet Muhammad said:

'When Eid-ul-Fitr arrives, the angels stand at the doorways and call upon Muslims: "O company of Muslims, go to the generous God, who gave you the good things and grants the great reward. For God ordered you to pray during the night, so you prayed, ordered you to fast during the day, so you fasted and obeyed your Lord, so now take your reward." And when they prayed the angels called upon them saying: "Indeed, your Lord has forgiven you; return to your home following the good way."'

Hadith

The Festival of Breaking the Fast is also a festival of alms-giving. Muslims who have not paid *zakat-ul-fitr*, the charity of the fast, during Ramadan should do so before the Eid prayer, with which the festival begins. This is the purification act which allows the poor and needy to participate in the festivities.

On this occasion of great joy and happiness, the Muslim first bathes and puts on new or best clothes, then assembles with fellow Muslims at the mosque or, if it is not large enough, outside. The

Opposite: *'Islam is brotherhood. Happy Eid, my friend'.*

night of Eid is traditionally spent in meditation and prayer. Families gather at the mosque to hear the news of the new moon or to watch out for the first sight of it from the courtyard or the minaret. Others spend the night at home in preparation for the feast day.

The festival begins with the festival prayer (*salat-ul-fitr*) about an hour after sunset. This is an essential requirement of the festival, and is similar to the Friday prayer (see Day of Assembly), consisting of two *rakas* (prostrations) in congregation and without *adhan* or *iqamat* (major and minor calls to prayer). By bowing and prostrating before God, the Muslim links the spiritual experience gained during the fast of Ramadan with the physical enjoyment of the festival. The sermon is read after the prayer, the subject chosen according to the occasion and time. Whatever the subject may be, however, it is traditional to speak about charity at some point during the sermon.

There are many customs associated with the Festival of Breaking the Fast and the Festival of Sacrifice, both of which are based on the pillars of Islam. These customs stem firstly from the rules of the Qur'an and the Tradition of the Prophet, and secondly from nationally determined variations in Eid traditions, such as dress and special dishes.

In Istanbul, early in the nineteenth century, cannons were fired from the castles in salute of Eid and ships would sound their sirens just before prayer time. An army parade would take place to the sound of martial music, then the sultan, on a decorated horse, would ride to the mosque to be received by the *imam* and the nobles of the society. On that day the nobles threw open their houses and all were able to join them in the festivity without any formal invitation. Nowadays, the cannon is still fired in salute in many parts of the Muslim world, and kings and presidents are driven to the mosque in limousines followed by a cortège of official cars, while soldiers line the route. After prayer, the government house or palace is thrown open and the head of the country receives visitors. In small towns and villages a representative of the establishment, a prince or a governor, may receive the people.

The Festival of Breaking the Fast often means more to Muslims living in western countries than it does to those in the East. It acts as a renewal of their pledge to the faith and the Muslim community, and creates an atmosphere of unity and togetherness. At Islamic centres in Europe and the USA several services are held on the first day of the festival, led by different *imams*. Muslims living far away from these centres come for the festival and linger at the mosque, meeting old friends whom they have not seen since the previous year's festival. Thus, in addition to being a time of spiritual renewal, the festival provides an opportunity for socialising and meeting others who, like them, live far from their home countries. In the courtyard of the mosque there is often a bazaar, with anything from artifacts to food on sale. Although the festival is a public holiday of several days' duration in Muslim countries, in the West one day's holiday, preferably the first day of the festival, allows Muslims to join in the Eid prayer at the mosque. As the first day of Eid may vary from area to area according to the sighting of the new moon, the first day of celebration is determined by the local community.

On the sub-continent of India, Pakistan and Bangladesh, Muslims living in cities assemble at the Jami'a Mosque, the Grand Mosque of the city, on the first day of the festival. Usually the mosque is too small for the number of worshippers, so roads around the mosque are closed to traffic, and the Muslims gather round about the mosque. Outside the cities Muslims gather for prayer on the outskirts of towns and villages, the assemblies often numbering thousands of believers at any given time.

The giving of alms and presents is associated with the first day of the festival. In Malaysia all members of the family go to the mosque where they make their donations and then offer Eid prayer, after which they go to the cemetery to visit the graves of relatives. On returning home more charity is distributed. In Tanzania, Kenya and Zanzibar, the head of the family distributes presents on returning home from Eid prayer. Children all over the Muslim world are given the best of worldly things on this day: money, new outfits and so on. For the poor it is the richest day of the year: not only do they receive charity, but they are able to participate fully in the festivities. For the others there is the satisfaction of having been able to help the needy to partake in the happiness of the celebration and being able to look forward to the possible reward in the hereafter.

Day of Arafat
The Day of Arafat, which falls on the ninth day of the twelfth month, Dhul-Hijjah, commemorates the end of the Qur'an's revelation to the Prophet on Mount Arafat, about twelve miles east of Mecca. The revelation ended shortly before the Prophet's death with the following verse:

> 'In the name of God, the Most Beneficent, the Most Merciful
> This day have I
> Perfected your religion
> For you, completed
> My favour upon you,
> And have chosen for you
> Islam as your religion.'

Qur'an 5: 4

Umar ibn al-Khatab was told that if this verse were revealed to any community, they would celebrate the day of its revelation to the Prophet as a festival. Umar replied that he knew the time and place that the verse was revealed: on Friday at Arafat. So both Friday and the Day of Arafat are festivals for Muslims.

The Day of Arafat is the climax of the pilgrimage to Mecca (hajj). The pilgrimage is the fifth pillar of Islam, and the observances are concentrated on the eighth, ninth and tenth days of the month of Dhul-Hijjah. These consist of a series of ceremonies, the most important of which are: circumambulating the Ka'aba seven times; walking between the hills of al-Safa and al-Marwa, outside the sanctuary; joining the assembly on Mount Arafat for the afternoon service on the ninth day; and offering sacrifices of sheep, goats or camels at Mina on the following day, the Festival of Sacrifice. Just as the worshipper must wash according to the prescribed ritual before prayer, so the pilgrim must be in the physical and spiritual state of *ihram* before making the pilgrimage. The state of *ihram* involves consecrating oneself to God, wearing the garments of *ihram* (two plain unsewn sheets) and shaving of the head for men. From this time onwards pilgrims may not use perfume nor indulge in sexual relations until after the sacrifice at Mina.

Attendance of the service on Mount Arafat on the ninth day of Dhul-Hijjah is the essential act of the pilgrimage. Pilgrims set out from Mecca after sunrise for the Mount, which stands in a barren plain large enough to accommodate the entire assembly of about two million pilgrims. On Mount Arafat Muslims examine themselves and declare their repentance. Camp is broken just after sunset, when pilgrims hurry to Muzdafila, about five miles away, where they spend the night in prayer and meditiation. The pilgrimages ends the following day with the Festival of Sacrifice (see below). Those who have completed the pilgrimage are known as *hajjis*.

Festival of Sacrifice

The pilgrimage to Mecca (hajj) culminates on the tenth day of the twelfth month, Dhul-Hijjah, with the Festival of Sacrifice (*Eid-ul-Adha*). The festival is also called the Great Festival (*Eid-ul-Kabeer*) as the celebrations last four days, a day longer than those of the other major festival of Islam, the Festival of Breaking the Fast. Other names by which the festival is known are the Festival of Immolation (*Eid-ul-Nahr*) and the Festival of Offering (*Qurbani Eid*).

This is the day of sacrificial ceremony for Muslims on pilgrimage, who offer animals at the small village of Mina on their way back to Mecca from Mount Arafat (see above) in remembrance of the will-

'Black is most beautiful!' Seven times the pilgrim circles anticlockwise round the Ka'aba.

225

ingness of the prophet Abraham to sacrifice his only son, Ismael, to God. Three stone pillars representing the spots where the devil tried to tempt Ismael into rebellion against his father, who was leading him to the place of sacrifice, are located in the vicinity of Mina. Traditional rites of the sacrificial ceremony include the stoning of these pillars by pilgrims, signifying the rejection of evil promptings. After stoning the first pillar, the pilgrims each sacrifice a sheep, goat or camel, following the example of Abraham, who offered a ram when God spared him his son Ismael.

Although the sacrifice is actually part of the observances followed during the pilgrimage to Mecca in accordance with the injunction of the Qur'an (Qur'an 22: 32–38), the festival is celebrated throughout the Muslim world. Every Muslim who can afford to do so sacrifices an animal on this occasion, some of the meat being used for the needs of the household, the rest being distributed amongst the poor and needy. The sacrifice is symbolic of obedience to the will of God and readiness to sacrifice one's desires, attachments and worldly possessions for God's sake if required to do so, just as Abraham showed his obedience by preparing to sacrifice his son, whom he loved, at God's command.

> 'In the name of God, the Most Beneficent, the Most Merciful
> It is not their flesh nor their blood that reaches God,
> It is your piety that reaches Him.
> He has thus subjected them to your service
> That you may glorify Him for His guidance to you,
> And proclaim the good news to the righteous.'
>
> Qur'an 22: 37

Muslims who are not on pilgrimage celebrate the occasion in their own towns and villages with great festivity and rejoicing. An animal is bought for the sacrifice and the night preceding the festival is traditionally spent in prayer and meditation. The day begins with the festival prayer, which is similar to the prayer for the Festival of Breaking the Fast (see above), and it is customary to speak about sacrifice at some point during the sermon which follows. Afterwards the animals are sacrificed in the name of God, and a portion of meat is given in charity as an act of purification which enables the poor to join in the festivities.

On the Day of Sacrifice Muslims also celebrate the Prophet's farewell sermon, which he gave on that day three months before his death, in the tenth year of *hijrah* (the migration from Mecca to Medina). The sermon sums up the principles of the Muslim community as laid down by the Qur'anic revelations and ends with an exhortation to Muslims to follow the teachings of the Qur'an and the Tradition of the Prophet.

'O people! Understand my words. I have left you something with which, if you will hold fast to it, you will never fall into error: the Book of God and the practice of His Prophet.'

Hadith

The Prophet then looked up to heaven exclaiming in a loud voice 'O God! I have delivered Thy message.' The crowd resounded with one accord, 'And thou hast!'

The Festival of Sacrifice is thus a time of rejoicing in the revelation of the Qur'an and thanksgiving for having been able to make the pilgrimage and sacrifice. Muslims reaffirm their faith in the Qur'an and the Tradition, and show their willingness to surrender their own interests and wordly belongings to God. The occasion is celebrated with the same great festivity as the Festival of Breaking the Fast, and celebrations may extend until the return of those who have completed the pilgrimage. Families prepare for their return by cleaning and decorating their houses, and on the day of arrival visitors from near and far come to greet the returning pilgrims.

New Year's Day

The Muslim calendar begins with the year (622 CE) in which the 'migration' (*hijrah*) from Mecca to Medina took place. The migration marked the success and spread of Islam.

In the first years of his prophecy, Muhammad's following was small and opposition to his preaching built up amongst the Meccans. As their hostilities increased the Prophet began to look for new grounds from which to propagate his message, and where he and his followers would be safe. However, an attempt to establish himself in Taif, about seventy-five miles south of Mecca, was unsuccessful. He was harshly rejected and attacked by the locals. On one occasion Muhammad, utterly exhausted and with bleeding feet, had to take refuge in a nearby orchard where he turned to God in prayer. Muslims still remember and repeat this prayer when faced with difficulties.

'O God! To you I confess my weakness, despair and people's lack of respect for me. O, You Most Merciful, You are the Lord of the weak and my Lord. On whom can I rely? Upon a stranger who disdains me or upon an enemy whom you have favoured over me? I can bear it if You are not angry with me for Your power is wide open to me. I beg by the light of Your face which has lightened the darkness and favoured this world and the hereafter, not to be angry with me. You I beseech, not for control or power, but for your sake.'

Muhammad returned to Mecca, where he continued to preach his religion. On one occasion at the Ukaz fair he got into discussion with a small group of men from the town of Yathrib. This town was the scene of recurrent civil strife between two Arab tribes and would benefit by the imposition of someone in authority. Thus the group saw Muhammad's cause as one which might unite the people of Yathrib. They listened to Muhammad's revelations of the Qur'an, accepted Islam and returned to their home town where they began to preach the new faith. After prolonged negotiations during which the persecution of Muslims in Mecca intensified and became intolerable, the Prophet ordered his Meccan followers to migrate to Yathrib. The Prophet joined them there later in the year, after which the city became known as Medinat-ul-Nabi (City of the Prophet), nowadays referred to simply as al-Medina (the City). The people of Medina accepted Muhammad as their guide and leader, and he organised the Muslims into a community who practised and preached their new religon. Aside from excursions, the Prophet remained in Medina from the time of his migration until his death ten years later.

New Year's Day is celebrated in the entire Muslim world by relating stories of the Prophet's life and spending extra time during the night in prayer. The occasion is not marked by a public holiday in most Muslim countries.

Muharram

The first part of the first month, Muharram, is an occasion when Shi'ite Muslims commemorate the death of Hussain (the grandson of Muhammad) and Hussain's little son, in the battle of Karbala.

The sudden death of Muhammad with no designated successor resulted in the development of dissident political groups within the community of Muslims he had established. The largest group assumed that the caliph (successor) should be chosen by the community from amongst the close companions of the Prophet. This was the origin of the Sunni sect, the followers of the *Sunnah* (Tradition), to which the majority of Muslims today belong. The other main group in the community held the principle of hereditary succession and maintained that the caliphs should be descendants of Muhammad through his cousin and son-in-law, Ali. These became known as the Shi'ite, the 'partisans' of Ali. Later still the Ummayad, the leading clan of the Quraysh tribe into which Muhammad was born, sought to take over the succession.

In the event, Abu Bakr, a close companion of the Prophet, became

Opposite: *At New Year all Muslims join together in praise. The eternal mihrab focuses the world's prayers in the direction of Mecca.*

the first caliph and Ali eventually became the fourth caliph against much opposition. He was murdered and the Ummayads then seized the caliphate, Muawiyah declaring himself as Ali's successor. Muawiyah's son Yazeed took over as caliph on the death of his father in the year 60 AH (679 CE), his succession establishing the caliphate as a hereditary system. Hussain, Ali's son, took a firm stand against this and refused to give his pledge of alliance to Yazeed. During his pilgrimage to Mecca that year, Hussain received a message from some of his supporters in Kufa, south-west of Baghdad, that they would fight in his defence should he decide to challenge Yazeed and attempt to establish himself as the rightful caliph. After completion of the pilgrimage, Hussain left Mecca for Kufa. Yazeed, learning of the situation, gathered an army and confronted Hussain and his followers on the second day of Muharram in the year 61 AH near Karbala, twenty-five miles north-west of Kufa. On the tenth day of the month (10 October 680 CE) the battle of Karbala took place. Hussain was killed along with his little son and his top aides the same day.

The Shi'ites commemorate this event by mourning during the first ten days of Muharram, at the end of which a passion play is performed which re-enacts the martyrdom and suffering of Hussain. Shi'ites today live predominantly in Iran, but also form a large minority group in Iraq, and can be found in the Arabian Gulf, the sub-continent of India and some East African countries. In some of these countries during the first ten days of the month, and in others throughout the entire month, both old and young dress in black. Special dishes, which vary from one region to another and which are not eaten at any other time, are prepared during this period. This tenth of Muharram became a symbol of mourning and sorrow, and is a public holiday for the Shi'ite community everywhere.

Festival of the Prophet's Birthday

The Festival of the Prophet's Birthday (*Mawlid an-Nabi*) is tradition-ally celebrated on the twelfth day of the third month, Rabi' ul-Awwal. This festival, introduced by the Abbasids of Baghdad during the fourth century of *hijrah* (tenth century CE), is the last of the festivals to have evolved. The Fatimids of Egypt are reported to have supported their claim for the leadership of the Muslim community by celebrating important events in the lives of the Prophet, his daughter Fatima and son-in-law Ali, and their two sons Hassan and Hussain.

On the anniversary of the Prophet's birthday people wear colourful clothes and delicious food is prepared for the occasion. The influence of the Abbasid and Fatimid traditions can still be felt in the Sufi marches, remembrance circles and religious chants, but festivities differ greatly from one place to another. In Malaya people gather together in main squares to listen to readings from the Qur'an and join in religious chants, which are followed by marches led by statesmen and leaders of society. In India, Pakistan and Bangladesh songs are sung in honour of the Prophet, usually after a lecture or talk describing the Prophet's way of life. Meeting places are decorated with coloured lights and flags, and traditional sweets are distributed.

The Festival of the Prophet's Birthday is a public holiday in only a few countries.

Festival of the Prophet's Night Journey and Ascension
This festival, which commemorates the famous night journey (*al-isra*) of the Prophet to Jerusalem and his subsequent ascension (*al-miraj*) to Paradise, is celebrated on the twenty-sixth night of the seventh month, Rajab. On this night, some eleven years before Muhammad's migration to Medina, the Angel Gabriel came to the Prophet and took him on a journey from Mecca to Jerusalem by means of the winged steed Buraq. Here Muhammad led all the prophets who had preceded him in prayer before commencing the second part of the journey, through the seven heavens.

During the second stage of the journey Muhammad was shown heaven and hell and spoke to all the prophets. Finally he was taken into the presence of God, who spoke to him about many matters and gave the commandment that all Muslims should pray five times a day, in a state of ritual purity attained by washing. Prayer, being the only direct link between man and his creator, is the central pillar and the nucleus of Islam, and the commandment given to Muhammad on this occasion was confirmed more than eighty times in the revelation of the Qur'an.

The tradition of the night journey and ascension is based on a passage from the Qur'an:

> 'In the name of God, the Most Beneficent, the Most Merciful
> Glory be to Him who took His servant on a journey by night
> From the Sacred Mosque to the Farthest Mosque,
> Whose precincts have been blessed,
> That We might show him some of our signs.
> For He alone hears and sees all things.'
>
> Qur'an 17: 1

Muslim scholars disagree in their interpretation of this passage, some taking it literally and others regarding it as a vision, however all agree on the important implications. Through this journey

Hijrah year	Muslim New Year	First day of Ramadan	Festival of Breaking the Fast	Festival of Sacrifice
1404 AH	7 October 1983	30 May 1984	29 June 1984	5 September 1984
1405 AH	26 September 1984	20 May 1985	19 June 1985	26 August 1985
1406 AH	15 September 1985	9 May 1986	8 June 1986	15 August 1986
1407 AH	5 September 1986	29 April 1987	29 May 1987	5 August 1987
1408 AH	25 August 1987	17 April 1988	17 May 1988	24 July 1988
1409 AH	13 August 1988	6 April 1989	6 May 1989	13 July 1989
1410 AH	3 August 1989	27 March 1990	26 April 1990	3 July 1990
1411 AH	23 July 1990	16 March 1991	15 April 1991	22 June 1991
1412 AH	12 July 1991	4 March 1992	3 April 1992	10 June 1992
1413 AH	1 July 1992	22 February 1993	24 March 1993	31 May 1993
1414 AH	20 June 1993	11 February 1994	13 March 1994	20 May 1994
1415 AH	9 June 1994	31 January 1995	2 March 1995	9 May 1995
1416 AH	30 May 1995	21 January 1996	20 February 1996	28 April 1996
1417 AH	18 May 1996	9 January 1997	8 February 1997	17 April 1997
1418 AH	8 May 1997	30 December 1997	29 January 1998	7 April 1998
1419 AH	27 April 1998	19 December 1998	18 January 1999	27 March 1999
1420 AH	16 April 1999	8 December 1999	7 January 2000	15 March 2000

Muhammad was raised to the highest spiritual state of which man is capable, and his status in God's sight as at least equal to that of any of his prophetic forbears was established. Muhammad was assured of God's help and guidance, and given proof of the unity of the universe, the unity of God's messages as revealed through the prophets, and the unity of mankind.

The festival is celebrated throughout the Muslim world. Mosques and minarets are lit in honour of the night journey, and Muslims spend the night relating traditions concerning the event, reading the Qur'an and joining together in prayer.

Night of Forgiveness
The Night of Forgiveness (*Lailat-ul-Bara'h*) falls on the fifteenth of the eighth month, Sha'ban. Muslims believe that a person's life for the coming year is determined by God during this night, which they spend in prayer seeking God's guidance. Many believers fast on the fourteenth of Sha'ban in preparation for the night. It is the custom in some parts of the world for Muslims to visit cemeteries to pay respect to their dead relatives, and the giving of charity is also traditional. The occasion is celebrated in some places with firework displays.

Table of Muslim festivals

Weekly (Friday)   Day of Assembly
1 Muharram   New Year's Day
1–10 Muharram   New Year Festival (*Muharram*)
12 Rabi' ul-Awwal   Festival of the Prophet's Birthday
26 Rajab   Festival of the Prophet's Night Journey and Ascension
15 Sha'ban   Night of Forgiveness
1–29/30 Ramadan   Annual Fast (*Ramadan*)
1 Shawal   Festival of Breaking the Fast (*Eid-ul-Fitr*)
9 Dhul-Hijjah   Day of Arafat
10 Dhul-Hijjah   Festival of Sacrifice (*Eid-ul-Adha*)

The table opposite gives the dates of the Muslim New Year, the first day of Ramadan and the two major festivals in the Muslim calendar from 1984 to 2000 CE.

11 Sikh Festivals

W OWEN COLE

Sikhism

Sikhism began with the ministry of Nanak, a *kshatriya* (warrior caste) Hindu who lived in the Punjab region of north India from 1469 to 1539 CE. Nanak became the first *Guru*, or religious teacher, of the Sikhs. He shared a number of ideas common to a group of north Indian mystics and teachers known as Sants: their use of the vernacular instead of Sanskrit as the medium of religious teaching, egalitarianism (including the acceptance of women disciples), the inefficacy of ritual, and the importance of the inner experience of God, to name but a few. This latter point was particularly significant for Guru Nanak who did not regard himself, and should not be explained, simply as the inheritor and refiner of a Sant form of Hinduism. He had an acute sense of being called and commissioned by God. Consequently, Sikhism is not to be understood merely as the daughter of Hinduism, but as a religion in its own right, divinely revealed. In one of his hymns Guru Nanak describes his religious experience:

I was a minstrel out of work,
The Lord gave me employment.
The mighty one instructed me,
'Night and day sing my praise.'
The Lord summoned the minstrel to his high court
On me he bestowed the robe of honouring him and singing his praise.
On me he bestowed the nectar in a cup, the nectar of his true and
   Holy name.
Those who at the Lord's bidding feast and take their fill of the
Lord's holiness attain peace and joy.
Your minstrel spreads your glory by singing your word.
Nanak says, through adoring the truth we attain to the
   all highest.

Guru Granth Sahib, p 150

The Guru's mission was not to create a new religion but to reawaken the world to the forgotten truth that everyone, regardless of class, caste or sex, could experience God and through his grace attain *moksha* (liberation). Before Guru Nanak died he designated and installed a successor. In all there were ten gurus, each of whom faithfully passed on the message given to the first, and sustained and developed the community which grew up in response to it. During this period, which ended with the death of Guru Gobind Singh in 1708 CE, three major decisions were taken which affected the Sikh movement fundamentally and resulted in it emerging as a distinct religion. First, in 1604 CE, Guru Arjan, the fifth leader of the Sikhs, completed the first compilation of a book known as the Adi Granth. This contained his own compositions as well as the hymns of his predecessors, together with works by such Hindus and Muslims as Namdev, Kabir, and Sheikh Farid. Authorised and authenticated copies of the teachings of Sikhism could now be available to local communities separated by considerable distances from personal contact with the guru. Second, the tenth Guru, Gobind Singh, created the *Khalsa* (Sikh brotherhood) in 1699 CE. By now the Sikh *panth* (the entire Sikh community) was large and scattered. Although the compilation of the Adi Granth had ensured some unity of doctrine, problems of organisation, allegiance and discipline remained. The solution was the Khalsa, which men and women entered not by birth but by a rite of initiation involving the making of vows and the accepting of a code of conduct. It also included the adoption of outward symbols, the wearing of the turban and the five 'Ks'. These are *kes* (uncut hair and beard), *kachh* (short trousers), *kara* (a bangle), *kirpan* (a short sword) and *kangha* (a comb). Lastly, in 1708 CE, on the eve of his death, Guru Gobind Singh declared that the succession of human gurus was at an end and conferred guruship on the Adi Granth which is now known as the Guru Granth Sahib, as well as upon the Khalsa which he had always regarded as an extension of himself. In effect it made the Sikhs a community whose life is focussed upon its scriptures ritually as well as doctrinally.

Sikhism is an intensely democratic religion. It has no priesthood and accords men and women equal status, in theory at least. It regards guruship as the essential property and characteristic of a self-revealing God. This revelation was communicated to messengers sent into the world to convey the message of deliverance to humankind. This is contained in the scripture and in the community which live according to its teachings. Ultimately the *panth* in an ideal sense is one with God who is often described as 'The One without a second'.

In an individual sense unity with God is realised through enlightenment, which is received by God's grace. This begins a process of spiritual growth which is nurtured through meditation (*nam simran*), congregational worship, and living in the company of other enlightened people, the Sikh community. Personal religion also takes on a social aspect through the principles of *kirt karna* (the ethic of honest hard work) and *wand chakna* (the giving of alms to anyone in need.) From these ideals all else in Sikhism emanates, the ideal result being a society in which the *varnashramadharma* (duty according to class and stage of life) of Hinduism is replaced by one in which there is only one *varna* (caste or class) – humanity, one *ashrama* (stage of life) – that of the householder, and one *dharma* (duty) – that of serving God through one's everyday life. One reason for the early appeal of Sikhism must be that it accepted the lot of the peasant, of necessity a hard-working family person, and commended this life-style, rather than that of the brahmin or the ascetic, as the ideal.

The festivals

In view of its links with Hinduism, it is not surprising that Sikhism should share the Samvat era and the annual calendar with it. However, instead of beginning with Chaitra, or the festival of Diwali at the end of Asvina and the first days of Karttika, the Sikh new year starts with Baisakhi (13 April). Until the leadership of Guru Amar Das there seems to have been no interest in special holy days, and Sikhism has never observed a weekly 'sabbath'. However at some time during his period of office Guru Amar Das commanded the Sikhs to assemble before him at Baisakhi and Diwali, the two most important festivals in the north Indian Hindu calendar. Whatever his motives, the consequence of Guru Amar Das's action was a requirement that Sikhs should choose where their allegiance lay – with the ways of the village or in the service of the Guru. To these gatherings Guru Gobind Singh added a third, Hola Mohalla, which coincided with the Hindu festival of Holi. These three celebrations, known as *melas*, are still observed by the Sikh community.

Baisakhi (13 or 14 April)
Baisakhi is the first *mela*: first in the calendar, for it marks the Sikh new year, and first in importance. On 30 March 1699 CE, Guru Gobind Singh, the tenth leader, ordered the Sikhs to gather in his presence at Anandpur. There he introduced his followers to a new concept of loyalty and initiation which he had devised, embodied

in the ideal of the Khalsa. The occasion marked the beginning of a new era in the history of Sikhism, noticeable outwardly by the adoption of a distinctive form of clothing – the five 'Ks' and the turban, (the latter usually being worn only by men) – and the use of the names Singh (by men) and Kaur (by women) as an appendix to the first part of the name to denote affiliation to the Sikh brotherhood.

There are three dimensions to Baisakhi. It is primarily a religious occasion, so the day will begin with bathing in a river, in the *sarowar* (the pool found at most *gurdwaras* or temples in India) or by taking a shower in one's own home. After private, individual or family meditation, the Sikh will then go to the *gurdwara* where the normal service will be augmented by talks and devotional addresses relevant to the events being commemorated. The cloth around the flag post and the flag itself (*nishan sahib*) will probably be ceremonially renewed on this day. It is also customary for new members of the Khalsa to be initiated, and sometimes for newly elected *gurdwara* committees to assume office.

Secondly, Baisakhi is a memorial festival. Not only was the Khalsa created on this day, it was at Baisakhi 1762 CE that the Sikhs, after consulting the Guru Granth Sahib, decided to respond to the plea of a Hindu brahmin whose wife had been forcibly abducted by the Afghan Usman Khan and took up arms on his behalf. Also it was during the Baisakhi *mela* of 1919 CE that the massacre of Jallianwala Bagh took place in Amritsar. Consequently, the speeches given at Baisakhi are frequently political as well as spiritual in their content.

Finally, at Amritsar, where the main Baisakhi gathering has taken place since the eighteenth century, sometimes despite the prohibitions of Mughal and British rulers, a large animal fair is held. Sikhs from many miles around the city will converge on it to visit the Golden Temple, join political rallies, sell livestock, enjoy the fun of the fair, and relax before the spring harvest is reaped.

Diwali (October/November)

Diwali is an all-India festival which Sikhs share with Hindus. However, the significance for Sikhs is quite different. Houses are 'autumn-cleaned', not in preparation for the visit of the goddess Lakshmi, but to remove mosquitoes and other insects before moving the beds indoors as the cold nights begin and winter approaches. Jewellery, household goods and new clothes are bought. Children enjoy sweetmeats and fireworks. Families and friends exchange presents. Candles and *devas* (lamps) illuminate *gurdwaras* and homes, lighting the darkness of the moonless Diwali night.

There are three events which Sikhs call to mind as they celebrate this autumn festival. It was at this time of year in 1577 CE that Guru

The Golden Temple, Amritsar. There is never a day when Sikhs do not visit it, but at Baisakhi and Diwali they come in their tens of thousands.

Ram Das laid the foundations of the city of Amritsar. Naturally the Golden Temple, its most celebrated building, is illuminated by hundreds of electric lights at Diwali. At this time also the sixth Guru, Hargobind, was released from imprisonment in the Gwalior Fort on the orders of the Mughal emperor Jehangir, who had earlier confined him there. Officers of the emperor had arrested the Guru for his failure to pay a fine imposed on his father, Guru Arjan. They may have been motivated by a suspicion that he was planning to commit treason and was raising a private army with which to launch a rebellion. Eventually the emperor himself investigated the charges and the Guru was released. However, in the Gwalior Fort there were also fifty-two Hindu princes, each of them innocent of any crime. The Guru interceded for them, refusing to accept his liberty if they were not given theirs. He was told that as many princes as could pass through the narrow passage to the outside world holding on to his cloak would be freed. The Guru ordered a cloak to be brought which had long tassel-like ends and the princes were able to leave holding on to this train.

Sikhs also remember that in 1738 CE, Bhai Mani Singh, the custodian of the Golden Temple, was martyred at Diwali tide. He had requested permission for Sikhs to celebrate the festival at the temple but this was granted only on condition that he paid a large sum of money to the authorities. This he hoped to be able to do from the offerings of pilgrims. However, the presence of a Mughal army deterred them and the obligation could not be met. Bhai Mani Singh was offered his life if he converted to Islam. This he refused to do despite being tortured, so at last he was executed.

Hola Mohalla (February/March)

Hola Mohalla is the most recent *mela* to be observed by the Sikhs. It dates from the time of Guru Gobind Singh and was first celebrated in the year after the formation of the Khalsa, 1700 CE. In that year the Khalsa assembled at Anandpur and took part in what can best be described as military manoeuvres. They were divided into two armies and engaged in mock battles. The Hindu festival of Holi was probably chosen as the time for this gathering for two reasons: it was a holiday and therefore a period when assembly would be easy to undertake; also it would wean Sikhs away from a Hindu celebration, as the Baisakhi and Diwali meetings already did, and so contribute to them developing a distinct indentity. This fits in with the philosophy expressed by the famous Sikh writer, Bhai Gurdas, (1558–1637 CE), nephew of the fourth Guru: 'Non-Sikh festivals should not be celebrated. Even if we observe the same day we do it in our own way.'

Anandpur is still the place where the principal Hola Mohalla festivities are celebrated. These take the form of wrestling or fencing tournaments, other sporting activities, and the enjoyment of fairground sideshows. A feature of the *mela* is the gathering of Nihangs, an order of Sikhs established by Guru Gobind Singh. They formed the most militant and fearless section of the Sikh armies in the troubled days of the eighteenth century and their successors today continue the martial tradition, wearing swords, usually blue turbans and having a special veneration for Guru Gobind Singh. The literal meaning of Hola Mohalla is 'attack and place of attack'. Its meaning is not lost in the present day *mela*, though the need to be prepared for battle has gone.

Gurpurbs

The other form of Sikh festival is the *gurpurb*, the birth or death anniversary of a Guru. Clearly these can be twenty in number, but not all are universally celebrated throughout the Sikh world with regularity. However, such occasions as a tercentenary will not be allowed to pass unnoticed and in *gurdwaras* associated with a particular Guru, his *gurpurbs* will be marked not only by traditional forms of celebration but by special events. For example at Bakala, where the ninth Guru was proclaimed, or at the Sis Ganj Gurdwara in Delhi, built on the site of his execution and martyrdom, processions, and many aspects of a *mela* will accompany the piety of the festival.

The principal characteristic of a *gurpurb* is the continuous, unbroken reading of the Guru Granth Sahib. This is called an *akhand path*. A succession of readers, women as well as men, will take their place behind the scripture and read it beginning at page one, so timing the operation that page 1430 is reached at the time when the celebration of the festival is due to start. The reading takes about forty-eight hours. Just before the end is reached the *bhog* ceremony take place. This begins with the reading of the Guru Granth Sahib from page 1426 to the end, followed by the first verse of the Japji, six verses of the Anand Sahib, the saying of the prayer Ardas, and the sharing of *karah parshad* (a mixture of flour, sugar, honey and milk). During the service which follows, hymns of the guru whose anniversary is being commemorated will be sung, and special speakers will explain them in lectures and sermons, and describe the guru's contribution to Sikhism and humanity. As usual the proceed-

Opposite: *A feature of gurpurbs is the continuous reading of the Guru Granth Sahib, timed to take about 48 hours.*

ings will be accompanied by *langar* (kitchen) which may be enjoyed by anyone who wishes to partake of the meal. In Britain it has been known for passers-by to be offered fruit so that they might share the festival. However, for cultural and climatic reasons, *gurpurbs* in a country like England appear rather sombre, not being accompanied by processions, bands, and entertainments as they would be in India.

Minor festivals

A brief mention must also be made of a number of minor occasions observed by some Sikhs:

Sangrand. This is the time when the sun leaves one sign of the zodiac and enters another. This should not have any particular significance for Sikhs, rejecting as they do the notion of auspicious occasions and astrology. However, Hindu practices are sometimes paralleled by services in *gurdwaras*.

Puranmashi. The full moon day which ends every Hindu month is also observed by some Sikhs, sometimes with all-night vigils and the singing of *kirtan*, (hymns taken from the Guru Granth Sahib). This is sometimes justified on the ground that Guru Nanak was born on a full moon. The service, therefore, is a monthly celebration of that event.

Lohri. This north Indian festival occurs in January at the time of the sugar cane harvest. Families and neighbours visit the homes of children born during the past year and sing songs. Meals, which include rice cooked in sugar-cane juice, are served and the chill winter air is warmed with bonfires. For Sikhs the festival has no religious significance.

Table of Sikh festivals

From the list which follows it will be seen that besides the *melas* already mentioned and the *gurpurbs* there are also a few fairs (*melas*) associated with other events or commemorating the anniversaries of famous Sikhs who were not *Gurus*.

January   Maghi Fair. This festival, held at Muktsar near Ferozepore, commemorates the battle of Muktsar fought by Guru Gobind Singh.

January   Death of Baba Deep Singh. The martyrdom of this scribe

Young Sikhs at the festival of Guru Tegh-Bahadur. They represent two of the sons of Guru Gobind Singh.

of the Sikh scriptures, who died attempting to recover the Darbar Sahib from the Mughals in 1760 CE, is commemorated at Amritsar.

January Chheharta Sahib Fair. This festival commemorates the sinking of six wells by Guru Arjan to supply the needs of the district, which is near Amritsar.

February–March Hola Mohalla Mela

March Mela at Dera Baba Nanak Gurdwara. This is an historical site, for a long time in the possession of the Bedi family, opposite Kartarpur where Guru Nanak spent the last years of his life.

13 or 14 April Baisakhi Mela

May–June Martyrdom of Guru Arjan. This occasion is universally commemorated.

June Death of Maharaja Ranjit Singh. This is commemorated in various towns associated with his reign, principally at Lahore.

July Birthday of Guru Har Krishan. The anniversary is celebrated at Delhi.

August Mela Baba Bakale. This is celebrated at Bakale near Amritsar where Tegh Bahadur was proclaimed Guru.

September Goindwal Fair. This festival commemorates the death (Immersion into the Eternal Light) of Guru Amar Das.

September Anniversary of the Installation of the Adi Granth (1604 CE). This festival is celebrated of Amritsar

October–November Diwali Mela

November Guru Nanak's Birthday. This festival is universally celebrated. The date of Guru Nanak's birthday is 15 April 1469 CE. However, the writings of the popular Bala tradition in the nineteenth century had the effect of encouraging the celebration of *gurpurbs* in November.

November Achal Sahib Batala Fair. This is held at Gurdaspur, where Guru Nanak disputed with the yogis.

December Martyrdom Guru Tegh Bahadur. This occasion is commemorated at Delhi.

December Martyrdom of Zorawar Singh, Fateh Singh and the young sons of Guru Gobind Singh. This is observed especially at Fategarh Sahib near Sirhind.

December Martyrdom of Ajit Singh and Jujhar Singh, sons of Guru Gobind Singh. This occasion is observed especially at Chamkaur Sahib where they died.

December Birthday of Guru Gobind Singh. The anniversary is universally celebrated.

Most *melas* and *gurpurbs* are fixed by the lunar calendar and may vary within the limit of about fifteen days from year to year.

12 Zoroastrian (Parsi) Festivals

MARY BOYCE

Zoroastrianism

Zoroastrianism was founded by the Iranian prophet Zarathushtra, known to the Greeks as Zoroaster. He lived probably between 1400 and 1200 BCE, at a time when the Iranian peoples were scattered as pastoral tribes over what are now the south Russian steppes, sharing many beliefs and customs with their close cousins, the Indo-Aryans, and like them worshipping many gods.

Zarathushtra brought them a new revelation: that in the beginning there had been only one God, Ahura Mazda (Ohrmazd), the 'Lord of Wisdom', wholly beneficent and just; and one other uncreated being, Angra Mainyu (Ahriman), the 'Hostile Spirit', ignorant and malign. To overwhelm him, Ahura Mazda created this world as a place where evil can be encountered and destroyed; and to aid him in this task he evoked the six Amesha Spentas, the 'Holy Immortals', from his own selfhood of goodness and light. With him they make up a divine Heptad, and together with his Holy Spirit they created this world in seven stages: sky, water, earth, plants, animals, man, and lastly fire, both visibly (in sun, moon and hearth fires) and as an inner force warming and animating all the rest. Each of the Heptad took one of the creations under his or her especial protection.

The doctrine of the Heptad is central to Zoroastrian theology and ethics. Man should constantly worship God and the Amesha Spentas, seeking through thought, word and act to bring them into his own being, so that he may himself become godlike and thus not only save own soul but help to redeem the world. Man should also, as chief of the creations and alone capable of deliberate choice, care for the other six, keeping them as pure and strong as possible, so that they may resist evil in their own instinctive ways; for, Zarathushtra taught, after the world was created Angra Mainyu attacked it, as Ahura Mazda had foreseen, bringing on it evils of every kind, physical and moral. He also made hell deep in the earth, where he had broken in. All souls are judged at death, the good going up to heaven, where Ahura Mazda dwells, the wicked down to hell. Angra Mainyu is often victorious in this present life; but in the end good will triumph and evil and death be no more. The Last Judgment will take place, and the resurrection of the dead. The earth will be cleansed by a great torrent of molten metal, through which mankind too will pass. The blessed will be reunited with their bodies, now made immortal; and Ahura Mazda will descend in glory to reign on an earth made once more perfect, as when it was created. This glorious New Day is called Frasho-kereti (Frashegird), the Making Wonderful.

The festivals

The Six Gahambars

These doctrines of Zarathushtra are celebrated each year through a chain of seven festivals, the holy days of obligation, neglect of which is a sin that will count at Judgment Day. Each festival is devoted to one of the Heptad and to his or her creation. The first six are known as the gahambars (meaning probably 'seasonal obser-vances'), and the seventh is called No Ruz (New Day), because it prefigures annually the happiness of Frashegird (see above). Tra-dition ascribes the founding of the gahambars to Zarathushtra himself. At first these festivals each lasted one day, and this was how they were still celebrated when Zoroastrianism was the state religion of the first two Iranian Empires, those of the Persian Achaemenians (c.550–331 BCE) and the Parthian Arsacids (c.141 BCE–224 CE). The Iranians then still used a traditional calendar of 360 days, divided into twelve months of thirty days each, and kept in accord with the natural year by an intercalary month being added periodically. In the fourth century BCE this ancient calendar was given a specifically Zoroastrian character, each month and day being dedicated to a divinity (for the faith teaches that Ahura Mazda evoked other lesser divine beings as helpers, after the great six). During the early years of the second Persian Empire, that of the Sasanians (c.224–651 CE), this calendar was reformed by the addition of five days at the year's end, piously called the Gatha days after the five groups of Gathas or hymns composed by Zarathushtra. Much confusion and distress followed this reform, with festivals being devoutly kept both on what were thought to be their true old days and on the officially sanctioned ones reckoned by the new calendar. Eventually contro-versy was ended by the duplicated feast days being joined together

Priests celebrating an Afrinagan service at a Gahambar in Bombay.

This photograph of a priest offers the opportunity to see a close-up of a face veil. They are worn in the interests of purity, to prevent breath reaching consecrated objects.

in one continuous observance, six days long. This was later reduced to five days, which is how the gahambars are still kept. Zoroastrians do not have a weekly holiday, so these long festivals, scattered through the year, have been much enjoyed.

Some time after the Arab conquest of Iran in the seventh century CE, a group of Zoroastrians left their homeland in search of religious freedom elsewhere. They settled under Hindu rule in Gujarat, in north-west India, where they were called Parsis (Persians). Those remaining in Iran are known as the Irani Zardushtis, or simply Iranis. After settling in India the Parsis made a calendar adjustment which caused their calendar, called Shenshai, to be one month behind the Irani one, called Qadimi (ancient). Both still have exactly 365 days, and so slip very slowly backwards against the natural year. Early this century some Parsis adopted the leap year of the Gregorian calendar, and fixed the beginning of their year, No Ruz, at the spring equinox, 21 March. This calendar they called Fasli (seasonal). It is now widely observed in the Irani community also. For the present dates of the gahambars and No Ruz according to these three calendars see the table at the end of the chapter. The Parsis by now form the larger part of the Zoroastrian community, and most Zoroastrians observe their festivals according to the Shenshai calendar.

Zoroastrians, for the past thousand years and more, have lived as minorities under Muslim, Hindu or Christian rule. Only their greatest festival, No Ruz, has been generally recognised as a holiday, being indeed retained by Shi'a Muslims as a secular festival of their own. But for many centuries most of the community lived in small towns and villages where they were in fact the chief inhabitants, working for themselves or their co-religionists, and so able to keep their own holy days. This is still true of some of the Zoroastrian villages in Iran, where the six gahambars are still strictly observed.

The chief religious observance at the gahambars is the Service of All the Masters (of creation) (*Yasht-i Visperad*). This, dedicated to Ohrmazd, is solemnised by priests at the fire temple, the service beginning at sunrise and lasting about three hours. As with all the religious services, its liturgy is in Avestan (the ancient language spoken by Zarathushtra himself). The intention of the service is to give thanks to God for his creations, and to sanctify them anew with sacred words and rituals. Devout lay people may attend, and in some of the old Parsi centres in Gujarat the celebrations of the first gahambar day centred on the fire temple. The big congregation overflowed into the temple courtyard and after the service fruits, bread and so on, which had been blessed during the service, were distributed among the congregation in a general communion. Other food would be cooked in the temple kitchens, and a feast would follow with rich and poor sitting companionably together. At other Parsi centres the consecrated food would be taken from the temple to where gahambar feasts were being held at private houses, or in a garden or orchard, with shared contributions of food and palm wine. Zoroastrians consider it a sin to fast, since this, they hold, weakens the good body given man by Ohrmazd, which should be kept strong and vigorous to combat Ahriman. They also believe that grief and melancholy are among the evils brought by the latter, to be countered as far as possible by joy and laughter; and so at all their festivals religious services are followed by feasting and merry-making.

In Irani villages the laity celebrate the gahambars chiefly in their own houses, for by ancient custom it is regarded as highly meritorious to endow a family gahambar. The service performed by the family priest in the home is the Gahambar Thanksgiving (*Afrinagan-i Gahambar*), which lasts about half an hour. The night before the women are busy preparing food, and they rise again before dawn to sweep and scour, for dirt too belongs to Ahriman, and holy days are observed with the most scrupulous cleanliness. At the due time the priest comes at the head of a procession: first the village elders, grave and dignified, some dressed like him in white, the colour of purity; then the younger men, and at their heels a pack of excited small boys; and finally a colourful group of matrons and little girls in bright traditional clothes, mostly reds and greens. The householder welcomes his many guests, who throng the central courtyard sitting knee to knee and facing an open portico, the *pesgam-i mas*, where all the family religious observances take place. Here the priest celebrates the short service and, when it is over, the consecrated food (usually bread, meat and seven kinds of dried fruits and nuts) is distributed to all those present. Some is set aside for the sick and bed-ridden, and if Muslim beggars have come to the house door unconsecrated food is taken to them straight from the kitchen, with warm words of welcome, for the gahambars are times for general goodwill and caring for one's fellow man. Then the priest leads the whole congregation off to the next house on his list. This continues throughout the mornings of the five festival days. During those days only necessary work is done and gaiety is fostered as much as possible. Older girls, who by custom do not attend the gahambar services, often meet at each other's houses in the mornings to sing, dance to the tambourine or play games such as blind man's buff; or they will go in a group round the little village shrines, praying and making offerings and then dancing and singing outside the shrine doors. In the afternoons and evenings there is much visiting

A traditional Gahambar dinner eaten off banana leaves, Bombay.

between houses and lavish festive meals take place, with wine and varied entertainments – dancing by boys and young men, singing, mime with dressing up, story-telling and the like. Such merry-making often goes on far into the night, for little time is wasted on sleeping during a gahambar.

The Sixth Gahambar and Farvardigan (Muktad)

The sixth gahambar is special, since it celebrates the creation of man himself, whose guardian is Ohrmazd. Moreover, it forms part of the chief holy season, lasting for eighteen days or more, which is observed to a greater or lesser extent by all Zoroastrians. It has for its crowning glory No Ruz; but there is a richness in its observances which arose at the third century calendar reform. Before this the sixth gahambar was celebrated on the last, that is, the three hundred and sixtieth day of the old year. That night was dedicated to All Souls (Fravashis), who were then welcomed back to their ancestral homes and bidden a ritual farewell before the sunrise of No Ruz. The calendar reform, however, introduced the five Gatha days between the sixth gahambar, celebrated together with All Souls, and

No Ruz. When the resulting confusions were resolved by the extension of all major festivals, the sixth gahambar came to be celebrated throughout the Gatha days, while, as the result of a double perplexity, the deeply cherished Festival of All Souls lasted for ten whole days and nights, as it does to this day. The Iranis call the first five days the Lesser Pentad (Panje-keh), the second five the Greater Pentad (Panje-meh), and the whole festival the Days of the Fravashis (Farvardigan). The Parsis use a Sanskrit term for it (Muktad) meaning the Days of the Released Souls. The Greater Pentad coincides with the sixth gahambar, which leads to an elaboration of observances but no incongruity of feeling, since Zoroastrians believe that the departed souls should be welcomed back with joy and asked to share in the happiness of their descendants.

In old Zoroastrian centres a special place in the home is prepared for the Fravashis by being thoroughly cleaned and freshly white-washed. At dawn on the first day of the Lesser Pentad gifts of welcome are set out there: flowers, fruits and a lamp, which is kept burning day and night throughout the festival; later specially cooked dishes of food are brought, to be blessed by prayers from the Avesta, the sacred book of the Zoroastrians. The flowers, and sometimes the foods, are put in vessels inscribed with names of the dead. City dwellers now usually use family tables placed in the halls of their fire temples on which the offerings are placed. The flowers (roses, jasmine and marigolds are favourites among the Parsis) are changed daily, and the temple halls are full of their fragrance and colour, the odour of incense and the continuous murmur of Avestan, as the priests solemnise the family services. The laity come and go throughout the day, the men often in white, the women in their loveliest saris.

On the sixth day the Gatha days begin, and the sixth gahambar. This is a very holy as well as joyful time and older lay people traditionally mark it by reciting holy texts or, nowadays, reading them from printed Avestas. Some read the appropriate Gatha on each of the five Gatha days; others are content with hour-long repetitions of the *Ahunvar* (the Zoroastrian equivalent of the Christian 'Lord's Prayer', composed by Zarathushtra himself). At the fire temples the priests solemnise the *Yasht-i Visperad* for the gahambar, and at night, at least once, a *Yasht-i Vendidad* for the Fravashis. (This is a long night office directed especially against the powers of evil.)

Meantime in Irani villages there are special domestic observances to mark this as the crowning gahambar. Little clay figures (animals, birds and the like) are made to celebrate the achieving of creation; these are white-washed and set in the *pesgam-i mas*; women bake cakes in all sorts of shapes, such as stars, ladders, and flat little men, and they too go into the *pesgam* to be blessed before they are eaten. The ordinary gahambar observances are also carried out with the usual festivities; but there is a growing sense of approaching climax, of the year ending. The devout often undergo a ritual purification at this time and recite, or ask the priest to recite for them, a general confession (*patet*) to free them from the past year's sins.

The night of the last Gatha day is devoted to bidding farewell to the Fravashis. In Gujarat the women carry the last food-offerings to the fire temple before midnight; there they are blessed at religious services and are fetched back before dawn to be set in a special room; the lanes are specially lit for the occasion and are full of brightness and bustle. In the Irani villages a fire is kindled on every roof, well before dawn, so that the darkness is lit by many small leaping flames. The last food-offerings are carried up on to the roof, and the fragrance of incense rises up with the chanting of Avestan. Then as dawn comes the Fravashis are felt to be slowly withdrawing, and when the sun appears they have departed for another year.

No Ruz

No Ruz is both an end, as the last of the seven great festivals, and a beginning, as the first day of the new year. It also symbolises both the end of 'limited time', with Frashegird, and the New Day of eternal happiness. The festival is characterised by a sense of renewal, by deep joy, and by active goodwill to all. These elements find outward expression in the wearing of new clothes, the exchange of greetings and gifts, with charity to the poor, and in family festivities. Most Zoroastrians try to be with their families for No Ruz; and in cities the festival, like the Christian Christmas, can easily take on a mainly secular character; but in conservatively religious families it is still kept as the holiest day of the year.

In such families everyone is up early, the children joyfully excited by their new clothes and presents, and there are special festive dishes for breakfast. Among the Parsis the whole family generally visits the fire temple to offer sandalwood to the sacred fire, pray, and give presents to the priests. There used to be a special No Ruz greeting exchanged by men as they met, with hands offered palm to palm; 'May we be one in strength, in righteousness! May Ohrmazd protect you! May we live long and happily!' In Iran men and women often exchange sprays of cypress or myrtle, since evergreen is a symbol of eternity. There the *Visperad* is solemnised at the fire temples in the early morning, as at the gahambars, and traditionally a list is sent to the celebrating priest from every house of all those living there, to be remembered in his prayers. No Ruz is a festival wholly for the living, foreshadowing the time when the blessed will enjoy eternal life. The other main religious observance special to No Ruz is the celebration at the fire temple in the early afternoon of a short thanksgiving service (*afrinagan*), devoted to the Amesha Spenta who guards the seventh creation, fire. Food which has been blessed that morning at the *Visperad* service is then shared in communion.

In houses the offerings in the *pesgam-i mas* include little boxes of fresh greenery, made up of seven kinds of seeds sprouted in time for this seventh festival (such as wheat, barley, rye). There are also eggs, another symbol of eternity, and poor children coming to the house for their No Ruz presents are given brightly painted eggs as well as fruit, nuts and gifts of money. There are many other visitors, as people come and go exchanging No Ruz greetings and being entertained with delicious food and wine. The religious and secular celebrations continue through the following days, and reach a new peak on the sixth day of the month. This is the 'old' No Ruz of the third century reform, which was considered then by traditionalists to be the greater festival. They evidently sought ways to exalt it, and it has long been celebrated, with much joyfulness, as the birthday of Zarathushtra. The Parsis call it Khordad-Sal, meaning either 'Khordad of the (New) Year', or 'Anniversary-Khordad'.

The first seven days of each month are dedicated to the members of the Heptad (Khordad being one of them) and perhaps for this reason the Parsis end their holy season on the seventh day. Traditionally the Irani No Ruz festivities continue till the twenty-first; and when it is a springtime celebration the thirteenth day of the month is celebrated in a special way: all the people leave their houses and spend the day in gardens, orchards or fields – picnicing, playing games, or simply enjoying the beauties of Ohrmazd's creation.

Name-day festivals (*jashans*)

All the twelve divinities to whom a month is dedicated in the Zoroastrian calendar also receive the dedication of a day (except Ohrmazd, to whom four days are devoted). When day and month dedications coincide, a festival (*jashan*) is celebrated for the divinity concerned. To keep these festivals is meritorious but not obligatory. All the Heptad thus have individual feast days, in addition to the more ancient gahambars and No Ruz; the Fravashis too have their *jashan*, when many people go to the *dakhmas* (funerary towers) to remember the dead, and offer prayers for them, and share a communion meal. Of the other *jashans* in honour of individual divinities the following are still generally observed.

Tir Jashan (13th of the 4th month)
This festival, also known as the Jashan of Tir and Teshtar, is in honour of two stellar divinities, and is a rain festival. It is chiefly observed by the Iranis who, within living memory, gave bracelets then to the children woven of seven coloured silks, symbolic of the rainbow. At the end of the festival they would climb to a high place and toss the bracelets up for the wind to carry away. Boys and girls still play with water, splashing in streams, and fortunes are told from tokens cast into a 'fate-pot' filled with pure water drawn from a stream and blessed with Avestan prayers.

Mihr Jashan (16th of the 7th month)
This festival, also kept chiefly by the Iranis, is a five-day observance in honour of the divinity Mithra (worshipped in India as Mitra, but regarded by Zoroastrians as one of the evocations of Ahura Mazda). It is celebrated as a harvest festival, when farmers make offerings of wheat, cotton and so on to the fire temple, and there are festivities to mark the gathering in of the crops.

Aban Jashan (10th of the 8th month)
This is a festival for the divinities of the waters, kept chiefly by the Parsis. The devout go then to a river bank or seashore, recite the Avestan hymn to the waters, and often cast flowers, sugar or coconuts into the streams or waves.

Adar Jashan (9th of the 9th month)
This festival is devoted to the divinity of fire. On this occasion many people go to the fire temples to make offerings of sandalwood or incense, and to pray before the sacred fire. Traditionally among the Parsis no cooking was done on the hearth fire that day.

Sada, the '100th-day festival'
The Iranis maintain also an open-air fire festival, which is probably more ancient even than the faith itself. It is held one hundred days before No Ruz; according to the fixed (Fasli) calendar in the depth of winter. The whole community contributes to the building of a huge bonfire near a spring or a stream; and as the sun goes down this is lit, to blaze up against the winter blackness and, symbolically, to warm the freezing water. In Zoroastrian terms this is in defiance of the evils of cold and dark. An *afrinagan* service is held at the great fire, after which merrymaking continues round it till the small hours.

Zartusht-no Diso or Sal-i Zardusht (*11th day of the 10th month*)
The eleventh day of the tenth month is held sacred as the anniversary of the prophet's death, with religious services devoted in his honour to the Fravashis. Nowadays the custom is growing of having a public discourse on this occasion, touching on some aspect of the faith.

Table of the Zoroastrian holy days of obligation as celebrated according to the three calendars, 1985–87

Festival	Shenshai	Qadimi	Fasli
First Gahambar	4–8 October	4–8 September	30 April–4 May
Second Gahambar	3–7 December	3–7 November	29 June–3 July
Third Gahambar	17–21 February	17–22 January	12–16 September
Fourth Gahambar	18–21 March	17–21 February	12–16 October
Fifth Gahambar	6–10 June	7–11 May	31 December–4 January
Panje-keh	15–19 August	16–20 July	11–15 March
Sixth Gahambar / Panje-meh	20–24 August	21–25 July	16–20 March
No Ruz	25 August	26 July	21 March
Khordad-Sal	31 August	1 August	26 March

Note: the Fasli dates remain fixed. The other two calendars recede against the Gregorian calendar by one day every four years.

Table of the obligatory and other festivals according to the Fasli calendar

21 March   No Ruz (New Year)
26 March   Khordad-Sal
30 April–4 May   First Gahambar
29 June–3 July   Second Gahambar
1 July   Tir Jashan
12–16 September   Third Gahambar
3 October   Mihr Jashan
12–16 October   Fourth Gahambar
26 October   Aban Jashan
24 November   Adar Jashan
12 December   Sada
26 December   Zartusht-no Diso
31 December–4 January   Fifth Gahambar
11–15 March   Panje-keh
16–20 March   Sixth Gahambar/Panje-meh

13 National and Secular Festivals
NINIAN SMART

It is not feasible to give a comprehensive list of secular and national festivals; instead I shall here attempt an analysis of some of the more important calendrical and other celebrations which lie for the most part outside traditional religious observance, but which may have something akin to a religious function, in solidifying identities, reaffirming values and refreshing the spirit of those who participate. In the first part I shall look to national festivals, because of the role which nations play in the modern world; and in the second part to secular festivals which are not so closely national in character. The structure of national secular festivals has been evolved chiefly in western (including Marxist) countries but the forms have spread in varying fashion to the so-called Third World.

In many respects nationalism has similarities to (and sometimes blends with) religion. Nationalism is the doctrine that each nation should have its own sovereign state if possible, or at least autonomy within a federation. It typically implies too that the nation-state is the group of ultimate concern, in that a citizen is expected if necessary to die for it in war, and may be executed for treason or incarcerated for offences against it. One is also expected to make sacrifices for it financially, through the payment of taxes. It is not surprising that the nation arouses great emotion, and that this can be reinforced by the state through various means – myth, ritual, ethical teaching, ideological or religious underpinning and so on. Our concern here is with the ritual dimension of secular society, but before discussing the anatomy of national rituals, and in particular festivals, a word about the mythic dimension will be in order.

National celebrations

For the modern nation (and, roughly, the national idea in its modern form derives from the time of the French Revolution), the most common form of identity is linguistic. Language itself may thus come to be held sacred, and so cultural festivals can develop which express its value – such as the Welsh Eisteddfodau. But typically the most important aspect of national identity is history. History indeed functions as myth – which is why the state is interested in having national history taught in schools. Such history stresses founding events and founding fathers, battles, great heroes (including literary, musical and other artistic heroes) and other significant events.

Thus typically we can find celebrations of the national dead (for example Armistice Day in some Commonwealth countries, Remembrance Sunday in Britain, Memorial Day in the United States, Anzac Day in New Zealand and Australia), of great heroes (such as Shakespeare's Birthday, Burns' Night, George Washington's Birthday), founding events (Thanksgiving, the October Revolution). There is also typically a National Day, which may coincide with one of these other celebrations, or may, as in the case of Britain, be connected with the royal family (the Queen's official birthday).

It is perhaps useful to dwell a moment on the logic of some of these celebrations. History, I have said, functions as myth. It does so because it gives form and content to 'our' identity. For the English, history is often thought of as starting most pregnantly with the Battle of Hastings, which signified a passage from pre-Norman to Norman times, and to the present royal succession. Thus if asked to list the kings of England one begins with William the Conqueror – the founder of a new dynasty. This helps to show that the English came truly into existence with the blending of Norman and pre-Norman, largely Anglo-Saxon culture. Not for nothing did some have nostalgia for an earlier time, hence the creation of the Arthurian legend. But national identity via consciousness of the past is not enough. Preferably the past should be seen as glorious, and the national substance is indeed enhanced both by successes and tragedies. Thus people who die in battle for their country are especially honoured, for though their deaths are a loss they are also a 'tribute', a 'sacrifice' on behalf of the nation. So the commemoration of the dead succeeds not only in expressing individual sorrows, but binding those sorrows to the cause of national freedom. And this in its own way increases the nation's substance, much as a god's power may be thought to be nourished by sacrifices. Positively, victories and other successes enhance the nation's glory, and these may be celebrated calendrically or *ad hoc* (Battle of Britain Sunday, VE and VJ Days). If victory coincides with the foundation of the nation-state, as is the case with American Independence Day on 4

July, so much the better. If the victory is of a revolutionary kind, it marks the transition from the old order to the new. The celebration of 14 July and the Fall of the Bastille represents such an event, which also in its very substance enshrines the notion of throwing off shackles and tyranny, and so the foundation of an order in which Liberty, Equality and Fraternity will be dominant.

The ritual at such national festivals is suitably solemn, and some of the trappings of traditional religion are either borrowed or imitated. The evolution of the national anthem in recent times is an interesting commentary on the secular uses of a religious form. The *Marseillaise* has élan and a powerful appeal to the mythic figure of *la patrie*. The United States anthem incorporates the iconography of the flag, among other things. The Soviet Union at first used the *Internationale*, a non-national hymn; but during the war Stalin caused a patriotic Soviet national anthem to be composed and adopted. The British national anthem combines religious appeal and a cheerful chauvinism.

But the musical side of patriotic celebration does not end with national anthems. There are often para-anthems, such as *Rule Britannia, The Battle Hymn of the Republic, The Horst Wessel Song,* and even *Waltzing Matilda.* More importantly the nineteenth century especially saw the rise of national musical traditions of a patriotic flavour, drawing often on folk motifs: consider the compositions of Rimsky-Korsakov, Giuseppe Verdi, Dvorak and Smetana, Chopin, Berlioz, Elgar, Grieg and Sibelius. To some extent secular musical events, such as the opera, thus become among other things quasi-religious celebrations of the national ego. The attempt to solidify such celebrations of the arts can result in events such as the Festival of Britain.

The period of nationalism has also seen the rise of sports as a mass phenomenon. Some, such as football (soccer), are genuinely international, but both internally, at such occasions as the Cup Final, and externally, during the World Cup or at international encounters, such popular sports help to celebrate national prowess. Again, the national anthems are woven into the surrounding ceremonial, or a quasi-religious flavour is generated in other ways (like singing *Abide with me* at the English Cup Final). Such patriotic expression is much less evident at individualistic sports, such as tennis and golf. The whole Olympic phenomenon, which is like an Indian *mela* with thousands and even millions (through the medium of television) gathering to watch the encounters between national teams, is a new secular festival of peaceful national expressions of *machismo* and human achievement. Sport, especially if it is regarded somehow as expressing the genius and spirit of a nation, can produce national events which become something like annual festivals: the World Series in Baseball, the FA Cup Final, the Lord's Test Match, the final of Australian Rules Football.

The nation thus finds its identity in historical myth, its substance in national heroes, from warriors to sportsmen, its ritual in national days, march-pasts and sports, and its solemnisation through music and poetry. In addition, much symbolic value is invested in the head of state.

Thus an important part of national ritual is the celebration of rites of passage of the head of state and, in the case of royalty, the family thereof. Thus in Britain the coronation of the monarch is a great non-calendrical celebration, to be repeated at significant later occasions (the silver jubilee and so on). Similarly the weddings of the monarch, of the heir and so on, become occasions of national celebration. Of course, most states are not now monarchical and so tend to have devised less traditional forms of celebration. In the United States the inauguration of the president is an important quadrennial event, and similar celebrations occur elsewhere. In Britain the annual opening of Parliament is a way of solemnising political continuity. The death of a head of state or other equivalent national figure can be expressed by a period of national mourning.

Some of the above celebrations do not merely have the flavour of religion but may actually incorporate it. Thus the coronation of the Queen in the United Kingdom was a religious as well as a civic ceremony, while other holidays may relate to a patron saint, such as Our Lady of Czestochowa in Poland, or Ferragosto in Italy (the Assumption of the Virgin Mary), or 16 December in South Africa which commemorates both the Covenant and the Battle of Blood River, a highly value-laden event in Afrikaaner history. Some of these more or less consciously relate to national identity, while others perhaps merely characterise the piety of the society in question (thus Ferragosto is less a celebration of national unity than a reflection of Italian Catholic piety, though primarily secular in its manifestations). In India, while Independence Day and Republic Day (the latter commemorating the call for independence by the Indian National Congress on 26 January 1927 CE) are celebrated in a secular manner, the other most important modern festival, Gandhi's birthday (Gandhi Jayanti), has an atmosphere of liberal Hindu attitudes, following Gandhi's broad religious outlook. Though seen as the father of modern India, which is strictly a secular state, he yet embodies the modern Hindu ideology of tolerance and pluralism.

Celebrations of national unity and the like can of course bear the same relationship to ideology as to religion. Thus Marxist states

India's Republic Day Parade in Delhi.

make use of May Day, for instance, not just as an expression of workers' unity throughout the world but more particularly as celebrating *this* people and *this* working class (in Romania the Romanian workers, in Vietnam the Vietnamese and so on). Similarly the use of Lenin's tomb as a kind of secular pilgrimage centre mirrors analogous traditional religious practices.

Sometimes festivals and parades are held not so much for the nation as a whole as for some ethnic group within it. Thus in the United States St Patrick's Day is a way of celebrating being Irish, with reminders everywhere, even in the beer which is dyed an alarming green; in Ireland itself the equivalent parades in Dublin and elsewhere have a directly national significance. Similarly in the United States of America there are other ethnic days, such as Columbus Day for Italians, an annual Puerto Rican parade in New York and so forth. Within the United Kingdom to some degree Hogmanay or New Year's Eve is a Scottish festival, while St David's Day celebrates Welshness, and the annual Festival of Notting Hill is beginning to give expression to West Indian identity within Britain.

Broadly speaking all the foregoing festivals and rituals of celebration have to do with national identities or ethnic character. But there are other secular festivals which are less clearly related to nationalism.

Other secular festivals

Certain festivals, such as May Day (or Labour Day), are consciously internationalist. This does not, as we have noted, prevent them from acquiring more particular national meaning. It is noteworthy that in the United States and Canada, Labour Day is the first Monday in September, rather than the first of May – partly due to hesitations concerning the socialist ideology associated with typical May Day celebrations. The United Nations attempts to promote calendrical events for worldwide observance, such as a Year of the Child, United Nations Day and so on.

Another class of festival days arises from the virtually complete secularisation of older religious days. Thus St Valentine's Day now celebrates personal relations between the sexes; Hallowe'en no longer celebrates All Hallows Eve, but rather is a means of giving children and adults some traditional neighbourly fun; Guy Fawkes Night (a blend of religious and political origins) is an occasion for fireworks; Mardi Gras in Rio, New Orleans and Munich is less a preparation for Lent than an annual mode of letting off social steam (rather like Holi in India); Christmas, although retaining a lot of religious overtones, functions for many folk in Europe and North America, mainly as a way of celebrating family relationships. Other days, like Fathers' Day and Mothers' Day, have spread in consumerist societies partly because commerce has an interest in promoting them.

Similarly there are local celebrations often arising from older local religious feast days, which now serve to celebrate local identity. In so far as for modern people the arts are a central kind of spiritual experience, music and arts festivals (such as Salzburg, Bayreuth, Siena, Cheltenham and Edinburgh) are analogues to older religious fairs. Since the mid-sixties, there have occurred in various countries enormous pop festivals, with a mixture of fun, music and spiritual intensity – the most famous being Woodstock. But here we are reaching the edges of the definition of 'religion', for arts festivals can be properly seen as primarily aesthetic. They have less of the intensity which characterises the more nationalistically oriented celebrations, though Bayreuth was conceived as a semi-religious celebration of Teutonic myth.

Educational institutions, which are the main bearers of traditional and national values, and which have in certain respects a secular-religious role in inculcating official conceptions of truth and virtue, produce various celebratory rituals, notably the graduation ceremony or (in the United States) commencement, which are annual means of sending forth the young to their next stage of life.

Of course, not all holidays can be counted as festivals, not even as secular ones. Thus Bank Holidays are occasions for businesses to close, and may be appropriate times for trips and other relaxations, but they have none of the special significance attaching to national and religious festivals and celebrations. They are (like Saturdays and Sundays for the mass of people) totally secularised spaces within the calendar for leisure.

Summary

We have noted how the most important class of secular festivals and public events are national in scope and spirit, because of the dominant position which the nation-state has come to have in modern living. We noted too how sometimes there is an overlap between the national spirit and some religious or ideological tradition. The most vital forms of national festivals celebrate origins (the founding of the nation) or great heroes and quasi-sacred events. We have seen too how sports have been appropriated as expressions of national sentiment and glory. Also important are rituals connected with the head of the state, and especially in the United Kingdom with royalty. Public events also are ways of solemnising the continuity of politics.

There are also secular festivals with some kind of religious origin which are nowadays more or less completely non-religious in character, such as St Valentine's Day and Hallowe'en. We have noted too that some more overtly religious holidays, such as Christmas, may in fact function secularly. There are, in addition to such post-religious celebrations, some more explicitly secular but international days, such as May Day. We also noted that cultural festivals may have a quasi-religious ambience, and how educational institutions provide a milieu for regular public observances and rites of passage.

It is worth commenting finally that within national frameworks there has arisen, especially since World War II, increased cultural

Opposite: *Celebrating May Day in Moscow*

Hallowe'en is no longer thought of as 'All Hallows Eve'. It is a day of fun for children and adults alike. Dressing up – or being disguised (from which the word 'guises' comes) is a feature of the festival. It is a time when mischievous spirits were thought to be abroad. In many parts of Britain and elsewhere the 'guises' call on houses and have to be 'bought off' or else some trick might be played on the occupants. This is all acted out in good spirit.

264

and ethnic diversity within formerly rather homogeneous nations. This means that the celebratory framework is likely to become more complex; this is already happening to the extent that in many countries some recognition of minority festivals has become necessary, as religious feasts take their place alongside secular national celebrations.

14 Observing Festivals in Schools

PETER WOODWARD

My first introduction to a primary school in Moseley, Birmingham, was an invitation to attend its week-long celebration of Divali. I arrived in the middle of the week to find a colourful, highly decorated entrance hall where children's delightful work overflowed from busy classrooms into the spacious corridors, and all the staff (except the headmaster) looked more attractive than usual in decorative saris and Asian jewellery. Most of the work on display related to Hinduism, but certain areas of the school featured Chinese lanterns and Islamic buildings in an attempt to encourage those children whose families came to Britain from China and Pakistan. This was a possible source of confusion, it is true, but not alien to the Hindu spirit of lively celebration and shared traditions that the staff wanted all the school to discover.

This was not just a pleasant example of topic work or an extended environmental studies project – all the children were celebrating some aspect of their culture and background; white children who had never moved outside Birmingham; black children who had come here straight from their Caribbean and African backgrounds; Asian youngsters from the Punjab and Bangladesh and others whose accents were Irish or Welsh; all were caught up in the excitement of the event, the celebration of an experience.

The wide varieties of age, ability, background and involvement meant that there were, in the celebration, different levels of understanding and participation; but for the children this was more than just learning – it was a sharing of culture, of religion, of life-style (food, clothing and story, particularly), of atmosphere. It was also an experience in which the staff of the school could share.

The British scene

How does the British educational system allow such a celebration

266

to happen? What of the much discussed 1944 Education Act with its Cowper-Temple clause insistence that religious instruction shall be given in every school in accordance with an agreed syllabus drawn up by a conference that represents (i) the Church of England, (ii) other denominations, (iii) teachers' associations, and (iv) the local education authority? Most of the early syllabuses drawn up for religious education were restricted to Christianity, and some still are (though denominational confessionalism is strictly excluded and rarely proposed). But few authorities today object if *additional* material of a relevant nature is introduced into schools, and most recent syllabuses, allow and encourage the inclusion of appropriate material from the world's great religious traditions. Not many are as thoroughgoing in this respect as the Bradford supplement and the Birmingham syllabus with its handbook material but the widespread pluralism of British society produces few objections from parents, teachers or religious organisations when *an effective balance* of multi-faith material is introduced.

School worship or assembly

The same picture holds true for school worship or assembly, which each school is instructed by law to hold every day for all pupils unless their parents choose to withdraw them (they have this right, though only a small number use it) or the building's facilities are insufficient to permit the whole school to gather in one place. In many situations the assembly is still an act of Christian worship; in other cases it might be a celebration of a festival from one of the main non-Christian traditions; alternatively it may be a less clearly formulated act of devotion to an unspecified deity to avoid causing offence to any of the communities present; at a different level again the assembly may be a secular celebration of a moral issue; or it may even become just a meeting point for the school where notices and team results can be announced and discipline enforced.

Both Christian and non-Christian festivals feature frequently, and it is interesting to see how the advent of variety has modified the nature of the contemporary assembly from what was once a straightforward act of collective worship into a teaching medium, in which information and insights, respectful attention and personal involvement, all have their own place.

Let me give as an example two Christmas assemblies held on separate days but in the same large hall that two church schools share, one an infant and the other a junior school. They are a joint venture of Anglicans and Methodists on the southern outskirts of Birmingham. Two fluorescent ultra-violet lamps had been installed and both audience and participants on the juniors' day were supplied with a star cut out of reflective card. At the appropriate time the main lights dimmed and the special lights glowed with an unearthly pallor that turned the actors into angels and the audience into a circle of twinkling constellations. The very practical set was transformed into a forum where heaven and earth could meet. At the infants' celebration stories from Sweden, Israel and ancient India all featured the coming of light into the world; the use of costume, music and mime drew from parents and children a response that evoked a real sense of encounter and devotion which everybody present could feel.

Both these schools are composed largely of white children, and many of their celebrations centre on Christianity. It is good to find, though, that a growing number of such schools are also selecting non-Christian festivals and using these either as a teaching medium or as a form of multi-cultural education. In either case there is a deepening of the pupils' perceptions of what it means to celebrate a festival, and sometimes this is enhanced simply by the fact that much of the material is unfamiliar – in just the same way as, in a different context, a vista of the Dead Sea when observed from nearby Masada adds a totally new element to the concept of inland water for those previously familiar only with boating lakes and inland reservoirs. By way of example, a primary school with a primarily white population in Acocks Green, Birmingham, will serve as a case in point. Here the celebration of Divali and the retelling of traditional stories about Rama and Sita were thoughtfully presented in a striking way. The colour that was missing from the pupils' faces was in no way absent from their acting of the events or the creative work that covered the school's walls.

The close working relationship that is evident here between classroom activity and assembly is invaluable if festivals are to relate to the whole of school life and not just to a tiny 'spiritual' corner of it. The links that are possible with other subject areas often prove particularly effective in exploring the meaning of festivals from different traditions: dress, story, crafts, food and science are all relevant. In this way the celebration of festivals can also be a gloriously creative means of 'celebrating the curriculum', a phrase that has different meanings in different contexts, but which is altogether appropriate in this one where the whole of the school's life, both academic and social, can be caught up in the sustained and joyful reinterpretation of a festival.

Multi-cultural areas

It is in the multi-cultural schools of the inner-city areas that the greatest impetus has come for the celebration of festivals. In many cases this has brought with it the development of a particular type of community participation in the celebration which is distinctive and memorable. Parents will prepare Asian or Caribbean foods and bring these into school for a Divali party or a Mardi Gras carnival-type festival. Eid cards may be made or bought and presented to classmates, again with a party or festive celebration. The Chinese New Year may involve the dramatisation of the Dragon dance – I remember vividly a scene in an infants' class in a Handsworth Junior and Infant School, Birmingham, where all thirty children danced together as the snaking tail of a magnificent, mythical dragon in his battle for the life the New Year would bring.

Commitment and objectivity

The impact and importance of the celebration of festivals from different religions and cultures lies in the balance it achieves between commitment and objectivity. For those of the faith involved, the festival will express something radically different from its meaning to the majority of the school staff and to most of the parents and pupils who come from other or no traditions. The former will celebrate with these 'outsiders' something they have elsewhere celebrated with 'believers'; the 'non-believers' will not be able to celebrate at all in the same way, but many will still find scope for rejoicing and entering into the spirit of rejoicing which they observe in their neighbours and friends. Some will feel able to do this without undue concern or anxiety that they are compromising themselves, but this will rarely be universal; it is in part the presence of those who have reservations that will prevent this type of celebration from ever being in school what it could be in church, temple or mosque.

The practice of celebrating festivals in schools

The type of Eid celebration that occurred a few years ago in a Balsall Heath primary school provides a good example. The Muslim festival of Eid ul-Fitr breaks the fast of Ramadan, and Eid parties were arranged for different classes in the school. These could not be held before the festival, since anticipating such events is not normally acceptable in Asian communities. Nor could they be held on the appropriate day, first because it was not certain on which day the new moon would appear and second because most of the Muslim children would in any case be away from school on the actual day of the festival. Instead the parties were arranged for an afternoon two or three days later, by which time the Muslims had returned to school and the immediate impact of fast-breaking was over; but the spirit of joy and accomplishment was still firmly in evidence. Relatives provided the food for the events, many parents and grandparents attended, and even though the proceedings were simple, with a few readings and recitations, speeches, good wishes, distribution of cards and sharing of 'goodies', the impact on the Muslim community of being able, and even invited and encouraged, to mark the event in school was tremendous.

For the staff and non-Muslim children the festival was an eye-opener. They met with parents and grandparents on friendly terms, they saw them in their best costumes, they caught the atmosphere of cheerful festivity that surrounded them at this time, and they perceived a different and novel side of the children's characters as they reacted to the presence in school of their families. The sense of dignity, of community and brotherhood that Islam fosters made an impact on the whole school that was both unexpected and enduring.

For the Muslims themselves there was an initial nervousness and hesitancy – it was the first time the school had celebrated such a festival in this way – but this soon evaporated in the cordiality of the occasion. Indeed many of the adults were increasingly happy to talk about their children and families, their festivals and their faith, although several found their English was too restricted for extensive conversation.

The main danger for the school here lay in their trying to do too much, too seriously, too soon. The staff have learnt from this and subsequent events, how slowly relationships have to grow if they are to survive and how important it is to avoid giving the impression of pressurising parents into positions for which they are not yet ready.

At the same time the community gave clear evidence that certain things mattered a great deal to them, and the easy way in which their caring attitudes and standards were conveyed to staff and others was a new and creative experience. In particular their joyful care for the Qur'an and their personal anxieties over the upbringing of their daughters were set in a very natural – and linked – context, which for the staff was an education in itself.

What happened here was a natural development of community life and celebration. It was not a formal school assembly, though the topic is, of course, highly suitable for just such a purpose. Rather it was an afternoon of informally structured activity in which most of the school could join in differing degrees. There was an educational element involved, but this was incidental rather than central. It was above all a happening, an event, in the life of the local community.

Source material

Celebrations like this raise a number of important issues in the life of the community, which are often ignored by those who compile assembly books for use in schools. These books usually intertwine two distinct strands: the presentation of information that can be communicated to pupils at an appropriate level and with varying degrees of interest; and the spiritual homily or moral instruction which frequently appears to be the justification for holding the assembly. Both aspects deal with the cognitive rather than the affective aspects of life, and the writers often seem to have an axe to grind.

This is particularly true of the 'anthology' type of assembly book, and is also a frequent occurrence in manuals that contain a term's assemblies ready made for the teacher to pick up and use just as they stand – an excellent device for emergencies but one full of hidden hazards in inexperienced hands.

It is all the more refreshing therefore to note contributions where an abundance of selections is provided from which the teacher must select and to which pupils may respond and react, but where the nature of their response is left open. When there is no presentation of a party line to which they should conform, young people will often surprise by the effective and positive nature of their response – though it may take a major act of faith on the part of their elders to stand back and leave them to it.

Signposts to good practice

What can we offer that will provide a positive pointer to good practice? If festival as described above is neither pure information nor message, neither formal assembly nor yet explicit educational content, then what is it and what does it have to offer?

Perhaps another example may help to illustrate the point. A number of Birmingham inner-ring schools have found a rich sense of fulfilment in Asian festivals, especially Eid ul-Fitr, Divali and Baisakhi, and have then moved on from there to ask what they can do to reflect the life and culture of the sizeable minority of pupils in these schools from a Caribbean or African background. One answer they have found has been to stage a Mardi Gras carnival-style celebration.

The ingredients of this pot pourri are very similar to those of the Eid celebration described above: story, speeches, parental and community involvement, and food, with an additional emphasis on music (steel-band style) and dance, reggae and calypso and with rather less concern for scripture and history. The overt links to religion are slight – though the idea of Shrove Tuesday merry-making in preparation for Lenten fasting has a sun-baked logic all its own – and one which is no less attractive than the more tra-ditional British 'pancake' philosophy! What is most strange is that the absence of such links with religion in no way detracts from the atmosphere of celebration found in more conventional 'religious' celebrations.

Key elements in the celebration of festivals and how these apply in relation to schools are discussed below:

Emotional response
A festival is a time of heightened emotions. Frequently the relevant emotion will be joy, as in Holi (deliverance of Krishna), Christmas (birth of Jesus), Eid ul-Fitr (breaking the fast of Ramadan); but it could equally well be awe (Yom Kippur and the days of Penitence, Holy Weeks and so on), repentance and self-discipline (Lent may figure here, though it is really a period of preparation for a festival, rather than pure festival itself) or sorrow (Good Friday, Muharram, the destruction of the Temple). This is saying something more than simply asserting that the festival is an emotional time. The emotion is heightened or deepened for a purpose, and it follows that the proper celebration of the festival involves an adequate enhancement of this emotional level. In a school situation this may be difficult, and even undesirable, to replicate. But unless there is some depth of feeling involved, the school's celebration will be inadequate, life-less and barren. A school celebration needs to be more than a clinical retelling of factual data and story. It misses the mark if there is no hint at all of the central emotion that marks out the festival from 'ordinary' days of the school year.

History and legend
A festival usually commemorates some incident in history or legend. There may be exceptions (harvest festivals could, arguably, be one), but they will be few. Historical incidents do, of course, have a tend-ency to become 'enlarged' with the passing of time and constant retelling, but though the element of history may be somewhat

uncertain, the gloss of time may give to the festival a glow of warmth and romance. But a festival that has lost its origins and become re-associated, emasculated or so contemporary in presentation as to be unrecognisable, is of little value to those who celebrate it. In an educational context it is all the more important that this element should remain firmly in view; and a celebration that concentrates on contemporary ritual to the exclusion of historical recall forfeits an invaluable and essential element.

Worship

A festival relates in some degree to worship. It is true that there are a number of secular celebrations where this will not apply, but the normal role of festivals in world religions, even those in Buddhism and Jainism, is to ensure that there is some acknowledgment of power or powers greater than the individual participant, and some form of worship. The problem for a school community here is the danger of hypocrisy, for many of the school (pupils and staff alike) will not join in this particular act. To feign would be deceitful and out of touch with the reality of the situation. In this sense the school community is often unable to celebrate a festival in the same manner as the community of faith, and would be well advised not to attempt to do so. At the same time the celebration would be incomplete if there was no reference to worship as the basis of the festival, and possibly if there was no opportunity for the minority, who are committed, to express their response to their faith in a meaningful way, while other friends look on and – in their own style – sympathise, share and participate, even though it be at some degree of distance.

Community activity

Festivals are never solitary events, but reflect the celebratory activities of a community. Concern with the historical work of an individual as the basis of a festival (for example those festivals commemorating the death of a Sikh Guru, the nativity of Jesus, or the birth of the Prophet Muhammad) may obscure this element; however it is important to ensure that any school-based activity reflects adequately the corporate nature of community celebration.

The annual cycle

Another aspect in the celebration of festivals relates to the annual cycle of which most festivals in the world's faiths are a crucial part. The individual festival is not an event on its own: it is part of a regular calendar which has been repeated and observed time and again. Each successive repetition builds on previous celebrations of the festival in the minds of the community, so that one re-enactment of Christmas or Passover recalls previous years' celebrations. The annual routine gives a sense of purpose, healthy repetition and regularity to the year, in the same way that the seven-day cycle does to the Jewish Sabbath and the five prayers of *salat* do to the Muslim's day. The festival's celebration provides a sense of fulfil-ment and completion, to each passing year and it is possible for any school to contribute something valuable both to members of the faith concerned and also to those who are outside the relevant tradition by drawing attention to the annual cycle. It is not so much a matter of factual information, useful though that is, as of catching the mystique of purpose and plan that lies behind the cycle, of being in touch with previous generations of celebrants in their routine of devotion. A school celebration which conveys something of this atmosphere is turning an assembly into an act of devotion without compromising the beliefs of either those within or those outside the relevant community – and that is a valuable achievement indeed.

Festival analysis

The Mardi Gras festival mentioned above was strong on emotion, community involvement and the role of the festival in the annual cycle. History and elements of worship were also involved, though in a less central manner. It would be interesting to analyse any school's assemblies, including the others mentioned in this chapter, in the same way. The value of such an exercise lies not in any introspective self-evaluation, which may be a dangerous exercise if over-stressed, so much as in the making of plans for a full and balanced assembly programme and for achieving what assembly is best fitted to do.

A recent visit to a multi-cultural primary school in Moseley for a Chinese New Year celebration was interesting because here, too, these five elements were all present in some way or other. The decorations on the walls, the role-play as dragons and lions, the attendance of parents and other members of the local community, and the distribution of sweets as pupils left the hall, all produced a heightened atmosphere where history and community met in the observance of this gateway to the annual festive cycle. Of worship as it is known in the West there was little, but that need not mean that worship (or the awareness of worship) was absent. For the few Chinese children present the celebrations may well have been worshipful, though whether *they* would have claimed that is open to question. The presence of heightened emotion – and this was an event filled with emotion – is not of itself, of course, sufficient to constitute worship, but the two often relate closely and the presence of one may indicate the real presence of the other – or sometimes compensate for its absence.

Assembly and worship

It may be that in this relationship we have another corner piece of the fascinating jigsaw puzzle which depicts the relationship of assembly to worship. These two terms used to be virtual synonyms for each other in the context of schools, but the arguments in favour of retaining and developing regular assemblies in schools no longer posit the need for the school to be a worshipping community. Instead assembly has become a variety of modified cocktails, some bland and smooth, others evocative and innovative, yet others vigorous and challenging, often with a scorpion sting in the tail. The worship element in this cocktail has not been universally eliminated, but where it has, its contribution can in large measure be replaced by a sensitive introduction of the element of heightened emotion. If this emotional response is coupled with the important consideration, which a multi-faith situation inevitably raises – that some of the community are within the appropriate tradition of faith (and a few of these may have a deep, personal commitment to it) while others stand outside and look in – a way may be opened up for young people to become aware of and develop an understanding of the significance of worship for people of different faiths and cultures.

Here is provided a way to circumvent the valid fear of dragooning people into worship or of pushing young people towards hypocrisy through making assumptions of a premature commitment. It is an approach which admittedly has other dangers (too many high spots too close together, divided loyalties within the community, assumptions about total commitment as opposed to partial belief and assent, and so on but it has the salient virtue that it can effectively open up an exciting and positive approach through festival to celebration. Is this perhaps an adequate justification for a continuing pattern of school assemblies?

Relevant examples here might include a harvest festival at a secondary school in the deep south of Birmingham; an inner-ring secondary school celebration of Divali when the lower school pupils acted as hosts for two classes of top junior pupils who would shortly be joining the ranks of those acting out the celebration; a community school Christmas 'happening' where a tutorial group presented their own understanding of what the festival means today. But for greater detail it would be better to turn back to the opening paragraphs of this article and read again how a primary school celebrated Divali: note the heightened atmosphere, the community involvement, the element of worship for those who honoured Vishnu at home, with an insight into Hindu devotion and culture for those who did not, the retelling of an old story and a flavour of the annual cycle of Indian festivals with its entrancing colour and magical quality. When these elements are present, festival becomes the ideal vehicle for linking together classroom, assembly and community in a meaningful celebration of that larger, unsung curriculum which, increasingly in our schools, is coming to be seen as the central core of daily life.

Bibliography

Babb, L A, *The Divine Hierarchy: Popular Hinduism in Central India*, New York, Columbia 1975

Dube, S C, *Indian Village*, Routledge and Kegan Paul, London 1955

Effendi, Shoghi, *God Passes By*, Baha'i Publishing Trust, USA 1945

Eliade, M, *Patterns in Comparative Religion*, New American Library, 1958

Gamble, Sidney D, *North China Villages*, Berkeley and Los Angeles, 1963

Gould, Cherry, 'Visiting India: Religious Education through Travel' in *Resource* Vol 5 No 1, 1982

Lewis, O, *Village Life in Northern India*, Vintage Books, London 1958

Mayor, A C, *Caste and Kinship in Central India*, Routledge and Kegan Paul, London 1960

Stevenson, Mrs Sinclair, *The Rites of the Twice Born*, OUP, 1920

Welch, Holmes, *The Practice of Chinese Buddhism 1900–1950*, Harvard University Press, Cambridge, Massachusetts 1967

Woodhead, H G W (ed), *The China Year Book 1939*, Shanghai 1939

The following books reflect something of the work of the Shap Working Party (see Preface).

World Religions: A Handbook for Teachers, Commission for Racial Equality, 1977

Comparative Religion in Education, J Hinnells (ed), Oriel Press, 1970

Hinduism, J Hinnells and E J Sharpe (eds), Oriel Press, 1972

World Religions at CSE or 16+, M Hayward and J Finel, Shap Mailing, 1982

Shap Mailing, published annually by the Commission for Racial Equality, which includes *Calendar of Religious Festivals*

Afro-Caribbean, Brian Gates (ed), Ward Lock Educational, 1980

Notes on the Contributors

Mary Boyce is a graduate of Cambridge University, where she wrote a doctoral dissertation on recently rediscovered Manichean hymn-cycles in Parthian. She was appointed in 1948 to a lectureship in Iranian Studies at the School of Oriental and African Studies, University of London, becoming Professor there in 1963. She spent a year, 1963–64, among the Zoroastrians of Iran, and since then has specialised in the study of their religion, both from texts and from contacts with members of the two living communities, the Parsis and Iranis. Her publications include *Sources for the Study of Zoroastrianism* (Manchester University Press, 1984) and *Zoroastrians, Their Religious Belief and Practices* (RKP, 1979).

Alan Brown has been Secretary of SHAP since 1982. Formerly a teacher, then a lecturer in an institute of higher education, he is now Schools Officer (Religious Education) for the Church of England's Board of Education at Westminster and the Director of the National Society's RE Centre. He is a trustee of the Chichester Project, for whom he has written *Christian Communities* (Lutterworth, 1982), and other works include *The Christian World* (Macdonald, 1984).

W Owen Cole is a writer on religion, the author of many books and articles including *The Guru in Sikhism* (Darton, Longman and Todd, 1982) and *Sikhism and its Indian Context 1469–1708* (DLT, 1984 He teaches Religious Studies and Multi-cultural Education at the West Sussex Institute of Higher Education, and is a former Chairman of the Shap Working Party on World Religions in Education. His wide teaching experience includes not only higher education, but also working in primary and comprehensive schools and as a part-time tutor for the Open University and the University of Leeds. From 1975 to 1979 he was Vice-Chairman of the Yorkshire Committee for Community Relations.

Riadh El-Droubie, journalist and author of several books on Islam, was born in Baghdad, Iraq, in 1935. After completing his high school education he studied engineering in the United Kingdom. As Editor of *The Minaret Educational Review*, he was closely involved in Islamic education in Britain and is author of several books on Islam for schools. From 1960 to 1978 he worked as Publications Manager and Assistant Editor of the *Islamic Quarterly* at the London Central Mosque and Islamic Cultural Centre, and now works in Saudi Arabia as Public Relations Manager of Sanders Associates, Inc.

Rabbi Hugo Gryn was born in Czechoslovakia and educated there, in Switzerland and in Hungary. During the 1939–45 war he was imprisoned in Nazi concentration camps. He resumed his education in England after the war and was ordained at the Hebrew Union College in Cincinnati, Ohio. He served as Rabbi to the Jewish community in Bombay and this was followed by a period of social and relief work among Jewish communities in North Africa, Iran and Israel. He has been Senior Rabbi at the West London Synagogue for the past twenty years. He is Chairman of the Standing Conference on Inter-Faith Dialogue in Education, a member of the SHAP Working Party, and active in the World Congress of Faiths as well as in a number of Jewish and inter-faith communal organisations.

Richard Gombrich was born in London in 1937 and educated at St Paul's School, Hammersmith, Magdalen College, Oxford and Harvard University. From 1965 to 1976 he was a Lecturer in Sanskrit and Pali, Oxford University, and from 1976 Boden Professor of Sanskrit and Fellow of Balliol College; also Emeritus Fellow, Wolfson College, Oxford and Hon Secretary, Pali Text Society. Publications include two books and many articles, mainly on Sinhalese Buddhism, among them *Precept and Practice* (Clarendon Press, 1971). His academic interests are: history of Indian religion, anthropology of religion and Pali philology. Other main interests include music, especially opera, cookery and photography. He is a frequent visitor to Sri Lanka.

Robert Jackson is Senior Lecturer in Arts Education at the University of Warwick. He edited *Perspectives on World Religions* (SOAS, University of London, 1978) and *Approaching World Religions* (John Murray, 1982), the introductory volume in the series 'World Religions in Education' of which he is General Editor. He has a research interest in various aspects of Hindu life in Britain. Publications in connection with this include chapters contributed to D G Bowen *Hinduism in*

England (Bradford, 1981) and *Hindus in Britain* (SOAS, 1982) written jointly with Helen Kanitkar. He has published various articles on religious education and he has contributed many programmes on world religions to BBC radio for schools.

Padmanabh S Jaini was born in a small Jaina village, Nellikar, in the Indian state of Karnataka. He received his high school education in a Jaina monastery, and graduated from the University of Bombay. He spent two years studying in a Buddhist monastery in Sri Lanka, after which he went to England, where he received his Ph D at the University of London. He was a Lecturer in Pali, Buddhism, and Jainism at the Benares Hindu University in 1952 and at the School of Oriental and African Studies, London University in 1957 and became a Reader at the University of London in 1965. In 1972 he became Professor of Buddhist Studies at the University of California, Berkeley. His major publications are in the fields of Buddhist and Jaina doctrines, and his most recent work is *The Jaina Path of Purification* (University of California Press, 1979).

Philip Hainsworth became a member of the Bahá'i faith in Bradford, Yorkshire, in 1938. He has served on national administrative bodies for almost four decades, being first elected to the National Spiritual Assembly of the Bahá'is of the British Isles in 1947 at the age of 27. After several years in Africa he was re-elected to the British National Spiritual Assembly in 1967 and is presently its Chairman. He has travelled widely in Europe, Africa and the Middle East, and represents the United Kingdom Bahá'i Community on many national bodies. During the past thirty-six years he has contributed regularly to Baha'i periodicals in the United Kingdom and East Africa and has written the sections on Bahá'i in *World Religions – A Handbook for Teachers* (CRE) and (I Believe (CEM); on *Initiation* (1978) and *Death* (1980) for the Lutterworth Educational 'Living Faiths' series. He was co-author of the popular book, *The Bahá'i Faith*, which appears on the Ward Lock Educational 'Living Religions' series (1980).

Douglas Jones professes a life-long interest in China. He was formerly Head of the Humanities Department in the Coventry College of Education, where he established in the 1960s courses in both classical and recent Chinese history, probably the first of their kind to be offered to training college students in this country. Currently Associate Fellow of the University of Warwick, his recent publications include works both on aspects of Chinese religion and on the history and settlement of Chinese communities in the UK. He visited the People's Republic of China shortly before Mao's death, travelling extensively there. He keeps close contact with Chinese communities both in London and in the Midlands.

Geoffrey Parrinder is Emeritus Professor of the Comparative Study of Religions, University of London. He spent twenty years in Africa, nine of them as senior lecturer at University College, Ibadan, Nigeria, after which he was Reader and then Professor at King's College, London, 1958–77. He was Charles Strong Lecturer in Australia 1964, Wilde Lecturer in Natural and Comparative Religion, Oxford 1966–69, Teape Lecturer, Delhi and Madras 1973, Visiting Lecturer at International Christian University, Tokyo 1977–78 and at University of Surrey 1978–83. He was ordained as a minister of the Methodist Church, England, in 1932 and is author of over thirty books on comparative religion, with translations into ten languages. His publications include *West African Religion, African Traditional Religion, Witchcraft, African Mythology, Jesus in the Qur'an, Avatar and Incarnation, Worship in the World's Religions, Mysticism and Sex in the World's Religions.*

Michael Pye, born in Shropshire in 1939, studied Modern Languages and Theology at Clare College, Cambridge (1958–61). For the next five years he was resident in Japan working as a teacher and writing a handbook on written Japanese. At the same time he developed interests in comparative religion which were pursued further through lectureships at St John's College, York, at the University of Lancaster and the University of Leeds. Among his publications are *The Study of Kanji* (on the Japanese writing system), *Skilful Means, A Concept in Mahayana Buddhism, The Buddha* and *Zen and Modern Japanese Religions*. A general work on Japanese religion is in preparation. Michael Pye is presently Professor of Comparative Religion at the University of Marburg, West Germany.

John Rankin was formerly Head of Religious Studies at the West Sussex Institute of Higher Education. Bishop Otter College, Chichester, is one of the constituent colleges and the home of the *Chichester Project* which he has directed since 1977. The project is concerned with research in Religious Education. He is a member of the Shap Working Party and former Secretary (1979–82) and Chairman (1982–85), and has published a number of books on religious education for middle and secondary schools. Among these are *Looking At Festivals* (Lutterworth, 1981), *Christian Worship* (1982) and *The Eucharist* (Lutterworth, 1984). He is also engaged in the production of in-service material for teachers of religious education in co-operation with the Open University.

Ninian Smart teaches at the University of California, Santa Barbara, and at the University of Lancaster, where he founded the Department of Religious Studies. He was formerly H G Wood Professor of Theology at Birmingham. His publications include *Reasons and Faith* (1958), *Doctrine and Argument in Indian Philosophy* (1964), *The Long Search* (1978), *The Science of Religion* (1974), *Beyond Ideology* (1982) and *Worldviews* (1983). He was director of two Schools Councils projects on Religious Education, was Editorial Consultant for the TV series on religion, *The Long Search*, was Gifford Lecturer in Edinburgh (1979–80) and has also taught for longer or shorter periods at Benares, Aberystwyth, London, Yale, Wisconsin, Princeton, Harvard, Dunedin, Queensland and Cape Town.

Angela Wood was born in London, spent her early school years in an international boarding school and part of her secondary schooling in southern Africa. She studied, taught English and broadcast in the Far East for four years, and took degrees in Religion and Curriculum at the University of London. She has worked for the Inner London Education Authority as head of Religious Studies for over ten years (currently at North Westminster Community School), is National Organiser for the Standing Conference of Interfaith Dialogue in Education and active in many other multi-ethnic concerns. She teaches at the West London Synagogue (adults and children), is involved in examining and moderating Religious Studies for two boards and has written a number of books for secondary schools. Her interests include new ideas and spiritual forms, food and children of all ages – especially her daughter.

Peter Woodward is General Inspector of Schools with responsibility for Religious Education in the City of Birmingham. Formerly he was a secondary school Religions Education teacher, then Senior Lecturer in Religious Studies at Borough Road College, Isleworth. One time Secretary and Chairman of the Shap Working Party on World Religions in Education, he is currently distributor of the annual Shap Mailing and Calendar of Festivals. He has contributed widely to publications on Religious Education. He is Chief Examiner for AEB Multi-faith O Level, Adviser to Central Television's school series, *Believe It or Not*, is heavily involved with in-service training for teachers, and an enthusiast for sport, travel and computers.

Index

Aban Jashan 254, 255
Adar Jashan 254, 255
Adults' Day 156
Advent 79, 81, 82–83
Afghanistan 36, 37
Africa 5, 76, 213
Afrikaaner 259
Akan 3
Akshaya-tritiya 143–145, 149
al-isra 231
al-miraj 231
All Hallows Eve 264
All Saints:
  Buddhist 53
  Christian 80, 82, 92–93, 99–100
All Souls Day:
  Buddhist 57
  Chinese 70–71
  Zoroastrian 250
American Independence Day 257
Ancestor worship 61
Annunciation 80, 82, 96–97
Anzac Day 257
Aoi matsuri 160
Armistic Day 257
Arrival of Sanghamitta 48
Asala 47
Asala perahära 47
Ascension Day 80, 81, 92
Ascension of Baha' U'llah 22, 27, 29
Ashadhi Ekadashi 113, 123
Ash Wednesday 81, 87
Assumption of the Blessed Virgin
  Mary 81, 94, 97–98
Atonement 4
Autumn Equinox 159, 164

Baha'i Festivals 19–30
Bahubali-mastaka-abhisheka
  148–149
Bairam (see Eid-ul-Adha)
Baisakhi (see also Vaisakhi)
  236–237, 238, 239, 244
Balkans 18
Bangladesh 223, 231
Basora (see also Sidhi and
  Satain) 120–121
Battle of Britain Sunday 257
Bean Scattering 152, 156
Bengal 17
Bhaia Duj 136
Bhatri Dwitiya 136
Bhogali Bihu 116
Bhutan 37, 38
Bihar 37
Birth of Bab 22, 24, 26, 30
Birth of Baha'ul'llah 22, 24, 26, 30
Body and Blood of Christ 93
Booths (see Sukkot)
Boys' Day 160
Britain 18, 84, 257, 264
Breaking the Fast (see Eid-ul-Fitr)
Buddha's Birth, Enlightenment
  and Death 45–47, 49, 50,
  54–55, 57, 58, 59
Buddha's First Sermon 47, 49, 55,
  58, 59
Buddha's First Visit to Sri
  Lanka 48
Buddhism 7, 31–59, 140, 159
Buddhist 1, 3, 7, 31–59, 156, 159,
  161, 168
Buddhist Festivals 31–59

Bunka no hi   166
Burma   35, 37, 38, 39, 43, 49–50, 58
Burns' Night   257

Cambodia (Kampuchea)   35, 37, 38, 39
Candlemas   102
Ceylon (*see also* Sri Lanka)   35, 36, 38, 39, 41, 43, 45–48
Chhath   136–137
Ch'i Hou Chieh   70
Chichibu Night Festival   152, 166, 169
Children's Day   160
China   4, 14, 18, 37, 38, 39, 41, 56–59, 60–73, 164, 213
Ch'ing ming   68–69
Chittrai   122
Chökhor   55
Chönga Chöpa   54
Christian   1, 2, 3, 4, 5, 6, 7, 17, 18, 74–103, 267
Christian Festivals   74–103
Christian Unity   82
Christianity   4, 6, 31, 39, 74ff
Christmas   1, 5, 18, 39, 77, 79ff, 82–86, 103, 261, 262, 267, 272, 274, 275
Christmas Eve   84
Chrysanthemum Day   164
Chung Ch'iu   72
Ch'ung Yang   72–73
Chung Yüan   70–72
Columbus Day   260
Communism   37, 39, 61, 63
Confucianism   60, 61
Confucius   61, 63
Conjunction of Nine Evils   56
Conjunction of Ten Virtues   56
Constitution Day   160
Corpus Christi   81, 82, 93, 103
Covenant: Baha'i   23, 24, 26, 30
Culture Day   166

Daksha-lakshana-parva   146–147
Dashera (Dassehra)   7, 130–133, 139, 141

Day of Arafat   223–224, 232
Day of Assembly   216–218, 222, 232
Day of Atonement (*see* Yom Kippur)
Day of the Covenant   24, 26, 30
Day of Thanksgiving for the Institution of Holy Communion   93
Death of Tsongkhapa   55
Declaration of the Bab   20, 22, 24, 26, 29
Descent from Tushita   55
Devuthna Ekadashi   137
Dharma Day   53
Divali (Deepavali)   4, 7, 106, 107, 111, 119, 134–136, 139, 141, 147, 236, 237–239, 244, 268, 269, 271, 275, 276
Diwali (*see* Divali)
Dola Yatra   119, 126, 139
Dolls' Festival   158, 160, 168
Double Ninth   72–73
Double Tenth   61
Dragon Boat   61, 69–71, 73
Durga Puja   130–133, 139
Durutu   48, 50
Dzamling Chisang   55, 59

Easter   5, 6, 18, 40, 61, 77, 78, 80, 81, 82, 86–92, 103
Easter Eve   83
Education Sunday   82
Egypt   4, 230
Eid al-Sukar (*see* Purim)
Eid-ul-Adha   212, 215, 220, 222, 224–227, 232
Eid-ul-Fitr   212, 215, 220–223, 224, 226, 232, 272
Eid-ul-Kabeer (*see* Eid-ul-Adha)
Eid-ul-Nahr (*see* Eid-ul-Adha)
Eid Ramadan (*see* Eid-ul-Adha)
Eid ul-Sagheer (*see also* Eid-ul-Fitr)   220
Ellul   208, 209
Emperor's Birthday   160, 168
End of Rains Retreat   42–43, 49–50, 52, 58

England   8, 9, 115
Epiphany   79, 80, 81, 86, 103
Eucharist (*see also* Holy
   Communion, Lord's Supper,
   Mass)   7, 75, 83, 90, 92, 93
Europe   77

Fall of the Bastille   258
Falling Asleep of Blessed Virgin
   Mary   80, 97
Farvardigan   250–252
Fast of Ester   209
Fast of First-born   206, 209
Fast of Gedaliah   208, 209
Fast of 20 Sivan   207, 209
Fast of Tammuz   207–208, 209
Fast of 10 Tevet   208–209
Fathers' Day   261
Feast of Feasts   80
Feasts of the Blessed Virgin
   Mary   94–98
Festival of Immolation (*see*
   Eid-ul-Adha)
Festival of Offering (*see*
   Eid-ul-Adha)
Festival of the Prophet's Birthday
   (*see also* Mawlid
   an-Nabi)   230–231, 232
Festival of the Prophet's Night
   Journey and Ascension
   231–232
Festival of Sacrifice (*see*
   Eid-ul-Adha)
Flower Festival   152, 159, 168
Flower Viewing   159, 168
Folk-religion   63
France   10, 18

Gahambars   246–252, 257
Gandhi Jayanti   117, 133–134, 139,
   259
Ganesha Chaturthi   128, 139
Ganga Dasa-hara   122, 139
Ganjitsu   153, 158
George Washington's
   Birthday   257
Ghana   3
Gion Festival   163, 168

Girls' Day   158, 168
Gishi-matsuri   167
Golden Week   160
Good Friday   88, 103, 274
Great Fast   80, 86, 102
Guga Naumi   126
Gurpurbs   240–242, 244
Guru-pancami   146
Guy Fawkes   261

Hallowe'en   100, 259, 262
Hanukah   170, 201–205, 210
Hanuman Jayanti   121, 139
Harvest   5, 72, 82, 152
Herd Boy and Weaving Maid   70,
   73
Heroes Festival   167–168, 169
Higan   159, 162, 164
Hinamatsuri   158, 160
Hindu   3, 10, 13, 104–139, 236,
   237, 239, 242, 259, 276
Hindu Festivals   104–139
Hinduism   7, 104–139, 234, 236,
   266
Hogmanay   260
Hoi   137, 139
Hola Mohalla   236, 239–240, 244
Holi   7, 118–119, 236, 239, 261, 272
Hollyhock Festival   160–161, 168
Holocaust Day   206, 209
Holy Communion (*see also* Lord's
   Supper, Mass, Eucharist)   8, 75
Holy Eucharist (*see also* Lord's
   Supper, Mass, Holy
   Communion)   93
Holy Innocents   86
Holy Liturgy   75
Holy Saturday   88–90
Holy Week   77, 81, 87, 88, 272
Hong Kong   39, 63, 70
Hungry Ghosts   57, 59, 70
Hypapante   80

Igloo Festival   158, 168
Immaculate Conception of the
   Blessed Virgin Mary   82, 96, 103
Independence Day:
   Jewish   206

Indian   257
  American   259
India   31, 32, 36, 37ff, 104ff,
  223, 230, 231, 234f, 259, 261, 268
Indian   4, 18, 104ff, 159, 236f
Indonesia   213, 219
Iran   213
Iraq   230
Irish   260
Isé   9
Ise Jingū O-taue Shinji   161
Ise Rice Planting   161, 168
Islam   4, 6, 7, 17, 18, 37, 39, 60,
  61, 101, 134, 211–233, 266
Israel   9
Italy   261

Jagannatha   123, 139
Jaina   140–149
Jaina Festivals   140–149
Jnana-pancami   146
Jaith-Ka Dasahra   122
Janamashtami   129–130, 139
Japan   1, 4, 6, 7, 9, 16, 18, 35, 37,
  38, 39, 41, 150ff
Japanese Festivals   150–169
Jashans   253–255
Jerusalem Day   207, 209
Jewish Festivals   170–210
Jews   1, 2, 3, 4, 5, 6, 17, 18, 75,
  170–210
Jidai-matsuri   166
Judaism (*see* Jews, Jewish Festivals)
July 14   258
Jum'ah   3

Kamakura-matsuri   158
Kanagat   130, 139
Kantō-matsuri   163
Karttika Ekadashi   137, 139
Karttika Purnima   137, 139, 148,
  149
Kathina Ceremony   43, 48, 50, 52,
  58
Keirō no hi   164
Kenkoku kinen no hi   156–158
Kenpō Kinenbi   160
Kenya   220, 223

Khordad-Sal   253, 255
Kiku no sekku   164
Kinrō kansha no hi   166
Kodomo no hi   160
Korea   37, 38, 150
Krishna Jayanti   129–130, 139
Kuan-Yin   58, 59
Kumbha Mela   115–116, 139

Labour Day   261
Labour Thanksgiving Day   166, 169
Lag B'Omer   207
Lailat-ul-Bara'h   232
Lailat-ul-Qadr   218
Lakshmi Puja   134–136, 138–139
Lammas   5
Lantern Festival   68, 73, 163, 168
Laos   35, 37, 38, 53
Lent   5, 79, 80, 86–87, 102, 263,
  272
Lhabap   55
Lights:
  Buddhist   45, 49, 52, 58
  (Jewish: *see* Hanukah)
Lohri   113, 139
Loi Kratong   52
Lord's Supper (*see also* Eucharist,
  Holy Communion, Mass)   7, 75,
  83
Losar   43

Magha Puja   53
Mahalaya   121, 130, 139
Mahashivratri   116–117, 139
Mahavira-jayanti   142–143, 144,
  149
Makar Sankranti   113, 139
Malaya   63, 219, 223
Mardi Gras   86, 261, 269, 274
Martyrdom of Bab   22, 26, 29
Mass (*see also* Eucharist, Holy
  Communion, Lord's
  Supper)   75, 83, 88, 90
Matsuri   150, 151, 152
Maundy Thursday   87–88, 93, 103
Mawlid an-Nabi   230–231
May Day   260, 262, 262
Mela   237, 239, 240, 258

Memorial Day 257
Mesha Sankranti 119, 139
Mid-Autumn Festival 72, 73
Mihr Jashan 254, 255
Mongolia 38
Mongols 37
Mönlam Chenmo 54
Moon Viewing 164, 168
Mothers' Day 261
Muharram 6, 8, 228–230, 272
Muslim 2, 3, 4, 6, 8, 17, 37, 270, 276
Muslim Festivals 211–233

Nachi Fire 161, 168
Naga Panchami 126, 139
Nanakusa 154
Natelis Solis Invicti 5
National Day (China) 61
National Foundation
  Day 156–158, 168
Nativity 83
Nativity of the Blessed Virgin
  Mary 80, 94, 96, 103
Natsu-matsuri 152
Navaratri 106, 130–133, 134, 139
Naw-Ruz 23, 26
Nebuta Festival 163, 168
Nenjū-Gyōji 152
Nepal 31, 37, 38, 39, 40
New Year 4
  Baha'i 20, 24
  Buddhist 40, 43, 45, 49, 50, 54,
    58
  Chinese 4, 56, 61, 63, 65,
    66–67, 73, 274
  Eastern Orthodox Christian 80,
    103
  Hindu 109, 119–120
  Jaina 142
  Japanese 4, 153–154, 158, 168
  Jewish (*see also* Rosh
    Hashanah) 4
  Muslim 227–228, 232
  Zoroastrian (*see also* No
    Ruz) 248–250, 253, 254, 255
Ngachō Chenmo 55–56
Nigeria 3
Night of Forgiveness 232

Night of Power (*see* Lailat-ul-Qadr)
Nineteen Day Feasts 19, 28–30
Nirjala Ekadashi 123–124, 139
No Ruz (*see also* Naw
  Ruz) 248–250, 253, 254, 255
Notting Hill 260

O-bon 153, 159, 162–163, 168
October Revolution 257
Ōmisoka 168
Onam 120, 127–128

Pakistan 36, 223, 231
Palm Sunday 81, 87, 103
Panje-keh 251, 255
Panje-meh 251
Parsi (*see* Zoroastrian) 245–255
Paryushana-parva 142, 146–147,
  149
Passing of Abdu'l baha 23, 27, 30
Passion Sunday (*see also* Palm
  Sunday) 87
Passover (Pesah) 2, 5, 6, 78, 92,
  170, 173, 179–184, 185, 209, 276
Pentecost (*see also* Whitsun for
  Christian festival) 5, 77, 78, 80,
  81, 82, 90, 91, 99, 103
Period Festival 166, 169
Pesah (*see* Passover)
Physical Fitness Day 164, 169
Pitra 121, 139
Pitri Paksha 130, 139
Poland 261
Pongal 113–114, 139
Poson 47
Poya 48
Presentation of the Blessed Virgin
  Mary in the Temple 80, 103
Presentation of Christ in the
  Temple 102
Puerto Rico 260
Puranmashi 242
Pure Brightness 65, 68–69, 73
Purim 170, 199–201, 209

Qurbani Eid (*see* Eid-ul-Adha)

Race Relations Sunday 82

Rains Retreat   41, 42–43, 48, 49
   52, 57, 58
Rakhi Purnima   126–127, 139
Raksha Bandhan   126–127, 136,
   139
Ram Lila   133, 139
Rama Navami   121, 139
Ramadan   2, 7, 212, 214, 215,
   218–220, 222, 232, 272
Ramakrishna Utsav   117–118, 139
Ratha-yatra   123, 139, 148–149
Remembrance Day:
   Jewish   206–207, 209
Remembrance Sunday   255
Republic Day   259
Respect for the Aged Day   164, 168
Rice Planting   152, 161
Ridvan   19, 22, 23–25, 29
Romania   262
Rosh Hashanah   171, 193–196, 209
Rosh Hodesh   171, 206
Russia   18, 37, 213

Sabbath   2, 8, 18, 41, 78;   Jewish
   (Shabat)   170, 173–179, 205, 209
Sacred Heart of Jesus   94, 103
Sada   254, 255
Saga dawa   54–55
Saint David's Day   260
Saint Joseph's Day   82, 99, 103
Saint Michael and All
   Angels   101–102, 103
Saint Nicholas   84
Saint Patrick's Day   262
Saint Peter and Saint Paul   82, 99,
   103
Saint Valentine's Day   261, 262
Saints' Days   98–100, 102–103
Sal-i Zardusht   255
Salono   126, 139
Samhain   6
Sangrand   242
Saraswati Puja   132, 139
Satain (*see* Basora)   120, 139
Saturnalia   79, 84
Seijin no hi   156
Setsubun   150, 156
Seven Herbs   154, 168

Seven-Five-Three   166, 169
Shakespeare's Birthday   257
Shavuot (*see also* Weeks)   5, 173,
   184–187, 209
Shemini Atzeret   191–193, 210
Shichi-go-san   166
Shinto   150, 151, 153, 154, 156,
   160, 161, 162, 163, 164, 166, 168
Shōgatso   153, 154
Shraddha   130, 139
Shravana Purnima   126, 139
Shri Panchami   116, 139
Shrove Tuesday   86, 102
Shruta Pancami   145–146, 149
Shūbun no hi   164
Shunbun no hi   159
Sidhi (*see* Basora)   120, 139
Sierra Leone   219
Sikh   1, 3, 234–244
Sikh Festivals   243–244
Sikkim   37
Simhat Torah   191–193, 210
Singapore   38, 39, 63
Skanda Shasti   138, 139
Snan-yatra   123, 139
Snow Festival   156, 157, 168
Sol Invictus   79
Solemnity of Mary Mother of
   God   94, 98, 102
South Korea   38, 39
Spain   213
Spring Equinox   159, 168
Spring Festival   63
Sri Lanka   35, 36, 37, 38, 39, 40,
   43, 45–48, 58
Star Festival   161, 168
Sukkot   170, 187–190, 210
Summer Festival   152
Summer Retreat   57, 59
Sunday   2, 3, 4, 8, 18, 41, 77, 78,
   80, 81, 82, 83, 92
Sunday of the Pharisee and the
   Publican   80
Sunday of the Prodigal Son   80

Taanit Behorim   206, 209
Tabernacles (*see* Sukkot)
Taiiku no hi   164

Taiwan   38, 63
Tanabata   161, 168
Tanzania   220, 223
Taoism   60, 61
Teej (Tij)   124–126, 139
Teng Chieh   68
Tennō Tanjobi   160, 168
Tevet   10, 208–209, 210
Thailand   35, 37, 38, 39, 43, 44, 50–53, 58, 63
Thanksgiving Day   257
Tibet   35, 37, 38, 39, 40, 41, 43, 53–56, 59
Til Sankranti   113, 139
Tir Jashan   254, 255
Tisha B'Av   208, 209
Toli Ekadashi   123–124, 139
Transfiguration   101, 103
Trinity Sunday   81, 92–93, 103
Tripuri Purnima   137, 139
Tsom Gedaliah   208, 210
Tsukimi   164
Tuan Yang Chien   69
Tu B'Av   208, 209
Tu B'Shevat   209
Tung Chih   73
Turkey   18, 220
Twelfth Night   79

Ugadi   120, 139
United Nations Day   261
United States   38, 77, 222, 261
Uposatha   3, 41, 48

Vaikuntha Ekadashi   138, 139
Vaisakha (*see also* Wesak)   7, 45, 50
Vaisakhi (*see also* Baisakhi)   111, 119, 120, 139, 236–237, 238, 239, 244

Vasanta Panchami   116, 139
VE Day   257
Veneration of the Cross   88
Vietnam   37, 38, 63, 260
Vira-nirvana   147–148
Visitation of the Blessed Virgin Mary   94, 97, 103
VJ Day   257

Waking of Insects   65
Wan Atthami   52
Weeks (*see* Shavuot)   5, 92, 173, 184–187, 209
Wesak (*see also* Vaisakha)   7, 45, 46, 47
West Africa   3
West Indies   5
Whitsun (*see* Pentecost)   18, 92
Whitsunday   6, 78, 92
Winter Solstice   65, 73

Yawm al-Jumu'a (*see* Day of Assembly)
Year end   168, 169
Year of the Child   263
Yo-matsuri   166
Yom Ha'Atzmaut   206, 209
Yom Ha-Shoah   206, 209
Yom Ha'Zikharon   206–207, 209
Yom Kippur   4, 170, 173, 187, 196–199, 210, 272
Yom Yerushalayim   207, 209
Yoruba   3
Yüan Tan   66–67
Yukimatsuri   156

Zanzibar   213, 220, 223
Zartusht-no Diso   255
Zoroastrian Festivals   14, 245–255